More Praise for *Long Live the Tribe of Fatherless Girls*

Esquire Best Nonfiction Books of the Year
O, The Oprah Magazine Best LGBTQ Books of the Year
Lit Hub Best Queer Debuts of the Year
Elle Best Books of the Season • *Paste* Best Memoirs of the Decade
Washington Post Best Books of the Month
Indie Next Pick • Indies Introduce Pick

One of the most anticipated books of 2019—*Entertainment Weekly*, *HuffPost*, *BuzzFeed*, *The Millions*, *Nylon*, *The Rumpus*, *Electric Literature*, *Lit Hub*, *Refinery29*, and many more

"A fearless debut that carries as much tenderness as pain . . . Devastating and funny . . . A eulogy and a love song. It's about girls and the women they become. And it's all compulsively readable." —Tessa Fontaine, *The New York Times Book Review* (Editors' Choice)

"The literary equivalent of sucking on a Warhead: at once nostalgically sweet, stingingly sour, and unnervingly satisfying." —*O, The Oprah Magazine*

"One of the best, most evocative titles of the release season." —*The Millions*

"Easily one of the best memoirs of the last decade . . . Gorgeous on the sentence level and flat-out breathtaking as a whole." —*Lit Hub*

"Haunting . . . Harrowing and charged with sharp edges, yet somehow life-affirming at the same time." —*Esquire*, "Best of the Year"

"Gripping and gloriously written . . . Searing, vivid, and deeply thoughtful." —*Elle*, "Best of Spring"

"Filled with desire and loss, love and forgiveness . . . An utterly unforgettable debut." —*Nylon*

"A deeply compassionate book . . . Madden has succeeded in creating a mirror of larger concerns, even as her own story is achingly specific and personal." —NPR.org

"[Madden] turns her life into art in this gorgeous reckoning." —*The Washington Post*, "Best of the Month"

"Truly stunning . . . Not many memoirs can get away with calling themselves page-turners, but T Kira Madden's sure AF can." —*Cosmopolitan*

"A dizzying and dazzling coming-of-age story . . . As hard to shake as glitter." —*Bustle*

"A memoir this fearless is bound to change readers' lives." —*Refinery29*, "Best of the Month"

"Gripping and beautifully written . . . Tackles race, identity, and trauma with skill and grace." —*The Today Show*, "Twenty Stories' Picks for the Month"

"Haunting, artful, and profound." —*BuzzFeed*

"A tough, raw literary voice." —*Entertainment Weekly*

"Striking and honest . . . LGBTQ+ literature is starving for this." —*Out*

"Luminous . . . Madden's incantatory prose is spellbinding." —*Los Angeles Review of Books*

"Like the greats, Madden writes with devastating clarity and lyricism, becoming a storyteller trustworthy enough to tell even the ugliest of truths. *Long Live the Tribe of Fatherless Girls* will make you want to remember, to want more. This story takes lots of glittery guts to tell."
—*Chicago Review of Books*

"One of the most transparent, candid, and heartrending collections of personal stories that is currently on the shelf." —*International Examiner*

"Raw and fearless . . . [Madden] honors fathers and mothers and families; the ways they love, and the ways they fail." —*Electric Literature*

"Madden is magic . . . She uses language new and strange but always devastatingly right." —*The Paris Review*

"A riveting and deeply personal work." —*The Advocate*

"One of my favorite reads in recent years. Madden's prose is sharp, lyrical, and gut-hitting, made up of sentences I want to read over and over again." —*Hyphen*

"Courageous . . . One woman's attempt to write down and rewrite her own history, so as to make space for more love." —*Asian American Writers' Workshop*

"A Lisa Frank-racetrack-Hawaiian shirt phantasmagoria that I couldn't get enough of. And, man, that last section—it'll knock you loose."
—Indie Next List citation (Molly Moore, BookPeople, Austin, TX)

"A stunning meditation on identity, adolescence, family, and forgiveness. Readers are rewarded with a climax as moving as the exceptional first chapters. This debut is fierce and unforgettable." —Indies Introduce citation (Emilie Sommer, East City Bookshop, Washington, D.C.)

"A stunner." —Kristen Arnett, *Refinery29*

"Harrowing and sad and funny and beautifully written." —Emily Temple, *Lit Hub*, "Lit Hub Recommends"

"A gorgeously written debut . . . Exquisitely captures the pain of growing up." —*Alma*, "Best of Spring"

"Pairs gorgeous writing with honest emotion . . . [A] must-read." —*Paste*, "Best of the Decade"

"Showcases the coexistence of familial love and complication with such shattering grace, understatement, and openness." —*Booklist* (starred review), "Best New Books"

"A deeply courageous work that chronicles one artist's jagged—and surprisingly beautiful—path to wholeness. Affecting, fearless, and unsparingly honest." —*Kirkus*

"Necessary . . . Madden weaves together an utterly human paean to belonging, to healing, and to loving and being loved." —*BookPage*

"[Madden's] story of how she comes to her queerness, her self, and ultimately her belonging on this earth is one that I think every queer person will feel deep inside their heart. I know I did, and I am grateful." —*Autostraddle*

"So vivid that readers can practically taste the flavored lip gloss and feel the thick glittery foundation of the early aughts on their faces, melting in the harsh Florida sunlight." —*Windy City Times*

"As graceful and rhapsodic as it is heart-wrenching." —*them.*

"Many readers . . . may find courage to confront, and perhaps recount, their own difficult stories thanks to Madden's brave undertaking to tell her own." —Bookreporter.com

"It would be easy to describe T Kira Madden's debut memoir as a coming-of-age story, or as a memoir about trauma, or a memoir of growing up biracial or queer. The truth is, the book is all of those things and more." —*The Rumpus*

"*Long Live the Tribe of Fatherless Girls* is sad, funny, juicy, and prickly with deep and secret thoughtful places. It is raucous and poignant at once and I recommend it highly." —Mary Gaitskill, author of *This Is Pleasure* and *Somebody with a Little Hammer*

"Harrowing and beautiful. What seems most miraculous about *Long Live the Tribe of Fatherless Girls* is the way T Kira Madden forges out of such achingly difficult material a memoir as frank and funny and powerful and surprising as this, her utterly gorgeous debut." —Lauren Groff, author of *Florida* and *Fates and Furies*

"Madden has come to break your heart *open*: to crack your heart wide, to spill out the heart's grief and pain so she can fill it back up with joy and beauty and love." —Matt Bell, author of *Scrapper*

"I've never read such a gorgeous and raw depiction of girlhood, the terrible vulnerability of adolescence, and the humiliation that often goes hand in hand with desire. Madden is fearless about diving deep into the darkest aspects of herself and her past, and that's what makes her work riveting and urgent. An absolutely necessary book." —Julie Buntin, author of *Marlena*

"This open, defiant memoir is the long-awaited daughter of Dorothy Allison's *Bastard Out of Carolina*. Madden captures the dangers and longings of a perilous girlhood with prose so vivid and sensuous we feel her past in our bodies. A mesmerizing piece of art I won't soon forget." —Claire Vaye Watkins, author of *Gold Fame Citrus* and *Battleborn*

"T Kira Madden is an acute observer of her family, her environment, and her own mind, and is generous despite—or perhaps because of—what she's endured. Her bleeding, gorgeous prose will get under your skin and leave you aching in love. Her first book is a triumph." —Sarah Gerard, author of *Sunshine State*

"*Long Live the Tribe of Fatherless Girls* reminds us beautifully that we are unshielded, that we are blessed with life only by a narrow and undecipherable margin. This book has grit and a feisty elegance I love, and I love the mess and tenderness here of being and having been a girl." —Noy Holland, author of *I Was Trying to Describe What it Feels Like*

"Madden's prose will hypnotize you as it wrings every drop of beauty out of her story. If you've ever known the predicament of having a magical and messy family, a female body, or the mixed blessing of a big heart and a keen mind in a troubled world, then you need this book as much as I did." —Melissa Febos, author of *Whip Smart* and *Abandon Me*

"What are the ties that bind us, the events that shape us? In this beautiful memoir, T Kira Madden confronts these questions, unflinchingly, with breathtaking honesty. Reminiscent of *The Glass Castle*, her unique vision and voice take us into the depths of her astonishing experience." —Mary Morris, author of *The Jazz Palace* and *Gateway to the Moon*

"*Long Live the Tribe of Fatherless Girls* is a wrenching story of longing, loss, and extraordinary coincidence—a debut act of courage and ferocious beauty from a formidable new talent." —Kimberly King Parsons, author of *Black Light*

"Madden perfectly captures the ache of a child trying to find her place. You may not be a competitive equestrian, a Floridian, or the mixed-race child of two parents who struggle with addiction; you may have never fallen in love with another woman; but everyone who has ever longed for more love will understand." —Rowan Hisayo Buchanan, author of *Harmless Like You* and *Starling Days*

"*Long Live the Tribe of Fatherless Girls* is a triumph. It's for anyone reading late into the night wondering, will I survive this? T Kira Madden tells us, as only she can, that the answer is yes. It's a journey through the dark heart of family love and the cosmic mystery of queer youth and you don't want to miss it." —Genevieve Hudson, author of *Pretend We Live Here* and *Boys of Alabama*

"This book is a dark powerhouse of yearning and reckoning that reminds us all of the girl we've spent our lives trying to grow out of—and all the ways we punish her for sticking around." —Tatiana Ryckman, author of *I Don't Think of You (Until I Do)*

"I loved this book for its big-hearted, aching renderings of sexuality, addiction, and family, for its exquisite attentiveness, and in the end for its hope that a family can grow to embrace all it's been and might become."
—Kristin Dombek, author of *The Selfishness of Others*

"A vivid portrait of queer awakening set against the devastating backdrop of addiction, loss, and, ultimately, triumphant reclamation. I finished this book blinded by tears and a deep appreciation for Madden's undeniable talent. She is a force to be braced for, and heralded." —Allie Rowbottom, author of *Jell-O Girls*

"Bubble gum pop, spray tans, lip piercings, and spiked orange juice are the sensorial ingredients of Madden's queer search for belonging. There are deep, ancestral ways of being and knowing at work in this book, casting spells and reciting incantations in the rat's mouth, in this place we call America." —Cyrus Grace Dunham, author of *A Year Without a Name*

"This is the book I wish I'd had growing up. It is a testament to the beauty and tumult of life's constant unfolding. Proof we are not meant to live in search of neat conclusions, but to embrace a state of being constantly shaped. Emerging from this book I felt kinder toward my younger self. T Kira Madden teaches us not to shy away from hard truths, for there are rich colors found in darkness. A reminder to treat ourselves gently as we grow." —Chanel Miller, author of *Know My Name*

Long Live the Tribe of Fatherless Girls

Long Live

Long Live the Tribe of Fatherless Girls

a memoir

T Kira Madden

BLOOMSBURY PUBLISHING

NEW YORK · LONDON · OXFORD · NEW DELHI · SYDNEY

BLOOMSBURY PUBLISHING
Bloomsbury Publishing Inc.
1385 Broadway, New York, NY 10018, USA

BLOOMSBURY, BLOOMSBURY PUBLISHING, and the Diana logo are trademarks
of Bloomsbury Publishing Plc

First published in the United States 2019
This paperback edition published 2020

Copyright © T Kira Madden, 2019

Photographs courtesy of T Kira Madden, 2019

Although this is a work of nonfiction, the names and identifying characteristics of
certain individuals have been changed to protect their privacy, and dialogue has been
reconstructed to the best of the author's recollection.

Bloomsbury Publishing Plc does not have any control over, or responsibility for, any
third-party websites referred to or in this book. All internet addresses given in this book
were correct at the time of going to press. The author and publisher regret any
inconvenience caused if addresses have changed or sites have ceased to exist, but can
accept no responsibility for any such changes.

Epigraph credits: page xv, excerpted from "The Glass Essay," in Anne Carson,
Glass, Irony and God, copyright © Anne Carson, 1995. Reprinted by permission of
New Directions Publishing Corp; page 232, excerpted from Katherine Anne Porter,
Ship of Fools (Boston: Little, Brown and Company, 1962).

ISBN: HB: 978-1-63557-185-1; PB: 978-1-63557-476-0; eBook: 978-1-63557-186-8

LIBRARY OF CONGRESS CATALOGING-IN-PUBLICATION DATA

Names: Madden, T Kira, author.
Title: Long live the tribe of fatherless girls: a memoir / T Kira Madden.
Description: New York, NY : Bloomsbury Publishing Inc., 2019.
Identifiers: LCCN 2018016519 | ISBN 9781635571851 (hardcover) |
ISBN 9781635571868 (ebook)
Subjects: LCSH: Madden, T Kira,—Childhood and youth. | Women authors,
American—Biography. | Racially mixed women—United States—Biography. |
Lesbian authors—United States—Biography. | Adult children of drug addicts—
United States—Biography. | Fathers and daughters—United States—Biography.
Classification: LCC PS3613.A28357 Z46 2018 | DDC 818/.603 [B]—dc23
LC record available at https://lccn.loc.gov/2018016519

2 4 6 8 10 9 7 5 3

Typeset by Westchester Publishing Services
Printed and bound in the U.S.A. by Berryville Graphics Inc., Berryville, Virginia

To find out more about our authors and books visit www.bloomsbury.com and
sign up for our newsletters.

Bloomsbury books may be purchased for business or promotional use.
For information on bulk purchases please contact Macmillan Corporate
and Premium Sales Department at specialmarkets@macmillan.com.

for my mother and father

You remember too much,
my mother said to me recently.

Why hold onto all that? And I said,
Where can I put it down?

—Anne Carson, "The Glass Essay"

CONTENTS

A NOTE FROM THE AUTHOR

While the material in this book comprises extensive research, interview content, photographs, and journals, much of it is based on memory, which is discrete, impressionable, and shaped by the body inside of which it lives.

PREFACE

or instance: the women. From the television commercial that's been looping for as long as I can remember, featuring the first song I ever memorized. In the commercial, white women in lime-green bikinis walk barefoot and elegant across the smooth deck of a yacht. Their steps have bounce to them; their thongs are amazing. The women flip their hair at the sun, and beads of seawater drip onto their shoulders, down the creases between their breasts. The droplets roll and glitter over their bodies like mercury from a smashed thermometer. A man sings: "Naturally you're lookin' good, you look just like you dreamed you would! You're having fun, you're at your best, and all it took was Just One Look! Florida Center for Cosmetic Surgery: just one look is worth a thousand words!" His girls are so pleased to be beautiful, his.

When I grow up, after I leave this town, I tuck in alone at night, listen to the garbage trucks lift and crash their arms through the New York freeze. I sip lukewarm water from a clay mug on my nightstand. Three A.M.—bewitched. Just last week, I had a father. He used to say, Sleep, child, need that beauty sleep. No child of mine could be so afraid of sleep. *He called me pretty then. Now he is dust—some teeth—a copper urn on my bookshelf, polished.*

My hands—they are never not shaking. I press them under my body. Breathe into my pillow until the world goes vague. When I drift off, it's the women who come first. It's the women wearing their happiness in a film of sweat, the honor of their position. And then it's me, a child. A girl pressing her hands against a television screen. She feels the women thrill through the static. She doesn't move. She stays like this until she hears him again, that little man on his boat, always there, still singing.

PART I

THE FEELS OF LOVE

UNCLE NUKE

My mother rescued a mannequin from the J. C. Penney dump when I was two years old. He was a full-bodied jewelry mannequin: fancy, distinguished. Those were the words she used. Her father, my grandfather, worked the counter day and night, slinked antique chains and strands of jade across velvet placemats, and felt the mannequin did no work for his numbers; *he's pau*—done. Grandfather said this with both elbows bent, a chopping motion. The mannequin would have to go.

In this part of the story, my mother and I live alone in Coconut Grove, Florida. We're in a canary-yellow apartment damned with beanbag ashtrays, field mice, the guts of flashlights and remote controls (*Where have all the batteries gone? Where do they go?*), and a shag carpet that feels sharp all the way under the shag. She's single, my mother, the crimson-mouthed mistress of my father, a white man, who is back home in downtown Miami with his artist wife, his two handsome boys. Soon, my father will move my mother and me into a porn director's apartment, and then to Boca Raton—*the Rat's Mouth*—to start over, but none of us knows this yet.

My mother, a Chinese, Hawaiian, pocketknife of a woman, shot a man once. She tells me this story all the time. How the strange man tried to crawl through her window, naked, choking out his cock as she slipped into a nightgown. She shot him in the shoulder with a boyfriend's .357 Magnum, his body spat out like a rag doll into the liquid black night. He landed in the street—too far to be trespassing—so she dragged him by the legs back on her lawn for more. The man was paralyzed for the rest of his life; he threatened to sue. My mother never once regretted this incident.

But this is how it was in Coconut Grove in the 1980s and early '90s. Bandits, robbers, glass stems on the sidewalk, bad men doing bad under the bridge. My mother had little to defend in that first apartment of ours—a few gems from her father, frosted Christmas ornaments, her Chinese jade, some cash—but then there was me. We needed a man in our home, a figure bigger than us, she said, to scare off all the other men who would come. All of this to say that the reason she rescued that mannequin, the reason she wrapped her arms wickedly tight around his waist, carrying him to the backseat of our Volvo where the top half of his body slung out the window, his bald head pat-pattering under the rain on our car ride home, all the reasons she did anything—the wrong things, the strange things, the dangerous, the sublime—the reasons she does any of it, still, is to protect me. Remember this.

I name him Uncle Nuke. He has marble eyes, real hair feathering out from his lash line, eyebrows painted with delicate streaks, thin as needles, curved. Little nail moons. He stands six feet tall and smells clean and metallic as the air before a Florida storm. Uncle Nuke wears a tuxedo, and under his clothes, my mother is learning to take advantage of his joints. With a simple twist-pop, she detaches his torso, places him in the passenger seat of our car, buckling him gently like another child. I like staring at the dome of his bald head from the backseat. It's chipped in places—silver, flecked. We're able to drive in the HOV lane with the extra body. *Three makes a family*, says my mother. *At least that*.

My father visits our apartment sometimes, at night, so late that my visions of him are smudged. There's the smell of him: Merit cigarettes, orange juice and vodka, money. The grind of his voice. The word: *father*. *This here is your father* and *Hello, I'm your father*. He slips up often and calls me *Son*. Mostly, when I conjure him then and remember him now, I think of gold. Gold horse bits on the buckles of his shoes; gold buttons on sailor jackets; a gold pinky ring; the gold chain necklace my grandfather gave him from the fanciest case at J. C. Penney. A trade, he said, for my father to wise up and make a commitment— *a Jew chain for the only Jewish man I've ever met*—to turn my mother into something honorable.

Before my father arrives at our apartment, my mother sits Uncle Nuke in a rocking chair near the front window. My mother likes him like this, in profile, the edges of his regal face chiseled out like a dream. Sometimes his legs lie in the corner of our living room, the trousers pressed, his knees locked into place. My mother and I like to change his socks at least once a week. We pull the bright patterns over his club feet, delicately roll the bands up his calves.

This man doesn't look like he belongs in our home. He looks like he belongs to a different era, someplace far away from here, a life with white dinner gloves, niceties, an engraved cigarette case—*U.N.*—that quietly clicks closed. My father knows all about the mannequin, his practical functions, the way he wards off intruders, but I wonder, still, what his shadow did to my father's heart when he drove up in his white

Cadillac—if it stoked something fierce enough inside him to make his temples quake, to whet his desire for my mother and me; if it was Uncle Nuke, not even a real man, who eventually made him unpack and stay.

When my father moves in, I begin crawling out of my bedroom at night to visit Uncle Nuke. We meet at his rocking chair. I coil up at his feet.

Where did you come from? I ask. I grip behind the joints of his ankles, breathing in. *I'm the one who loves you now.*

I press my cheek into the patent leather of his shoes. My mother has my father and I have Uncle Nuke. In the morning, I wear the red indents of his shoelaces across my face like a map.

I can't bear the thought of leaving Uncle Nuke. Not for school, or for walks to Biscayne Bay; I don't even like to leave whichever room he's in. I, too, learn to work his joints. Before school, I twist off one of his hands, hiding it in my lunch box. I hold the hand as much as I can throughout my day, a horseshoe grip around the bulk of fingers.

What's wrong with the kid? I've heard my father ask. *She doesn't get her weird from me.*

She likes to hold him is all, says my mother. *You know kids—you have two others. They like to hold on to things, don't they?*

Here is a memory that still comes to me: I am small, too small, thimble legs in a yellow dress. My parents are getting married tonight. There are steep steps in the lobby of the Omni Hotel, and I am expected to walk down these steps with grace, to flick flowers. My mother wears a Chinese wedding gown, a beaded headpiece like a bird of paradise. She says, *You can do this*. She smiles the biggest smile of her life. My grandfather is wearing his best cuff links, veiny green jade, proud at last. He walks me through the steps I will take, *Count. You can count, right? Everyone will love you.*

They do. I make my way down the stairs with *Oh*s and *Ah*s of delight, the pop of flashbulbs. The bastard child.

My parents seem very much in love. I am old enough to know that. They dance little steps, around in a square. They smear cake and lick it. My father's lips part as he squeezes my mother by her waist, their slow song tickling the water in my glass, and I am jealous of the both of them.

At home, in the half-dark, I tell Uncle Nuke all about it.

I say, *I guess we can keep him. If we have to.*

PENCIL

A diary entry, age nine: If I were a pencil sharpener, I would be miserable and lonely. I would be a small blue pencil sharpener. My only friend would be the scissors, which are black. Sometimes, people put a yellow stick in my mouth and I have to bite until it gets sharp.

WHY YOU LIKE IT

I wanted love the size of a fist. Something I could hold, something hot and knuckled and alive. What I wanted was my freckled cheeks printed on cheap paper, stapled at the ears, the flyers torn from telephone poles and the scales of palm trees, a sliver of my face left flapping in the wind. I wanted to be the diametric opposite of who I was; am. To get gone. I wanted limbs dangling from the lip of a trash compactor, found by a lone jogger who would cry at the sight of my ankles, my beaten blue knees with their warm fuzz of kiddie hair.

Did I want to die? Not really, no. I wanted the beauty of the doomed. Missing girls are never forgotten, I thought, so long as they don't show up dead. So long as they stay missing.

* ✳ *

I am nine years old in 1997, and I read magazines. I clip out so many images and faces that the remaining paper looks skeletal, like the threads of a crumbling leaf. My favorite magazine is called *TigerBeat*, with lips so glossed on the cover the paper looks wet. The clippings line the perimeter of my room, scotch-taped around the edges, gleaming.

The magazines have girl parts inside and boys with shining chests and words that tell me how I should or should not act, how to make lifelong friends. This is how to make him wait; this is how to get crushed; this is how to line your panties.

Are you lonely?

Sure, I'm lonely, I write to myself, on the electric IBM Wheelwriter my Grandma Yukling gave to me. Grandma goes by Rose now, because her American co-workers at the bank told her it was easier to say. *Rosebud—more memorable*—they saw it in a movie once, and so she used it.

Grandma Yukling-Kam-Rosebud taught me to set the typewriter margins when she came and visited from Hawai'i. She told me to write an *autobiography*, because it's a good thing—*sometimes*—to remember your life. Instead, I've been writing about a girl named Joni Baloney. Joni is exactly like me except she's white and athletic and people tend to grope her. She's bullied at school and chomps on sandwiches under an exotic, drooping tree. She can't help her preference for baloney. In chapter 2, boys rip off her underwear at recess and take turns wearing the damp cotton over their heads, so Joni Baloney runs away, pantyless, and joins a traveling freak show, rocketing horses off high-dive boards. Joni wears bikinis and makes it big and that's that. I can do things like that when I write—pluck any thread of want and weave a whole world.

I have a new favorite section of *TigerBeat*—the pen pal ads—because these kids seem lonely, too. The ads feature square blocks of photographed faces with little stories about each kid, a home address below the story. Anyone can send mail directly to the addresses, no parents necessary, a feature that will soon be discontinued.

A couple of weeks ago, I wrote a letter to the magazine with a picture of myself. I wanted to look wanted. I handed my father a cardboard camera and clenched my jaw so the marbles of my temples would show. I covered my braces with my lips. When we picked up the photos from the drugstore, I felt proud of the stillness in my eyes—the absolute focus. In most of the pictures my hair is slicked back, but even without hair, I am still a girl.

To the magazine I wrote, *Hi Hello my name is T Kira but please DEAR GOD forget the T. I am* obsessed *with riding horses and I like to palm the tassels that hang from my grandmother's drapes and yes I would like a real camera for Hanukkah and yes I would like an instrument, any instrument, for Christmas and yes I do like the smell of a gas pump but really what I would really, really love is a pen pal, yes, and Thank you.* I promised to write back. I promised to keep secrets. I wrote many lists like this but only chose the best parts to send. Small, sweet facts. I spritzed the envelope with Cucumber Melon body spray, sprinkled glitter all over the wet bull's-eye of sweet.

I see it in the checkout line at an East Boca convenience store. I'm at a Palmetto Park strip mall with my mother. My father is next door at the bar, but he doesn't know that we know it. *We'll stop for groceries,* my mother had said, picking me up from school, *and check for your magazine. And let's make a bet—will Daddy's car be in the lot?*

Daddy's car is in every lot, or driveway, whenever we play this game. Whenever we come looking. It's amazing, I think, really something, how my parents share this telepathic connection. A few months before the convenience store, my mother took one of my father's golf clubs to his Jaguar. The cracks spread over the driver's seat window until the glass went soft looking, like chiffon. Since then, I wonder why we continue playing the Bet Daddy's Car Game.

My mother places cartons of juice on the rolling belt of the checkout line. Behind the black cage wire of the magazine rack, I see it. The dimpled smiles of the Hanson brothers; Leonardo DiCaprio, tugging down the V of his shirt; each Spice Girl lined up in a row. I yank it off the shelf and please, just imagine it, opening something this beautiful with your own face inside. Your own shape shining on real paper. You could trace me with a pencil if you wanted to.

I show my mother, and then the grocery clerk, and then my mother again. *Look, look, it's ME!* My mother grabs all the issues off the shelf, but I tell her to put them back. *People won't see it if we buy them ALL.* I hand her the one magazine.

You're smart, she says, *I'll keep you.* She pets the top of my head.

Can we go in the bar and show Daddy?

He's busy, she says.

It's true—he always was.

That night, I read my ad aloud to myself under the covers, with a flashlight. I pretend to be a stranger finding me, folding a dog-ear over to remember my black-and-white face—a very interesting girl. I check and recheck the words to make sure my address is printed correctly beneath my picture—7127 Baybreeze Court, Boca Raton, Florida, 33428. I wait for a pebble-tap at the window, a flashlight pulsing in a Morse code I will instantly understand, telling me to get moving, to come outside, to leave quietly. My bag is packed in my closet—it's been there for months. I wait for any knock of the living.

Hundreds of letters arrive. Every day, after school, my mother pulls right up to the mailbox for me. We are supposed to have uniform mailboxes here in Boca, rounded and silver like bullets, but my mother does not believe in uniform. Instead, she purchased and installed a spray-painted hummingbird mailbox the color of a sunset, with wooden wings that spread two feet wide. I pull the bird's beak to open the mouth of it, and letters burst from its tin stomach. I gather the letters in my arms, between my legs in the car; I press them to my chest.

Each letter comes in a different envelope, a new shape and bulk, different arrangements and patterns of stamps. Each smells like it came from another world entirely, and I do my best to imagine each country, state, bedroom, glass of milk. My favorite stamps have exotic animals printed on them. My favorite stamps come from Madagascar.

What's Madagascar? I ask my father one night. My father knows everything.

He spins our globe in his hands until the Earth looks small. He lists off the oceans, the tiny seas. He sips his drink.

Here, he says, pointing. *Right here. This little chunk of land in the water.*

And kids live there? I ask. *Kids like me?*

Kids live everywhere, he says, and I'm terrified. Until this moment, I have never even considered children my age living outside the Mainland. That's what we call the United States in my family. Everything except Hawai'i is the Mainland. My Grandma Rose is from China, and Hawai'i, but in my mind she has always been curled over and ancient. Pink foam rollers in her hair, fingers like ginger root. Never, ever a child.

Most of my letters come from other girls in elementary schools. They tell me about their P.E. teachers, some hobbies, what their parents make them for dinner; they include the loopy initials of their crushes. Honestly, I'd expected more. I write back to as many as I can, but too many come. I keep the unanswered in the bottom of my dresser, the ones that do the least for me. Whenever I drop a new letter into the dark of that drawer, I open the drawer very quickly, looking away, blinking back the guilt of it.

And then there are the men. The men mostly write about their dreams. They dream of gangrenous toes and a God with pierced ears and Bill Clinton dressed in a nightgown. Sometimes, they confess things to me: *I want to move to California. I feel like a failure and was born a failure and will never not be a fat, old, failure. I'd like to learn to play the piano and leave my wife.* They can trust me, they write, and I believe them. I have always been talented at keeping secrets. So far, it's been my only job.

One man always asks me questions about riding my horses and how that must feel. To tame something so wild and dangerous, like a gun loaded right between my legs.

Jet, *like the plane,* is my favorite of the men. He wasn't the first man to write me, but I like his letters best. Jet has called me interesting, and sweet seeming, and a *different kind of pretty.* He believes that O. J. Simpson is a madman gone free. My mother doesn't trust O. J. either, so I immediately believe in this Jet.

Jet tells me he lives on a houseboat, but his address lists a street in Virginia Beach. He owns three yellow labs named after dead movie stars—no other family. Jet is fifty-one, my father's age, and he writes in tiny, lowercase letters—always a runny blue ink. He uses crisp, narrow envelopes that smell like something sour.

What do you think about most often? he recently asked me.

My ponies, I wrote. *And my heroes. Dominique Moceanu and the rest of the Magnificent Seven, but especially the white Dominique. I think about flying. I think about Drew Barrymore and how it would sound for Leonardo DiCaprio to say my name. I think about fax machines because those things are crazy. Mostly, I think about JonBenét Ramsey. She's my number one hero of all time.*

Jet tells me that I can call him J-Daddy and that this name is reserved only for me. Reading this feels like the first glint of something grown-up in my life, a slice through my stomach clean as a kite through the sky. *Reserved only for me.* I repeat these words. I address him this way in all my letters because I want to be *his*, and because he wants to be *mine*, and because nicknames sound so very adult. I write *Hello, J-Daddy,* and *My Dearest J-Daddy,* and *My Darling Dearest Daddy* with all capital *D*'s, *I want to know everything about everything you've ever done and I want to know how you did all of those things and were you scared when you did them?*

I've stopped writing everybody else back, except the girl in Madagascar. The drawer has thickened so much it's difficult to close. If you want to know the truth, marrying Jet feels like the only thing left to do.

Doris Day, Judy Garland, Rita—these are the names of his dogs. Jet loves glamour. He promises that one day he'll show me the classic films of our lives, promises that once I see the actresses' faces blown up in Technicolor, once I see the smoke of their cigarettes genie up and out of the screens, their slender wrists, their backless silks, I will understand what it means to be a woman. This is something I am dying to know.

I have a future with Jet, and that seems to be something all girls are supposed to have. I hear this word all the time at school, at home: *Future. How about your future? Time* magazine recently published a story about cars driving themselves on roads paved with magnets, but I can't imagine myself inside one of them. Before Jet, I imagined myself murdered by twenty, or off with Joni Baloney in a tent somewhere, nowhere in this future.

Now, I think maybe we could grow old together on his boat. I can see us holding each other through the darkness of Y2K, surviving. The world will rise with water, and I will learn how to swim. Maybe this future-me will even wear glasses. *Our future*, Jet writes. *You and me. You are my future.*

Lately, my mother walks around the house all night long while I'm trying to sleep. *Ignore her when she does that*, my father says, *she's just zombie walking, restless legs*, but when he's out at night, which is usually, I like to lead her back into her bedroom like a horse into a trailer. I say, *Shhhh, shhhh*—it's just us. My hands tuck the blankets around her frame; my fingers comb through her hair. She stares right through me and says, *What kind of person will you be?*

Jet has been very specific about our plans to meet. I cannot tell anyone about it, and I suppose that makes it better. I know my father will not like J-Daddy, but perhaps, I think, my mother might come around. Maybe Jet will tell her about his childhood, and about his dogs, the way he holds them at night when they're too frightened to sleep, all the things he has told me. He could tell her about our real love, describe what it means for me to be an old soul, how he is the only one who has ever, truly, clearly, seen it.

We'll live on my boat, Jet's been writing, *and travel the whole world.*
I get seasick, I write, *I get it real bad.*
Not with me, he promises.

All I have to do is get out to the beach. Jet will drive his boat down the coast to Florida; he wants it that much. I will watch *Natural Born Killers* with my mother, our favorite movie, maybe sit at the typewriter and send Joni Baloney to the pyramids in Egypt, or the Academy Awards. My mother will say, *So where's your father tonight? Want to make a bet?* But I won't take her up on our game, not tonight, no. I'll say, *Go to sleep, MomMom*, and wait for her to take her pills, the medicines, the smokes and bottles she and my father keep locked away in their bathroom. At two A.M. I will call a local limo company from my new landline. I'll walk down the driveway in my satin blue pajamas, meet the driver under the stars. *To the beach!* I'll say, handing over the wad of cash I've been saving from my allowance. *An interesting girl like you must have very important places to go*, the driver will say, opening a door for me. We'll drive. I'll stick my head out into the salty heat until it crisscrosses my hair.

At the beach, I'll see it: the ocean glittering like a sheet of foil; Jet's boat, lit up, windows blushing in the night, anchored. The sand will be cool by now, damp and hard between my toes as I run toward the water, toward the figure of a man splashing out of his boat, toward the lame waves frothing at the pier. We'll meet in the water, Jet and I, and he'll pick me up in his arms to carry me the rest of the way to his boat, our home, where music spools out of his radio. Jet will finally get to see the way I look when I laugh, and he will hear me sing his favorite lyrics, impressed that I know *many* words to *many* songs. I am cold, and he can see that through the satin, so he wraps his right arm around my chest and presses his other hand into my hand, and I say,

Look at the difference of our hands, look how you could crush me, in my voice that has always been little. He is moved by this statement, and takes my whole face in his grip. I open my mouth for him and, for the first time, feel what it is. He tastes like something adultlike but new—crushed leather couch, cinnamon—too perfect to ruin.

When I think about it, I write in a letter, *I touch where I'm not supposed to, and when I touch like that I want all the lights out in my room so that I cannot see where it is I am touching.*

There is a reason why you like it, Jet replies, *and that reason is shame.*

Do you know what it means to be a grown-up? This was one of the first things Jet ever wrote to me. *You'd have to be very adult in order to answer such a question.*

Do I know?

My mother found the letters when we were packing to move. A new house: bigger, grander, white with eggplant trim; behind the front door, a swimming pool. She approached me in our laundry room. I can still see the both of us: my mouth hanging open with its metal and springs, my mother's hand opening and closing a fist. She didn't know where to situate her anger, where to store it. She still hasn't found the proper place.

My mother lay the white envelopes on the dryer. Her chin, too steady. Even now, when I see piles of mail, I swear I can smell the floral pinch of detergent.

There are bad people in this world, she said, *and bad people always want the good ones.*

But he's my pen pal, I said.

No more letters after we move, she said. *Not unless they're to Hawai'i, to Grandma, and I'll read them first.*

She cupped her hands around the back of my neck. My mother. I can still feel her there. Water dribbled from my eyes, and I nodded my head yes. Jet and I might find each other again after middle school, or high school, or maybe a summer in between. But in this moment, with the weight of my head held firm, I knew I didn't need him. Jet would have to wait.

Do you know what it means to be a grown-up?

How much I wanted it before I knew.

EVEN THE DOGS

It's four A.M. on my father's birthday, and he's in his red-sleep, the kind where his skin pulses the color of roast beef and his wedding ring looks ingrown. This is his don't-wake-me-for-three-days kind of sleep, the face-down-on-the-tile kind of sleep, which is where he is now, naked, on my parents' bathroom floor.

I said wake the fuck up, ass-blob. My mother pushes her bare foot into his back until it leaves a yellow-white imprint. A dead-body color. My father moans, and the sound drools out onto the tiles. His eyes wink on like lagging televisions. My mother curses in Chinese—*you fucking fat cow!*—the only Chinese phrase we both still use.

Why does he sleep on the floor like this? I ask. *Your bed is so nice.*

One day you'll understand how good a floor can feel, she says.

It's true: their bed is nice. I sleep in it sometimes. Night terrors don't leave me alone come three A.M. lately—the shadows of limbs behind my windows, visions of blown-off faces with dangling eyeballs—and my parents are always awake, up to something, alive.

He plays dead because cold tile feels good to fucking fat cows after double fisting Sambucas all night with strippers, says my mother, each word louder than the one before it.

Sometimes, Mom buckles me into the car in the middle of the night to collect my father from these strippers. That's the word she uses: *collect*. My father is always in need of *collecting*. The strippers seem sweet to me. They swing their shoes by the straps, tap their nails against my mother's car window, saying, *Come on, Chinadoll, relax, it's nothing.* They call my father *Big Boss*, or *Mad Man*, depending on the night.

My mother walks over to the bedroom closet. She claws into my father's hanging clothes and tosses each item at his body—limp, cotton skins.

Both of you, get dressed, she says. *We're going for a drive.*

My mother drives without saying a word. No music. No radio. I am curled up in the backseat, surprised to see that my father's face is not asleep but alert. His eyes are wet and wide in that orange glow of night-road, that perfect combination of street lamp and moonlight that casts a terrific sadness, or wildness, on any face in its spell. I wonder if he and my mother will touch each other.

Where we going? he says. I have never heard my father's voice— which is usually brass and gravel and all New York—go soft.

My mother doesn't say a word. She stays focused on the road, fingers gripped around the steering wheel, leaning into it. She's in another world, I think.

Honey? Hello? You hear me?

We are headed to the Florida Everglades, a one-hour drive from our house in Boca Raton. I know this because every school in South Florida takes a field trip here, and every kid hates it. On our class trip, we wore mosquito masks and earplugs and rode through the murky

waters on an airboat. The whole thing smelled like a scum-skinned
fish tank. A giant fan blasted as our boat moved through tall grasses,
gators swiveling around. I didn't learn anything.

Now, in the car, the grasses are thin, bleached bodies in our head-
lights. I touch the backseat window with my toes, as if I might be able
to feel their scrape. There are no other cars, no signs or signals.

How you doing back there, kid? My father moves his arm back to
give me three quick pats on the cheek. He does this when he's in
trouble—loves me like this. It's his way of reminding my mother that
he can function in the world in more ways than one. He can be a father,
a family man, and also the *Big Boss*.

I don't say a word either. I love my father more than anyone, for
reasons I have yet to understand, but I feel more loyal to my mother.
This is what I write about in my diary most days, though I haven't
stacked up the logic. All I know is that I want my father to enjoy our
car ride together, but I will also bite his hand if it comes near me again.

You know, honey, if the kid wasn't in the backseat—
My mother looks at him now, though she still says nothing.

I'm just sitting here thinking to myself: Self, if the kid wasn't here and all—
She smiles, slanted and deviant.

People would find me, you know, he says. *The Everglades—typical.
Police would troll this place first. If the kid wasn't here . . . you know your
kid is in here, right? She's no dummy even if you think so. She's watching
all of this. She's old enough to talk. Can somebody fucking say something?*

If the kid wasn't here. I am used to these words.

We finally pull up to a wooden fence, a damp field. In the middle
of the field there's a basket the size of a small car. Beside the basket, a
striped sheet of reds and purples rippling far across the grass like
a bloody sea.

What's all this now?

A balloon ride.

I don't do heights.

Happy birthday, you fucking fat cow.

What we are is up in the air. My mother stands in the corner of the balloon basket, all on her own, loving it. She closes her eyes and stretches her arms to feel the first hot slab of sunrise. She looks so peaceful here, just like this, and I know she would jump if she could, if she could do it fast enough, before getting caught and dragged back in by her sneakers. She could tilt her weight headfirst and leave us here—simple. Years later, when she swallows a bottle of pills and survives the overdose, I'll wonder if she considers this moment on the balloon—the sun, clear air, *Kealani*—what could have been a sure thing.

Can we quiet it down a sec? says my father. *I need a sec. I need to relax.*

Can't, captain, says our balloon man. He wears overalls. Tiny, fish teeth. His name, we learn, is Dwayne. Dwayne turns a valve to get the fire going every couple of minutes. It's a deafening blast, meant to keep the balloon warmer than the atmosphere, meant to keep us afloat.

I have never seen my father afraid of anything, but here he is, knuckles bulging like popcorn, his chest thumping wild. He stares down, and then up, and then back at me, shaking. The day stings against my arms.

I need something to drink or I'll be sick, says my father.

Aye, aye, captain. Dwayne opens the mouth of a cooler, uncorks a bottle of champagne into the dirty rag in his fist. He pours the gold liquid into a plastic chute until it dribbles over. He hands it to my father, who chugs it down. The foam catches on the scratch of his chin.

What is this? Pepsi?

It's what we've got, sir.

I need a drink.

Sir, it's all we have.

I'll drink the fuel, says my father, looking up into the flames. Dwayne laughs a vibrating cackle and pats my father on the back. Dwayne is the only one laughing. I look at the fuel tanks in the center of the basket. I count them.

Up here, the only sound from below is the dogs. After the valve is opened, after each burst of heat, the dogs bark in unison all over South Florida. I can't tell if they feel terrified or empowered by our sound, but somehow I feel safe with them down there, in time with our flight, listening. I look at the Everglades, the strands of water swerving up to the highways, like something ophidian.

If I screamed, would the dogs hear that, too? I ask.

Prob'ly not, says Dwayne. *It's the pitch is all wrong.*

I know this, of course. I am a very quiet girl. Even the dogs would miss me.

Nice birthday gift your honey got you here, Dwayne says to my father. *Renting out the whole gig like this. Pretty penny.*

I got money, says my father. His face is shining with sweat. He rests his forehead against his arms crossed on the edge of the basket, lifts it, sets it down, lifts it, sets it down. I grab his wrist and dig my thumb into the soft underside of it, something he has done for me before, on boats, when I am yakking into the deep blue. *Let it out*, he has said, *chum the boat.*

Got the life, don't you? says Dwayne.

Guess so, says my father.

Some life we got, says my mother.

I have a pony, I say.

We've got money, says my father.

In twenty minutes, it's time to land. The winds have picked up, and our balloon is headed south, toward Miami.

Can't you just turn it around? asks my father.

You can't steer a balloon, says Dwayne, *you ride Mother Nature.*

Dwayne focuses on dials, flips switches, and ties cords around a hook to open some vents in the balloon. He wants to level out the air temperature, he says, until we fall. Ropes slide in and out of his hands.

Chase car will come get us, he says, *wherever we land. God's judgment from here.*

God is dead, says my father.

Can't we ride it all the way into the ocean? says my mother.

I can't swim, I say. *Remember?*

They don't.

As we descend, the dogs get louder. I think I hear every single one of them. The wind carries us west in rapid jerks, and my father sinks down inside the balloon until he is sitting, clasping his knees.

We won't make a field, Dwayne says. *Hold on.*

We float down to a cul-de-sac where every house is painted in a Candy Land palette. I pick a favorite house—mint colored, like my Auntie T's—and squeeze the wicker as we inch closer and closer to it. Dwayne leans with his ropes. *Incoming!*

Our basket skids across the shingles of the minty house's roof. The shingles flip like the scales of a gator. A few ping off. We bonk off the cullis as Dwayne tugs at more cords, lets more air in and out of our balloon. He does not panic as a man exits the house in his bathrobe.

The hell you doing, landing on my house!

We hit the man's lawn with a thud. The basket begins to tip as the envelope of the balloon gets caught up with another wind. My mother laughs maniacally, clapping her hands. My father opens the basket door and collapses on the grass.

Who's paying for this roof? the man screams. *Look at this roof!* The bald sheen of his head is amazing.

Happy birthday, my mother says to no one.

Good excuse for a home makeover! says Dwayne.

I want to go again, I say.

I hop out of the basket and find my legs. I watch my father crawl his way across the lawn, dry heaving, pulling clumps of grass between his fingers. As a boy, my father made a black cape with a chain around the neck and wore it everywhere: the dentist's office, the dinner table, school, Temple. The neighbor kids teased him so badly his mother threw it away.

He stands up, wipes the dirt from his pockets.

JUST ONE LOOK IS WORTH A

THOUSAND WORDS

The mole is brown and speckled and sprouted with a few wired hairs. It's on my left hand, just above my wrist, the size of the diamond on my mother's ring finger. It matches her mole—she reminds me of this—as she holds her delicate hand out next to mine, comparing.

But my mother's mole looks elegant, a black beauty mark.

I hate my mole.

I hate every new part of my body that curves and bumps and swells and darkens as the years go on.

One night, alone in our kitchen, I pull the largest, sharpest knife from the block. I don't know why I choose a knife so big. I suppose I like the severity of it. I rest my hand on the cutting board on the island in the center of our kitchen. Without thinking much about it, I catch the knife at the base of the mole, gnaw onto my lip, brace for it. When the knife cracks down onto the wood, the mole is not gone—it's dangling. It's grey now, dead looking, like a single

Sno-Caps candy. I cut the rest of the way. I am very professional about this operation.

I press wads of paper towels to the wound. I press, press. When I take it off, the blood and hole where my mole used to be glimmers like a garnet under the kitchen lights.

One month later, the mole grows back. It's a different color this time—cream.

Then the speckles come back. The hairs.

But we matched, says my mother. *How could you hurt yourself like that, and take off the way we matched?* She had cleaned up the blood. My mother did.

The next time, I use a smaller knife. In my bathroom.

I'm found out in the car, my hand dripping blood all over the taupe leather seats.

What the hell is wrong with you?

Blood stained the carpet of our Jaguar. It stained my dress. It was so red. Beautiful, like lace, the way it spread out.

The scar on my hand is subtle.

WOMANLY THINGS

Penelope does not want to be a ballerina anymore. She wants her name shortened to Lee, her clothes more threadbare, used. She's my new friend Misty's older sister, and lately she's been playing the guitar for us—Fiona Apple, the Cranberries—her hair twisted in a long, slick braid, her words too big for either one of us to understand. Lee just began high school—five years older than we are—so Misty and I have taken to spying on her, asking every kind of question. We take our mental notes.

Because Lee likes to eat stir-fry, we eat it, too. She likes to balance baby corns like Jenga blocks, so I do this, too. When she begins writing songs, Misty and I write some, too. Lee's songs are about aching for and missing random stuff. The past, her innocence, a bag of jelly beans, camp. She strums an acoustic guitar pressed against her bare stomach, whisper-humming the words with her eyes squeezed closed.

Misty and I write about Jewish boys becoming men, the echo range of seashells, a secret place in the sky. We write about blonde girls and their supreme blonde beauty and about how nobody will ever love us because we are neither blonde nor beautiful (*When I see you, my heart melts down / Down so far I sink to the ground / But when I see you with that dumb blonde / I scream to myself, What have I done wrong?*). Misty is white, with a real kid-like body, and we both suffer from freckles. We sing about this until our throats crack like radio static. We call our two-person act Kotton Kandy. We rename each other *Sparkle* (Misty) and *Shimmer* (me), promising to get out of Boca one day, pay for matching boob jobs, and forget who it was we were.

Lee listens to each one of our songs, nodding her head. She records us on a video camera with her hand balanced beneath a padded strap. She tells us we have *potential*. We believe her so much we keep writing, rehearsing, harmonizing, performing outside her bedroom.

You've got to really feel the music, she says. *Feel it like you're inside of it.*

Misty and I take turns calling the 800 number for The Box music video channel, punching in serial numbers to request Britney, Christina, Mandy, Jessica. We suck on Warheads and wait for our girls to appear, carefully learning their hair flips and choreographies, the shapes and characteristics of their belly buttons.

On her boom box, Lee blasts a song about going down on a man in a theater.

This is Alanis Morissette, she says. *Take notes on this attitude. Take notes on the feeling.*

Later, when I ask my mother what it means to go down on someone in a theater, she tells me it's a way that two people share popcorn. Everybody does it.

Back home, on my Uncle Whack's black box of cable, I've found something I quite like. On channels 590–595, naked people fuck each other. They say this word all the time on the channels. They say *Fuck my face*, and *I'm going to fuck you stupid till your brain shoots out of your ears*, and *Get over here, my little fucktoy*. Once, after school, Misty and I took turns saying the word—*fuck*—the first time for us both while we hung from the school monkey bars. We whispered it at first, repeated it back and forth until we built some momentum, and after a minute or two we were screaming it—*FUCK!*—until we laughed so hard it felt like ghosts were crying out of our faces.

When I'm alone, though, I can't stop thinking about *It*, that burn that makes me want to turn the television off but also keep it running forever. I discovered *It* around the time of Jet's letters, and then again, recently, in the bathtub, the showerhead turned all the way to level three. *It* is all I can think about lately; I can't seem to stop. It's like a fist grabs hold of my brain, squeezing it, until my own thoughts pop out and suddenly I've got somebody else's crazy thoughts. I like to go until it hurts.

I tell Misty none of this. *It* only happens alone. But when I get to folding my pillows in half and straddling them at night, sometimes I hear the pike of my Grandma Rose's voice. The first time I tried to swat a mosquito from my arm, she pinched me by the chin, screaming *That could be your grandfather!* Every fly is somebody dead and sacred. Every cockroach is watching. I wonder if my ancestors know about the showerhead, the hairbrush, the pencil, the pillow lumps, the candlestick, the toothbrush; if they're screaming *Ai yah!* from a spider web somewhere beneath my bathroom sink.

Lee goes to a special art school and hangs out with other former ballerinas. The metallic spandex and blossoms of tulle are long gone, only present in the framed photographs her mother hangs on the wall in a perfect, chronological row. Some of Lee's friends have short hair, shaved like a boy's, and Misty and I have never seen any grown girl (who's not a *mom*) with this kind of hair before, and we laugh about it, ask Lee why her friends do it. Why the baggy pants? Why this look? Why don't you all wear glitter on your eyes like high schoolers are allowed to do? You're supposed to look sexy, we say. You're supposed to wear tight, womanly things—things that hug you in all of your womanly places.

Misty is still a ballerina. I show up to her classes in East Boca and wait behind the glass. I attend every recital and *Nutcracker* performance because it's nice to support my friend, but it's even nicer to watch her teacher, Jaqueline, kick-kick her legs in a leotard. I can see every dent of her body under that skin-like fabric. I can even see her breathing.

Whenever Lee brings her friends over, Misty and I sled down the staircase on linen couch cushions. We usually get snagged somewhere in the middle and tumble the rest of the way down. Lee takes our cushions under her armpits and leads us back up to Misty's room. She looks sad in the doorway the way adults often do, and she says, *Can you please just leave us alone tonight? Can you guys just listen to Hanson or take your quizzes or write your songs? Anything?*

Misty and I love the Hanson brothers. We love their high-pitched voices, their shoulder-length golden hair. *I wonder what kind of conditioner they use*, I say. My hair is cut like the top of a mushroom so that it fits neatly beneath my riding helmet, and because I refused to brush my hair—it was not my choice. I think these boys look more womanly than me.

I kiss Misty's posters on the wall, and she says, *Ew, get your slobber off my Taylor!* We move on to our magazines and take the quizzes in back to learn what category of *flirt* we could be. Between each quiz, we play a round of *Our Game*. In *Our Game*, we try to predict our sexual futures. We tell each other what our future boys and men might look like—*I'm going to lose my V-card to a boy with long, long hair, like Hanson*, I say. *A boy who is cute, but also, pretty*. We predict where these boys will take us. Where they will kiss us one day. Where they will *fuck* us. *Rapids Water Park*, Misty says, *for my V-card. I want it in the lazy river, on a doughnut tube, under the water where nobody has to know*.

When I am not watching channels 590–595 in my parents' bedroom, when I am not thinking about Monica Lewinsky and her wet cigar, when *It* hits, I've been returning to an airplane with the Wicked Witch of the West. I'm enjoying my flight, seat reclined, drinking an orange soda from a plastic cup, until the Wicked Witch tells me I've had enough. She pulls a piece of sharp metal from beneath my seat, some sort of *necessary safety appliance*, and she lifts my uniform school skirt, shoves the metal up between my legs. After that, she wraps a fresh diaper around these parts until the tape slices into my hips. I want to suck the mole off her face. The Witch opens the emergency door, as if to admire the view. She tells me to *come, come*, look out at the world, before she pushes me out of the plane and into the sky. I go soaring off into the bent horizon of blue, and eventually land in a field of sawgrass, ass first, the metal piece impaling me under my diaper, stabbing out my insides. It feels good. I spit up ribbons of red into the grass. The Wicked Witch tells me I'm a very sweet girl, that I've done a fine job. She rubs my back in small circles.

When my hands stop, when I yank my eyes open, it takes minutes to blink away the color green. *I'm so sorry*, I say, to no one in particular, waiting for that witch to die out with my ceiling full of stars.

One school night, during *Our Game*, Misty and I hear Lee click open the front door for her friend Paula. We stand at the top of the stairs to say *Hello*. Paula is the pretty-boy type, I think. Her parachute pants hang below the knobs of her hipbones, and she's not wearing a bra. *Go back in your room*, says Lee. She is more stern than usual, more guarded about this friend. She takes Paula's hand and leads her to the couch. She flicks off the lights. *Go to bed, okay?*

We go to our room. Ears up against the door. We want to know what Lee and Paula are talking about more than we've ever wanted anything. A few minutes go by before Misty says, *Let's get some ice cream*. I like this excuse.

Yes, I say. *I need it now*.

We open our door and tiptoe down the stairs. Lee and Paula are still on the living room couch. Their limbs are interwoven like cat's cradle strings. The television turns their skin deep purples and blues, though we cannot see what it is they are watching. What we see is Lee's heart-shaped face on Paula's shoulder, and then Paula's hand on Lee's head, and then a lift, a look, their two noses coming together, fingers rubbing the baby hairs around their ears. They kiss for a long while, and I think I must be dreaming. Misty's eyes go wobbly with shine, and she jerks my hand, leading the way back up to her room.

Back to Our Game, she says. *I want a French boy, in Paris. He'll take me on his scooter and we'll eat fancy bread and cheese and we'll fuck slowly to a Brandy song.*

During a fifth-grade field trip, our class goes to the movies. We see *Forces of Nature*, starring Ben Affleck, who is afraid of airplanes, and Sandra Bullock, who is much braver than that. I sit between Misty and Duke Freeman, who goes by Devilish Dukie, and my mother sits behind us as a chaperone (all the class moms take turns, but the kids like when it's my mom; she's the *chillest*, and she even let us watch a bootleg VHS of *Titanic* in our hotel room—naked scene and all—when we took a class trip to Disney). Duke looks like a Hanson brother. His lips are a deep pink, his hair like corn silk. I want any excuse to talk to Duke during the movie, so when Sandra and Ben are somewhere on the road, I reach over into Duke's popcorn bag, lean into his ear, and ask, sincerely, *May I go down on you?*

Duke does not understand my request, but, somehow, my mother hears it.

After the movie, when we are back home, she tells me not to share popcorn anymore.

Popcorn, and Alanis Morissette, she says, *are best enjoyed when you're older.*

I mention Paula and Lee the morning after we watched them from the stairs. *What do you think they were doing?* I ask Misty. *Do you think Paula slept over?*

I don't think they were doing anything, she says.

We never got the ice cream, I say.

You watch too many movies, she says. *You get confused.*

I ask about the incident for weeks, almost every day, until Misty tells me to stop asking. *I wrote my sister an e-mail about it*, she says, *just to make sure.*

Did your sister write back?

They're just friends, Misty says. *Best friends.*

Like us?

We never see Paula again, but from then on, when I write our love songs, I write them with Lee and Paula in mind. I want to live inside that feeling, fumble my way through it, the way Lee taught us. I think about that haircut, my craving for ice cream; their hands had such purpose. I think about the look just before the happening.

SHOW NAME

Uncle Whack isn't really my uncle, and his hair isn't really white. He bleaches it to look this way, shaves the sides of his head clean to get a stripe of skunkish Mohawk. He's my real Uncle Kai's best friend, and they are trying to get sober together; they are keeping their hands busy. Uncle Whack's the one who rigged up the illegal satellite dish on our roof and the "black box" with an infinity of cable. He shoves playing cards into the box, sometimes a spent matchbook. *This trips the system*, he says, *Abracadabra*.

My two uncles like to hammer up on our roof while I'm trying to study Latin. They mow the lawn, scrub our water tanks. They pour jugs of chlorine and chemicals into our fountain out front until it looks carbonated. My mother is proud of her little brother and his friend. She knows they're trying to be good, and clean from dope, which is something she also wants very badly for herself. When my uncles are not fixing up the house for cash, they're making calls for my father. In our living room, all of them scream at people on the phone and sell stocks for someone named Jordan Belfort. This is something I won't understand until the day I do.

My parents are leaving town again. *So mega lucky*, say the kids at school. *Rich parents, all those vacays. Do you get back souvenirs? Pets?* But I'm never really sure where they go. Last month, I know my father went to South Africa to visit my half brothers, who live in Johannesburg with their mother. I know this because my father got into some sort of trouble on the plane. Some men in suits decided that smoking in the sky is dangerous, a menace, and banned it just a few days before his nineteen-hour flight. At the fifth hour, my father snuck a smoke in the airplane bathroom with his head in the toilet, flushing every few seconds to suck the evidence down. He returned home with some stories about this incident, and a mousetrap-sized metal dulcimer for me.

What would you say to Uncle Whack taking care of you this week, huh? Does that sound like fun? Uncle Whack can take you to Blockbuster. I bet he'll even watch you ride! My mother is using the voice she uses when she wants something. It climbs up and down octaves—a sing-song, composed, *motherly* pitch.

But where are you going now?

A romantic getaway, okay? Don't worry about that, okay? We need mommy-daddy time. And next week, Daddy will take you to Vegas.

Okay.

I don't want Uncle Whack to watch me ride horses. Riding is the only thing in the world that's my own. I took my dad for a ride only once, in North Carolina, around my birthday in July. He slung his right leg over an Appaloosa named Trigger, hooked his Gucci leather loafers into the western stirrups, and let me adjust his heels. I led him up Smith Mountain in a winding trot. My father smoked with his lips while both hands gripped the saddle horn, which I found particularly impressive.

Son, he said. *What do I do about, how do I go about, how do I—I forgot to wear underwear.*

Pick a side and move it all over, I said. I didn't know what it meant when I said it, but I'd heard this question and answer before with other men, on other trails.

My father wore a face bunched in pain for the rest of the trail. He couldn't keep his toes up, his shoulders square; he looked completely amateur, sloppy, bumbling. When I think about riding, this is what I love most: I have a power, a strength, a language with animals big enough to kill a person, easy. It's the one thing that I have.

Are you paying Uncle Whack to hang out with me? I ask.

He needs the money, my mother says. *He's on a good track, doing the good work. One day at a time.*

What about Uncle Kai?

He's not ready, she says. *Not responsible, not yet.*

Auntie T?

Auntie T isn't coming back for a while.

Fine, I say. *If we do grown-up stuff. But only if.*

My parents give Uncle Whack very clear instructions like they've been practicing for this moment all their lives—*Parenting*—to show somebody what it is they know.

She doesn't like to be left alone, says my mother, *especially at night. She has night terrors. Chronic nosebleeds, but she knows how to handle it. She can cook soup for herself, and mostly she'll read all day. Letters, too. You'll have to take her to the barn to feed her horses; you'll have to help her take her boots off—pull by the heel; you'll have to make sure she wears a helmet. You'll get it. And whatever you do, obviously, don't let anyone in this house without a warrant. Lock up. The alarm code is 7-11.*

When I'm older, I'll understand that this is around the time the FBI became interested in my father and his friends. My uncle. Jordan Belfort. Soon, our family will make headlines. But right now, I nod and say, *We are very private people, yes,* the way I've been taught. My father winks at me. He hands Uncle Whack a wad of cash, thick as a hockey puck, folded over in half. *Careful with her,* he says. *She's good.*

Uncle Whack is twenty-six years old, and I think he's the oldest friend I'll ever have. He wears blue basketball shorts with tiny pin-prick-sized holes all over them, pulled down to just above his knees. Above that, plaid boxers lumpy with his white tee. His face is a perfect boyish circle, dimpled in the cheeks, and sometimes he wears a side-ways baseball cap over the skunk-do. He doesn't look like any of my men on black box channels 590–595.

Got it, Mad Man, says Uncle Whack, giving a salute.

Almost forgot, says my father, handing him the keys to our car.

Careful with my Jag, he says. *I know people who'd take care of you if anything happens to my Jag. Yeah? Yeah?* He points to Uncle Whack and play-punches him in the chest. We all laugh along. Uncle Whack slings my father's bags over his shoulders—Louis Vuitton printed leather, matching—and straightens his back like a butler as he walks my parents to the limousine parked on our black yawn of driveway.

Next week, Vegas! screams my father. *Get ready, baby!*

I wave from the front door.

Did you know a rat lives inside our Jaguar? I ask.

Did you know is my favorite game to play with Uncle Whack. It makes me sound informed, knowledgeable.

Nah, ma, that ain't true. He tosses his baseball cap on our pink leather couch, then dives into it.

Did you know that rat attacks are real? The last one happened in New York in nineteen-seventy-something. Nobody believes me about the rat in our car because it lives in the backseat, but one day it's gonna rat attack me with a rat pack and my eyeballs will get chewed out by the time my parents get on the Sawgrass Expressway.

Damn, ma. Why you always so twisted? Uncle Whack pulls a pack of Parliament Lights from the waistband of his boxers. He bites into a filter, lights up, blows the smoke up into our skylight. A band of wavy light streams down on his body as if he's a saint.

Did you know smoking will kill you? I say, *But your body can and will repair itself within five years of your last cigarette?*

What are you, ten? Chill with that shit. You read that in the Cyclopedia?

Last week, a major anti-smoking organization came to our school and taught us about the dangers of tobacco. We sang a song about cigarettes to the melody of Peter Pan's "I Won't Grow Up," as a group of PTA parents and teachers filmed us on camcorders for a potential television commercial. *I won't light up!* we sang, *I will never smoke a day, 'cuz tobacco is EVIL, it'll take your youth away. 'Cuz cigarettes are awfuler than all the awful things that ever were, I'll never light up, never light up, never light up—not me!*

At the end of the day, a blonde dreidel of a woman passed around a pack of Salem Lights and told us all to sniff them and let the consequences spill over our hearts. I never wanted to let go of that pack. I wanted to absorb that woody, muscled smell. I wanted to be the blonde-permed Sandy at the end of *Grease*—zipped in black, tight and shining as a seal—desired and getting it once she chewed out that cigarette with a stiletto twist, as if it were a natural instinct, one she'd known all along. I pulled a Salem from the pack and ran it back and forth under my nose like a harmonica, feeling every bump of paper on my skin. I considered stealing it—*pocket? Caboodle?*—but the dreidel woman snapped at me to pass it on and so I did.

Did you know I'm going to be famous? I say. *A famous No Smoking advocate.*

Uncle Whack thumbs at the remote, and then another remote, and then a third. My father likes this setup: a six-foot big-screen TV, with three smaller TVs on top of it. This way, he can watch several games at the same time. Uncle Whack flicks ash into my father's ashtray on the couch.

So, whatcha wanna watch on Daddy Whack's black box?

I do not tell him the truth.

At the barn, Uncle Whack is afraid of the horses. I show him how to palm carrots into their mouths, fingers webbed away from the teeth, but Uncle Whack keeps his distance. He adjusts his hat, turns it forward and back, saying, *Nah, ma, I don't do big dogs.*

What's your guy's name? he asks.

I have four of them, I say. *But this one's my favorite.* I kiss my pony on the nose. *Nicky is his home name, but his show name is Cloud 9.* I'm convinced the temperature of Nicky's nose can predict the weather. Today, I feel rain.

What's a show name?

Your home name is, like, stupid. It's who you are at home. Alfie or Frisky or Wrinkles—usually kind of embarrassing. Your show name is the one you use in horse shows, and big stadiums, when you're all braided up and exactly who you want to be. They're jazzier. Better. My horses are

Cloud 9, Velvet Slippers, and Bid's Glitter Man, see? Tulip is my mini-pony, and she doesn't have a show name because she'll never grow up or be famous.

Uncle Whack rolls his eyes. I can tell he's not taking me seriously.

Wanna help me tack up? I ask.

Can I sit while I do it?

I guess.

I clasp Nicky into the crossties in the aisle of the barn. I ask Uncle Whack to hand over my bounce pad, my saddle. He flinches when I tighten the girth around Nicky's barrel-belly, saying, *Damn, yo, that's rough.* He loops the leather martingale around his own neck and smiles, *Giddyup, it's Uncle Whack!* I don't think he's ever been around horses before.

I remove Nicky's halter and wrap my arm around his head before I say, *Watch this*, plunging my fingers into his gums, behind his molars, his mouth grinding grassy foam onto my shirt as I lift a snaffle bit over his tongue. There is nothing exciting or impressive about putting a bridle on a horse, but I want to show Uncle Whack that I'm not afraid of teeth, that I can be firm and deliberate.

Did you know I brought Nicky to school for show-and-tell?

I think I heard about that, says Uncle Whack.

I took him on a course around the playground and we jumped the seesaw, back and forth. It was groovy. The school news did a whole segment on me.

Is that what fancy school's like these days? In the Rat's Mouth? Kids bringing their ponies to school and shit?

I'm going to Nationals this summer, you know, I say. *In Chicago. Then the Olympics, obviously. I'm kind of a big deal. I'm going to be the next Margie Goldstein Engle. Even she says I've got something special.*

That's 'cause you're a kid, says Uncle Whack. *Everyone talks up kids like they're special.*

I reach my left toe into my stirrup iron and swing myself up and over Nicky's body. No leg up, no mounting block. I want my fake uncle to know I am strong. In the ring, I warm up quickly: two-point, trot, canter. We move in tight circles. I jump courses without counting my strides. I want speed, not precision. When we fly, I yank on Nicky's mane, dive forward, ducking; I forget about form.

Uncle Whack is sitting on a lawn chair near the front of the barn. His legs are propped up on a tack box. He's not even looking at me. He's looking into his lap, checking his beeper.

I dig my spurs into the sides of Nicky's body. *Go, boy.* We build until the two of us are tight and furious as a storm wall. He froths at the mouth and neck; he can read me. We jump and jump and jump and jump until the insides of my legs burn with that feeling I can never seem to put away.

Her name is Lacey, and she's the kind of girl worth taking home to mom. She's got small feet and she's not afraid of anything; she's like a gypsy the way she moves around from couch to couch. A peach on her that you wouldn't believe—Lacey. No last name.

This is what Uncle Whack tells me anyway, or maybe some of it is what I've gathered about Lacey from the words I clip out and keep from their conversations, things I may have even imagined from their code-talking. I keep the words in a list in my journal below the title, TOTAL FACTS KNOWN ABOUT LACEY, NO LAST NAME.

The thing is, Uncle Whack says, *Lacey lives in Tampa.*

The thing is, he says, *I need to see her.*

From the way Uncle Whack speaks to Lacey on our landline, I think she must have broken his heart. I've overheard my mom use this voice before, at night, with my father—that desperate, animal breathing between unrelated phrases—*Please, Would you?, Stay.* On the other end, I hear Lacey's sighs rattle the receiver in a wet-sounding static. She speaks slowly, *Oh, Wendall, Don't,* and that's about all I hear from her. Uncle Whack counts facts on his fingers, recalling small things they have in common—*the show with the lady with the vase on her head; the man at the fair! The way he popped his son?*—phrases I can only assume are inside jokes they once shared, years ago.

Lil Kiwi, he says, hanging up the phone. *You mind if I call you that?*

I guess I don't mind, I say.

He lights a smoke and scoots his feet up on the couch. His knees tuck in as if he were a little kid, wanting something.

It's just that I never know what to call you. T Kira, T, TT, Takara. T Kira is kind of a hood-ass name for a prep school Chink, you know that? Uncle Whack pulls this name, *Lil Kiwi,* from an armband my friend Jenny made me. She cut a ribbed sock straight across in two neat slices to make a stretchy band of fray. She colored it highlighter green, bedazzled a few stones, and scrawled LIL KIWI in the jagged graffiti letters she's been practicing.

This is your rap name, she'd said. *I'm Bana, short for banana, and you're Lil Kiwi. Together we can be some dope-ass rapping fruit. No more of that Jewey Jennifer shit.*

Uncle Whack pulls on his smoke and offers me a fist pump.

I need you to be cool about something, he says. *You're cool though. Aren't you?*

Uncle Whack offers me three promises if I say yes to Tampa. We can go to Busch Gardens and ride as many roller coasters as I want;

he'll buy me the best, fanciest dinner in the world—*a real date, me and you*, he says; Lacey will take me shopping, and style my hair, and trim my nails, *whatever girls do with girls.*

I don't want to do girl things with Lacey. I don't want to see Lacey's face, or get to know the inner workings of Lacey, or hear Lacey speak to Uncle Whack in her breathy, papery voice, *Oh, Wendall*, gripping his hand, or kissing his eyelids, or cupping a flame to his cigarette, *You know you shouldn't smoke, darling! It's bad for you!*

But then there's this thought, the thought that makes the roof of my mouth tingle, that makes me feel different around Uncle Whack than the way I feel around my dad, or Uncle Kai. What it is—so simple: He will learn to love me. He will learn to love me before he gets to her. *Let's go*, I say. *I'm cool.*

We drive northwest to Tampa in my parents' Jaguar, with the top up.

The rats will get us more easily this way, I say. *They're scared of the wind.*

I don't play like that, says Uncle Whack. *The wind? My hair? No bueno.* He slicks back the skunk stripe with more hair gel. He looks extra polished—jeans instead of the basketball shorts, a shave that makes his chin look like a new sponge. He looks so nice it makes the hairs on the back of my neck go wired, and it also repulses me.

When is Lacey going to meet us? I ask.

I don't know yet, ma, he says. *Gotta wait for the beep.* He taps his beeper a few times, hooked on his belt loop, to remind me that it's there. He lights a cigarette with the red snail coil of the car lighter.

Is she really the right girl for you? I ask. *For real, for real?*

Always has been, he says. *Cross my heart and hope to die.*

It smells different up in Tampa, on the other side of the state. Swampier, I think. Billboards with goopy fetuses on them dash by. Alien-looking creatures that I want to squeeze in my hands like putty. *I have a heartbeat*, they read. *Do the right thing.*

When do we get to go on our date? I ask. It's getting dark, and the mere fact of evening makes my body buzz with current.

Lacey hasn't come through yet, he says, *so let's hit up some grub.*

Uncle Whack drives us to a freight train, plugged right into the ground.

I used to come here all the time, he says. *Choo choo!* He pulls his arm like he's a conductor, but I don't laugh. He opens the door for me. *M'lady.*

We sit facing each other in a small booth on the train. White tablecloths. A single rose in a plastic vase. Older couples sit around us in baseball caps—the Dolphins, the Canes, the Heat.

You ever try a steak before? Uncle Whack asks me. *Filet mignon? Best of the best?*

I don't think so, I say. *Mostly I eat a lot of pigs. And Campbell's soup. And lobster.*

Well, tonight's the night, he says, clapping his palms and rubbing them together. *I got the Mad Man's cash, and a hot date!*

We'll share a filet, he tells a waitress. *Rare.*

When the steak comes, I watch Uncle Whack slice it and fork a cube on his tongue. I watch him chew with his mouth open, the way

I am always told not to do, with fleshy fibers of red flashing between his teeth. A pool of oily blood shines around the meat, and I slice off a piece of my own. I take it between my teeth, then into my mouth. I suck the juices, bitc. The saltiness sticks in my molars as I grind my jaw and slice some more.

This is the best moment of my life, I say, looking at him. I mean it.

After dinner, Uncle Whack pulls us into a Red Roof Inn. The red neon letters look like cartoon daggers. *Can we stay somewhere else?* I want to know. *I don't think I like it here.*

We're not rolling up to the Ritz, ma, he says. *You're not with mommy and daddy.*

There are two beds inside the room. A brown, sticky carpet between them. When I sit on the foot of the bed, I feel the other half of the mattress rise up. The ceiling is covered in a popcorn plaster, and I imagine a chunk of it falling into my mouth in the middle of the night, choking me. I do not want to die in a Red Roof Inn.

Look, a TV, says Uncle Whack. *You're used to those.* He flips through the channels—a rainbow of static, a weather report, Nickelodeon, a lion tearing up a zebra. *Fun!* he says. *Make yourself comfortable so you can sleep, okay ma?*

I go into the bathroom to change into my lavender silk pajama set. I look in the mirror, examine my crooked bangs, the holes in my ears pierced too high up, the hair sprouting between my eyebrows. My buckteeth peek out so far from between my lips that it's difficult to close them. I do not want to look like a baby anymore. I do not want to die in a Red Roof Inn.

When I walk back into the bedroom, Uncle Whack is counting the wad of cash on his bed.

Listen to me, he says, sitting down. *I've got to go find Lacey now. That cool?*

That is not cool, I say. *That is definitely not cool.*

I won't be long, he says. *You'll fall asleep and I'll be back. You'll wake up tomorrow and Uncle Whack'll be right here, ready for the roller coasters, okay? You like that Kumba ride, don't you? That big blue?*

I feel it in my throat first. The tight knot that always unfurls itself into a shakiness all over my face. From there I can never stop the tears from coming, and I hate myself for it. I slam my fists into the mattress.

Don't leave me, I wail. *Please, I love you, don't leave me.*

It's okay, ma, he says. He moves over to my bed to hug me. He pulls my face into his chest. *Shhhhh, it's okay, girl. Damn, damn, you're just a kid.*

I kick myself under the covers and tell him I'll never speak to him again. I'll tell my parents that he kidnapped me for ransom as soon as I can find a phone. I'll run away. I'll drown myself, facedown, in the motel bathtub. *La la la*, I sing. *I'm not even listening to you.* The thought of him leaving feels worse than any other time I've ever been left; I didn't know this one was coming.

I'll be back soon, he says, *promise*, and the door slams before I can take any of it back.

The next morning, I wake up to Uncle Whack smoking in the corner of the room. His eyes are swollen, staring out the window, and his skunk stripe is dangling down on the side of his head. His beeper is on the coffee table in front of him, dark and still.

How was Lacey? I ask.

She didn't come through, he says. He won't look at me. *Maybe today. Maybe at the park. Come on, get dressed.*

Uncle Whack delivers on exactly what he promised. He lets me ride all the roller coasters I want to ride—the Kumba, the Montu—twice, and then three times, over and over again. I hold his hand in the line for every ride, and stand next to the wooden height requirement signs to show him that I'm okay. On the Congo River Rapids ride, we get so drenched our shirts suction our bodies. Uncle Whack checks his beeper constantly, but it's not hooked on his belt loop anymore; it's tucked away in his pocket.

So where's the famous Lacey? I ask.

She's caught up, he says.

We stop at a concession stand. Uncle Whack buys me a turkey leg and a pack of Sour Punch Straws that I zip up in my fanny pack. We sit down at a picnic table under an umbrella, and I gnaw the meat off the bone, offer him a bite.

Can we see the giraffes? I say. *I hear they have purple tongues.*

Sure ma, he says.

I had a good time on this trip with you, Wendall, I say.

I'm your Uncle Whack; don't forget it. He looks more serious now, his eyes covered by thin, black glasses. I can tell by the shade of his nose that he's been crying under there.

Okay, Wendall, I say.

This'll stay a secret between us, right ma? he says. *Tampa and all.*

Yes, Wendall.

Listen, I love this girl.

It's true that I'll keep this secret, always, until now. Secrets are the only kind of love I know. It's also true that my parents will never ask much about what we did. Years from now, I'll ask whatever happened to Uncle Whack, and my mother will say, *I remember him. The nicest boy.*

I open my fanny pack and take out a Sour Punch Straw. I bite into it again and again until the foot-long candy is just a few inches of gritty sugar hanging out of my mouth.

You can't eat strawberry flavored shit if you're Lil Kiwi, he says. *That ain't right.*

I don't want to be Lil Kiwi anymore, I say.

Oh yeah? Then who?

Call me Sandy, I say. *It's my show name.*

The next week, as promised, my father takes me to Las Vegas. Our connecting flight is in St. Louis, and we're delayed; there's a storm coming through. My father is irritable in the airport, shaking his foot, tapping his pinky ring against the armrest. He points over to the smoking lounge. It looks like a giant ice cube from across the terminal—a glass square with eerie cloudiness. *You can handle it, right?* says my father. *You're a big girl now.*

I clamp my mouth closed as we walk into the room. I do not want to be poisoned to death in the St. Louis airport. I sit next to my father on a bench, and we're surrounded by other people with their own brands of smokes, their own newspapers and headlines. I want to talk to each and every person, ask where they're going, but everyone, including my father, is quiet. They puff. They read. The streams of smoke break, then lift. It looks like ballet—this evidence of adulthood. My father wraps his arm around me like he's proud, and I rest my head in his armpit, open my mouth, breathe in the gray air as deeply as I can. I hold it. Breathe out.

There are old, splintered, wooden seats back at our boarding gate. The wood is soft; it gives way to my thumbnail. The wood is scattered with initials and drawings—hearts, stars, and forevers—and when my father goes to the bathroom, I sneak the keys to his Jaguar out of his sports jacket pocket for my own message. I want to carve my name into the armrest to honor this day, the day I was woman enough to sit inside the smoking room, but I'm afraid to get caught before our flight; I'm afraid of proof; I think someone might arrest me.

I grip the keys in a fist and bring it down. Push and drag it.

CRY BABY

His name is Quince Pearson. Quince has black hair, expressive hands, an infomercial smile I will never have. He's the star basketball player, but we share an Honors history class because Quince is not afraid to be smart, to crinkle up his forehead and consider the past. My heart burst last week when Quincy did a presentation on Euripides. He unzipped his khaki uniform shorts at the front of the classroom, scissor kicked them off his ankles till his belt buckle clacked against the wall. We all stared at Quince's Abercrombie boxers, his pale, hairless legs, as he said, *Eu-rip-a-dese-pants-off! That's how you wanna remember this dude!* I think Quince is the most creative person I've ever met. He is eleven going on twenty.

Today, my homeroom teacher, Mrs. McBoner, wheels over our classroom television and fumbles to click it on for the morning announcements. Her name is really Mrs. McBride, but we've renamed each of our teachers and given them upgrades—Ms. Clit, Mrs. Tear-My-Condom, Dr. Gooch, Ms. Dyke-Hoochie. The TV snaps on and off, switches channels, because some kids in class installed computer programming into their wristwatches and this allows them to control the TV. Sometimes, during a test, one of them will turn the TV on mute, raise the volume to the max, then unmute so the speakers blare some kind of *Days of Our Lives* romance scene. This made Mrs. Tear-My-Condom cry on behalf of Mr. Tear-My-Condom being dead, and her suspicion that he was reaching out to her in this small, tacky way.

I'm in middle school now, and my best friend's name is Clarissa Donoto. She's in the seat next to me, taking notes on the morning announcements. We're best friends because Clarissa is also tormented and, together, we torment other losers. She's got a scraped-off dinner plate kind of face—round, blemished, pale—but she's the smartest girl in school with the bubbliest handwriting. Today a boy named Harry sits behind her bouncing his sneakers on her metal desk basket until her double-chin jiggles. *Fat Fuck! Fat Fuck! Fat Fuck!* he whispers, leaning his lumpy, pink face into the back of her hair, but Clarissa is used to this by now—a pro—she never cries; her eyes don't even leave the TV screen.

The high schoolers on television read from a sheet of paper. They make stupid jokes and talk about Dan Marino's legacy and how he will build us a new football field made of state-of-the-art Astroturf. His son attends our school, but he doesn't even play football—he's into drama.

Surprise, surprise, the high schoolers say on the screen, *a middle school dance this weekend! No uniforms necessary. It's goin' down in the gym!*

I reach over to grab Clarissa by the shoulder, but she gives me a look like, *Ugh, Stop.* Clarissa is my only friend, but she is also trying to move up. Outside school, we sing every word of *Rent*, tell secrets, and look up pictures of Bonsai Kittens with the bedroom lights off; her mom makes us baked ziti and classic Italian desserts; I attend Clarissa's soccer games. But in school, our friendship is cautionary. Clarissa grew up with members of the A-crowd, the *most* popular, and when they start on me she's allowed to join in on the chanting, *Your underwear is showing, Queera. Get bent!* I know where I stand: I wear a soup thermos with a strap around my neck, a back brace; I have an imaginary boyfriend named Brahman; I roll a suitcase filled with books because my equestrian posture is still considered *precious* and can't handle any excess weight. My nose bleeds onto my desk at least twice a day. I want Clarissa to move up, and I'm no good for that. It's an arrangement I understand—a deal I would, and eventually will, gladly take for myself.

It's 1999 and our prep school is one of the first in the country to issue mandatory laptops to every student. They're called *Study-Pros*, and they're wired to a group of men in the library called the *Tech-Center* who observe and control how we use them. If we get distracted in class, clicking around on Napster, a member of the Tech-Center will often move the arrow of our mouse directly to the "X" like some phantom conscience. Recently, a member of the Tech-Center called my father to tell him I had downloaded porn videos onto my Study-Pro after school hours, when I didn't think it counted. My father told him to go fuck right off.

We call the Study-Pros *Craptops*. They look like baby tombstones, cold to the touch, a gritty silver with blue rubber bumpers and handles. Because the school says they are indestructible, each class has made it their mission to destroy them. There's nothing more thrilling than watching the A-crowd hurl their computers into the school lake and then onto the asphalt of the pickup loop, where high schoolers run them over in BMWs. The only way they stop is if the president's Maybach creeps up. The president of our school—a huge, booming man with pants too short—has a chauffeur drive him from building to building in order to keep us in line. He'll be investigated for fraud and money laundering just after we graduate, claims he will deny, but right now, this is still his school, his ways.

Clarissa and I are waiting outside the drama building for our moms to pick us up. She's just finished a Key Club meeting, and I've just exercised one of the school horses, an asshole gelding named Kale, who lives here on campus.

Do you think I could e-mail Quince? I ask her. *About the school dance?* I step on top of my Craptop in my riding boots and jump a little. This is about as much as I can do without feeling guilty.

You're loco, she says. *We're not even supposed to go to this thing. Dances like this are not for people like us.*

Maybe I should just tell him how I feel, I say.

What about Brahman? she laughs.

Get out with that.

Boys are supposed to ask girls. Don't be desperate.

It could go good with Quince. I can write a good e-mail.

I can't do this right now, says Clarissa. *The girls are coming soon.* Clarissa promised her psych homework to the A-crowd, typed papers on the groupthink in *12 Angry Men.*

My parents say I should always express myself, I say.

Do not touch your Craptop, says Clarissa. *That would be so fucking embarrassing.*

The A-girls trickle out of the building across from us. They gather under a palm tree, unbutton their skirts and let them drop to the grass like dead birds. Beneath their uniform skirts, the girls all wear tight, cotton shorts with slits up the sides. The shorts are called Soffes, and my mother won't buy them for me because everybody else wears them. She says they look cheap, and *why would you want to wear the same shorts as these skank-ass white brats?* Clarissa swings her pink JanSport backpack over one shoulder (two shoulders would be social suicide) and waves me off. *Do not!* she says, between her teeth, as she smiles and skips toward the girls.

Years later, my mother will tell me that she prayed to a higher power every day that maybe, just once, she might find me standing with the other girls at the school pickup loop, laughing. *Don't be alone,* she would repeat in the car. *For once, don't be alone. Let those girls talk to her. Let her act like a skank-ass Boca bitch if that's what it takes, just don't be alone.*

The next morning, before school, my Study-Pro lights up with an e-mail from QPearson88. *B my date 2 the dance?* it says. *2 shy 2 ask. Meet U there.*

I have a date to the middle school dance, I tell my parents. My father is lying on the living room couch, propped on an elbow. He drops his roll of newspaper on the floor, his sports bets scrawled over it in blue and red smears. He says, *Who? I mean, who's the lucky guy? I mean, I'll chop his balls off.*

I love when this happens in the movies, on TV, in the books I read: a boy comes for a girl and then the father suddenly loves the girl more, steps up, becomes protective. No boys or men have ever desired a fatherless girl. I have always wanted this complication.

Don't say that! I laugh, swatting him in the arm. He takes me down to the couch with him in one swift yank. On my father's four TVs, four different announcers give us some stats. Dad says the Raiders will pay my college tuition one day if we play our cards right.

What's this? What're you saying? My mother's sitting on the floor in the corner of our living room, next to the television pyramid, organizing stacks of CDs for her new catalog-ordered player.

Mom, you won't believe it.

Believe this, she says. *Watch!* She punches in a number—57—and the player glows blue, spins all the glittering CDs around like a fan. Michael Bolton's voice seeps out of the speakers. *Like magic!* she says. *It's like a goddamn computer, this thing!*

Enough with the Michael Bolton! screams my father.

And Rich Gannon passes, it's the Raiders! screams an announcer.

I have a date to the middle school dance! screams me.

Wait for another! screams my mother, punching in a new number. *Enough with the Wilson Phillips!*

My mother stands up and grabs hold of my hands. We dance to our song—*Some day somebody's gonna make you wanna turn around and say good-bye!*—in front of the televisions.

Where'd you two even come from? says my father. He can't help but smile. *Not from me.*

My mother wants to dress me for the middle school dance. She drives me to the Boca Raton Town Center mall, pulls our car up to valet. *Limited Too? or dELiA*s?* she asks, giving me a nudge, because these are the stores of my dreams, the stores I haven't been old enough to shop in yet. These stores sell Spice Girl lollipops and the lowest pants and the finest glitters that don't rain off.

Inside Limited Too, my mother chooses a baby-blue tank top with clouds on it. She holds it up between her fingers—the V-neck cutout, a white sparkling shoelace that ties the V tight. She walks me to a dressing room and hands me a black miniskirt with two baby slits up the sides. It's too tight on me, and too short, but my mother says, *Celebrate those legs!* as she pulls me out from behind the dressing room curtain. I can barely move my thighs in the skirt, so I shuffle my feet. *You don't ride horses for nothing!*

It's too much, I say. The Backstreet Boys sing through the store speakers, and I feel embarrassed, like a little girl, just listening to the way they want it while I'm wearing this outfit. My legs are scarred and pale from my half-chaps, from all the stiff boots and pinching stirrup leathers over the years. Even worse—they're hairy, especially my knees.

You're just used to that long, fugly uniform skort, she says. *You look hot like this, trust me. Quince will DROP DEAD.*

Will you let me Nair for this? I ask. *Please?*

I'll think about it, she says. *It is a special occasion.*

After the mall, my mother drives us down to Fort Lauderdale, to my uncle's shoe warehouse. My other uncle, Uncle Bert, works the forklift inside. The warehouse is a giant, chalky-smelling place with leaning mountains of white shoe boxes. They each have our name—*Madden*—printed all over them. Some of the shoes are new, but others are damaged discards—two left feet, a nail in the insole—and sometimes I'm allowed to climb up and pick from these piles.

My Uncle Bert hops off his forklift when we pull up to the side entrance of the warehouse. He licks his fingers and smooths down his mustache. He looks like my father if my father were to quit shaving and wear tube socks and take up the Grateful Dead. He's my favorite uncle. *Did I hear my favorite girl found a date to the middle school dance?* he says.

With Quince Pearson, I say.

That's not just any date, says my mother.

Quince Pearson—I think I've heard of him, says Uncle Bert. He pulls a soft pack of smokes from the front pocket of his plaid shirt.

'Bout this tall? Yes. *Handsome?* Yes. *Best taste in girls?*

Uncle Bert, stop! I laugh. I can't stop laughing. I am eleven years old, and I can finally joke about love. Stand up inside it.

Uncle Bert lets me climb the shoe mountains for the rest of the day. *Find the perfect dancing shoes!* he says. *Better be dynamite!*

I love opening each box under the humming, ginger glow. I love the crackle of tissue paper, the smell of suede and glue. I can barely fit into even the smallest of the shoes, but I still know every term, what I like and what I don't like—*the choke is all wrong, the toe spring is perfect*— because this has become one of the many languages of our family.

All the VJs and pop stars on MTV have made my uncle's shoes extra famous, so the A-girls recently asked me for a new white, chunky sneaker called the Bobbie. *If you deliver*, Addison Katz said, *we'll be your very best friends*. I came to the warehouse, and Uncle Bert helped me collect and label the Bobbie boxes, each and every size. My mother wrapped them in expensive paper, pressing each crease with a gentleness that wrung some kind of sadness inside me. The next day, when I handed over the gifts next to our school lockers, the girls tore open the boxes, tied up the laces, and left the wrapping paper crunched in the halls. They never spoke to me again, but the shoes are worn in by now.

On the floor of her bedroom, my mother does her best to curl my hair with hot rollers. My hair is too short for this, an ear-length bowl, so we decide to move on. She surprises me with a box of tiny, plastic rhinestone flowers that open like clams and snap on to strands of hair, and she clips them all over until my head looks like a cluster of stars. Tonight, she lets me remove all the orthodontic bands from my mouth. I spit my plastic lip bumper into its case, slide my headgear out of its molar-hooks, and now my mouth is only partially metal. My two lips meet for the first time in a year. My mother swipes a berry-colored powder across my cheeks and some sky-blue eyeshadow, to match my shirt.

I walk down the hallway toward my father on the couch. He stands up—something he seldom does. *You look beautiful*, he says, without sarcasm. *I'll be damned.*

My parents drive me the five minutes to school. I've never seen it at night before, and suddenly it feels bigger, more dangerous, like what I imagine a college might look like. *Go find your man!* screams my mother, as I shut the car door. I wave them good-bye, walking backward, until the taillights on their new Mercedes shrink and die out.

I like the hallways when they're like this, dark and gaping. Usually I have to be careful of somebody coming up behind me to unzip my suitcase or smack a sign on my back, but right now, in this moment, I'm the most beautiful girl in the hallway. I am night blooming in my cloud shirt and black, leather platforms with my very own name inside. I am a girl, with a date, attending my very first dance.

Queera! says Clarissa. She arrived with the A-girls but promised to sneak back out of the gym and find me in the halls. She looks nice, wearing a slinky rhinestone dress and a crown of butterfly clips. Her

black curls are gelled into a bun and she looks skinnier tonight; I
wonder if she's been eating. Weeks ago, when she bent over to use her
locker, a boy named Ian screamed *Slim Fast!* and the whole hallway
roared. Since then, I've only seen her suck down plastic tubes of fat-
free yogurt in the cafeteria. Sometimes, she and the other girls chew
on granola bars and spit the brown pulp back into plastic cups. All the
taste, no calories.

How do I look? I ask, taking a deep breath.

*Your skirt is totally split up the side, you know that right? How very
Con-tramp-o Casual of you.*

I look down and Clarissa is right—my skirt must have ripped when
I was climbing out of the backseat. The front and back are connected
by only a few thick threads. My whole thigh is showing, along with
my tie-dye Limited Too underwear.

Well now-the-fuck what? I say. *My parents aren't coming back for
hours.*

You're such a boner-killer, you know that? she says. *Come on.*

Clarissa leads me to a classroom, Mrs. Vag's. The lights are still
on. Student government runs late here, and Clarissa is in charge of
the key. I've run for student government twice—*Don't be saddened,
Vote for Madden!*—but never made the cut. Both times, my mother
baked campaign cookies for the entire middle school that everyone
devoured, mumbling, *Who knew she could make cookies without fortunes
inside?*

Inside Mrs. Vag's room, in this kind of light, Clarissa's glitter and
charcoal makeup looks exaggerated and clownish. I wonder if I look
the same. She walks over to Vag's desk and picks up a stapler. *C'mere,*
she says, getting on her knees.

I walk over to her.

Take the shoes off, she says, *I can't even reach your ankle.*

Shoes are the one thing I have on girls my age. Most girls in Middle are allowed one pair of starter heels for dressy occasions—strappy, kitten things only a half inch off the ground, the kind of shoes my veiny-calved grandma might wear. I've been wearing platforms and clogs most of my life—sample styles stuffed with padding—with cheetah patterns, leather tassels, sawtooth soles. They don't match our uniforms, but they're not banned from school yet.

Clarissa works from the top and works her way down and around, snapping the jaws of the stapler quickly, efficiently, like she's done this before. She *pop pop pops* the metal teeth like bullets. She pulls the fabric together and squeezes. She reloads the stapler and works until my whole side looks silver.

An improvement, she says.

Clarissa can be cruel, a real bitch. She lies and taunts and she can't be trusted, not yet, but here's the thing: she loves me more than any other friend I've ever known. There is a tenderness between two people who desire so much more than what they can have, who reach for the cards they have not been dealt, two girls who will soon be ridiculed for exposing their hairy backs at a bar mitzvah service—*Did you goats escape from the petting zoo?*—who will spend the next few years quietly shaving each other down the spine in an empty bathtub, bleaching each other's mustaches, helping each other vomit up cheese fries and pastries; these little tasks that seem, to us, to so many young girls, like the very membrane between a life of being seen and no life at all. My love for Clarissa is so strong it changes the temperature of the air around us—that's how it feels—which is precisely the thing about losers, the thing that binds us here on Mrs. Vag's floor, and the thing that will bind us even after we change, grow up, become new people, meet other former and current losers: losers stick together. We recognize one another. Eighteen years from this moment, when I watch Clarissa walk down the aisle on her wedding day, her skin is flawless as skim milk in a white, backless dress.

There are laser lights, black lights, and strobe lights. The gym is foggy and loud. The DJ blasts everyone's new favorite song, "No Scrubs," and the crowd sings along with their hands cupped around their mouths, *Wanna get with me with no money? Oh no!*

I recognize only some of the kids on the dance floor. The kids from my classes, the Honors kids, sit on the bleachers, chewing at hangnails. Clarissa and I scan this group, looking for Derek Jacobs.

Do you think he kept his highlights in? she asks, and we grab each other by the elbows, snort-laughing.

Derek sits in front of us in German class, and lately Clarissa and I have been untwisting our Milky Pens, running the pastel-colored ink through his black, curly mullet. Derek is a genius, and he doesn't care what anyone thinks of him, and so we hate him. At twelve years old, he will be the youngest certified engineer employed by Microsoft. At fourteen, he will be the first person implanted with a microchip on national television. He will be honored by Oprah and Bill Gates. At eighteen, he'll die in a motorcycle accident.

Are you ready for a new hit? the DJ asks. He instructs us to make a circle in the center of the room; he wants to see us *move it move it*. He plays Juvenile's "Back That Azz Up," a song Clarissa recently down-loaded and played for me.

Do you see Quince?

Not yet, says Clarissa. *I'm sure he'll find you.*

The A-girls form a circle. It's more shocking than I'd imagined, seeing everyone in their weekend clothes, no button-ups or sweater vests or pleats. The bass thumps wild, and Clarissa and I watch the girls take turns crawling on the floor, then moving flat on their stomachs. They slam their fists on the glossy gym wood as they hump up and down with their groins. They make faces like they're in pain, or maybe it's just that they're feeling really good. I squeeze my thighs together.

That's called the Cry Baby, says Clarissa. *My sister told me about that move.*

The boys take turns approaching the designated Cry Baby from behind. They move on top of the girls in a push-up position. They roll their bodies and hump the girls, and the girls keep banging the floor with their fists, kicking their legs like they're about to start swimming. Everybody is fake crying, fake rubbing their eyes in exaggerated twists. Quince Pearson is one of these boys. I watch him hump the crying Skylar Fingerhut, the crying Claudia Greenberg, the crying Beth Diaz, the crying Harley Pelletier. After some time, one of the adult chaperones pulls Quince off of Addison Katz, shakes her finger. *No, no, no, that's enough.*

Do you think he's as nervous to see me as I am to see him? I ask Clarissa.

Of course, she says. *And wait till he sees your outfit!*

I've never danced before, I say. *Nothing like that.*

We'll practice, she says. *Don't worry.*

Now that the crying is over, a new circle has formed. One boy has taken off his tie, and he wraps it around another girl's neck. When he does this, the two of them sway into the center of the circle. The girl bends over, plants her hands on her knees. She gyrates her butt up and down as quickly as possible, flinging her crimped hair around in a circle. It's almost like the hula, I think, if hula were to be danced while bent over, to angry music in English, by horny white people. The girl snakes her tongue out of her mouth and taps the front of her braces with it. She flicks it in and out while she grinds. The boy holds on to her hips and pulls her butt into his body. At one point, he lifts his hand above her bent-over back. He moves this hand up and down, up and down, like he's petting a dog or flattening dough. When everyone has applauded and screamed, *Nasty! Hot! Get it, Danny!* it's the girl's turn to take the tie and choose the next boy. She wraps it around Quince Pearson's neck. I watch them dance like that. The pizza dough move, the ass bouncing, her left leg hooked around his back when they face each other, still humping.

Clarissa pulls me into the gym locker room. It's so bright in here after the black lights that I have to blink it off in the mirror. My blue mascara and blue eye shadow are gooping, stinging. *Open your eyes, Chink,* says one of the girls coming out of a stall. *Oh, that's right, you can't!*

I am used to these comments—I don't even remember when I began hearing them—but I have a white father and an uncle who makes shoes for white, beautiful celebrities, and I've known my Hanukkah prayers since I was a baby, and mostly, I don't understand why other people can see something I can't. This difference about me.

All hail power to the Earth, power to the Water, Goddess of the Stars and the Flames, Ni-How-Bru-Ha-Ha-Alikazam-O-Kamikaze.

Jesus Christ with the Wicca, says Clarissa. *You are so embarrassing.*

Clarissa knows the drill. I wear a pentacle necklace and make up spells when people give me the most shit. The sterling pentacle screws on to a small cobalt bottle. I tell people the bottle is full of blood, but it's usually cranberry juice or some kind of essential oil my mom gives me for my nosebleeds. Once, I cast a spell on Ms. Dickhead, and she fell down a flight of stairs the very next day. I felt bad about that, cut off a lock of my hair and buried it as some sort of penance, but ever since this incident people tend to walk away when I start the chanting.

Seriously, says Clarissa, *you need to practice before you go back out there. Show me what you got. You watched them, right? Show me.*

Clarissa instructs me to bend my knees as much as I can. She uses her hands to help arch my back. She positions my legs so that they're farther and farther apart. I try my best to do what I saw. I place one palm on each knee; I bounce up and down; I rock my head back and forth until my hair with its rhinestone clips goes flying. I find what feels like a steady humping motion.

You look like you're having a total fucking seizure, says Clarissa. *But I guess it's not that bad.*

I keep going. I rock my body back and forth. *Like this?*

Oh my fucking God. A voice. It's Addison Katz. A few of the girls follow her inside the locker room. *What the freak are you doing?*

I stand up. *Dancing*, I say, *like you. I'm here with Quince Pearson. We're dates.*

Oh really? says Addison. Her blonde hair is pinned into a knot on the back of her head. Spikes of it stick out so that it looks like a child's drawing of a sun. Two thin, golden strands hang gelled beside her cheeks, and it's all unmoving, bound by glitter hairspray. She's wearing a bandana as a shirt. *Well in that case*, she says, *you need to sex it up a little.*

Addison and the girls tell me to try the Praying Cry Baby. They tell me this is done in a kneeling position, fists pumping in a tantrum. They tell me to rub my eyes with hard wrist-twists, toss my hair even harder. They tell me to cry like the hottest baby that ever cried.

Quince will bust his zipper, Addison says. All the girls nod. Clarissa looks to them—nods, too. We leave the bathroom in one big group, ready.

Back in the gym, the glow sticks have come out. Everyone is sucking on them, and their teeth glow dirty blues, pinks, and yellows behind their braces. All of us girls walk through the crowd, holding hands, until we make it back to the center circle. Some of the boys have laced larger glow sticks between their fingers. They move their hands around their bodies and above their heads so that the glow sticks leave figure-eight-shaped trails.

Club Boca up in herr'! the DJ spits into the mic. *Are you ready to shake it?*

He begins playing another song I've heard before. It's called the "Thong Song." Quince Pearson jumps into the center of the circle, raving, his face glowing lime green inside the hoops of light.

Show Quince what you've got! says one of the girls. *Now's your chance!* and I feel a push.

I move into the center of the circle. Quince looks at me, but instead of grabbing my hand, or taking me in for a hug, or giving me one of his glow sticks, or spinning me around to hump me from behind, or patting my dough, or wrapping his tie around my neck, his eyes bulge and rim white. He backs up out of the circle and into the crowd. Sisqó sings about dumps like a truck and thighs like what. I know this is my chance. I know that to back away, to press myself back into Clarissa's arms, would mean even more ridicule, being called a fucking wimp. I *am* a fucking wimp, but this could change all that. I know this could be the last time I am ever asked to a dance.

The moves feel more natural with a bass throbbing under my feet, with Sisqó's words of encouragement. I dip my butt as low as I can go, pretend to wax the gym floor with it. I push my palms into my knees like I was told, balance my weight, vibrate every muscle as hard as I can manage. The staples in my skirt ping off onto the floor. They scratch at my thighs, open the torn slit, but I don't care, I want to get down, I want to get my freak on. The crowd screams, hollers; I drop on my knees and pump the damp air, thrusting my hips back and forth. I cry baby, cry. I feel sexy. I feel seen. For the first time, I feel seen as someone sexy. I lean my body forward and flat onto the floor. I give the crowd what they want. I pound the ground with my fists, kick the rubber toes of my platforms. I hump the floor like a dog humps a stuffed lion—deliberate, fast. The song fades out. Something slower leaks in. K-Ci and JoJo and a few piano keys.

Even though I'm dizzy, I pick myself up to stand. Everybody has wet, glowing faces and tears in their eyes. They point at me, bending over, waving away their laughs till they say, *It hurts, it hurts, oh my god, I can't.* Quince Pearson has his face buried in a seventh-grade girl's shoulder, and I can't tell if he's laughing or crying or both.

Clarissa bursts through the circle, takes my hand.

Bleachers, she says.

We thump up the steps to join the other Honors kids.

I thought it was good, I say. *I felt it.*

Let's forget that ever happened, she says. *Let's not even talk about that ever happening.*

We watch the girls weave their fingers around the boys' necks for the slow dance. The boys rest their hands on the girls' butts, or just above them. They all stand in place—they don't move a single step—they simply shift their weight from left leg to right leg, swaying a little. It's unimpressive, I think. It's not dancing at all.

Did I blow it with Quince? I ask.

No, she says. She's quiet for a pause after that. *He told me he feels too shy or something. He said something to one of the girls like he'll ask you to dance when he's got more courage. When the time's right.*

Clarissa won't look at me as she says this.

Maybe he can't even handle me, I say.

I think that's it, she says. *I think that's it.*

My father picks me up at ten o'clock. He's trying to be sober this week, so he's staying close to home, smoking more, yelling less. He lights the end of a new cigarette from the butt already in his mouth, flicks that filter on the school lawn in a scabbed trail of light.

How'd it go with Prince Charming? he asks.

I love it when my father asks me questions. These moments come in slivers; they're bright and fleeting, and, when I catch the insides of them, I feel like the most important man in the world is really listening to me, and with the power of one of his nods or *Uh huh*s, or *Sure*s, or laughs, I, too, am important. My father will always have that way about him. But tonight, my throat feels so lumpy and hard I don't want to talk much.

He got too shy, is what I say.

My father turns up the radio. It's a Jim Croce song, his favorite.

You ever listen to the words here, son? he asks.

Operator, oh could you help me place this call, sings Jim.

No, I say.

You should, he says. *It's a sad, sad story.*

The truth is, I waited and waited for Quince Pearson to ask me to dance. I waited on the bleachers long after Clarissa was picked up, until there were only a few people left on the dance floor, until it was only Quince and Candy Schwartz, their arms wrapped tightly around each other, her thumbs hooked on the back belt loops of his cargo pants. I waited until I saw them kiss on the lips, until I stomped down the steps in my platform shoes and tapped him on the shoulder, *Hi, Quince, Hi*, until he looked at me in a sad way still lined with kindness, cocked his head, and said, *Hey there . . . what's . . . up?* I waited.

I open the window of the car, stick my hand out into the hot wind. I like the resistance of it. We're miles from the ocean, but I swear I can hear the crash of all those littered waves.

You can keep the dime, sings Jim.

That's the most important lyric, my father says. *Remember that part*, he says. *After all the calling and calling for his sweetheart, he doesn't even want to get through in the end. Love's barely ever worth it.*

At home, my mother sits on the living room floor with a joint in her mouth and the red velvet chocolate box where she keeps her *stuff*. She punches numbers into the CD player, jumps up when I walk through the door.

Hi, baby! she says. *How was it? How was Quince? What happened to your skirt?*

Ripped, I say.

My mother knows me best. She knows everything by just looking at me, even when I don't want her to, even when I steady my eyes and fake it.

Take off those shoes, she says. *To hell with middle school dances. We'll have our own dance. We've got the CD player!*

I kick my feet until my shoes thud against the wall and then the floor. My father picks up one of the eight remote controls from the coffee table and sits down on the couch. I watch my mother give him that *Don't even think about it* look and he understands, stands back up.

My mother punches in a new number. Takes a hit. The robot player spins and spins. The speakers thump something disco, chords hot and elastic. The three of us dance in a circle, facing one another on the gum-bald carpet, snapping our fingers, throwing the dice. My father lets me stand on his feet as he shuffles and grooves. He holds me tight. He dips my body backward till the room tips over. He says, *One day, you won't even remember this night ever was.*

BUGS

I discovered them in a Cracker Barrel bathroom. The bugs, that is. Ruthie Mitchell's mom took us to a Cracker Barrel off the Sawgrass Expressway for a *real-life experience*, for a *change of scenery*, and we like this. The triangle peg game, the slopping grits, the rocking chairs, Dolly Parton singing through a tinny speaker. We could be other people in this place—adults on a highway in the cool bruise of night, taking shifts to drive a million miles north to find Jesus, or husbands, or any other world outside our middle school.

But in the bathroom light, in the mirror, I see it. Something moving on my head. Just a fleck, really. No fatter than a poppy seed. I lean in closer to the mirror. Dolly is singing about her coat of many colors, and I move both palms to either side of the part in my hair. I push down with my hands to flatten the hair like a sponge, and I see them, bugs, skittering away from the light, away from my part, running down to my ears.

I don't mention my bugs to Ruthie Mitchell or her mother for the rest of dinner. I don't want to ruin our adventure; I don't want to be a bad guest. Instead, I eat my chicken-fried steak and I nod to everything they both say and I am quiet, very quiet, in the car ride home to Ruthie Mitchell's house situated right on a cemetery. I wait until we turn on *Airplane!*, until the two girl scouts beat each other to heaven, swinging each other by the pigtails, and then I say, *Your house, Ruthie. Do you think it's haunted, seeing that people are buried in your yard?*

Maybe, she says. *I mean, probably.*

I think my head is haunted by some critters, I say.

Mrs. Mitchell calls my mother immediately. She checks Ruthie in the guest bathroom, their bodies bent over the sink. *Bugs*, she says. *Bugs everywhere.*

Who has more bugs? I ask.

Why should it matter? You've both got them.

I think Ruthie must've given them to me, I say. *Because I don't live dirty.*

Really, I'd had a feeling about the bugs for months. I'd never seen them, but one day, in art class, Gleb Ankari screamed *Lice!* pointing right at my head. I scratched at the scabs already hardening on my scalp, and started crying. Lucky for me, I could tell our art teacher also hated Gleb, who always drew cartoon tits and ass—*It's ART!*—and gave him a Saturday detention for harassing me, the shy girl with a chronic itching problem.

We'll call you Alligator Girl, my father once nicknamed me, *like a superhero name, or a freak show star!*—I got the head-to-toe eczema from him.

When my mother arrives at the Mitchells' house, Ruthie warms a baby bottle in the microwave. She curls up in a beanbag chair in the living room, sucking milk from the bottle. She's worked up, Ruthie Mitchell, my thirteen-year-old friend; she barely wants to say hello. *Ruthie's got the bugs, too*, I say, *and she's pretty upset.* Mrs. Mitchell tells my mother I've got a pretty bad case, the worst she's ever seen. *You didn't notice until now?*

I don't live up my daughter's ass, my mother says in the car, *How would I notice?* My mother shakes her head. *Has she noticed that her daughter sucks on a bottle?* We both laugh so hard our car swerves off and edges into the thick, Florida grass.

Day One: My mother brings home a Publix bag of stinky chemicals from the drugstore. She sits on a lawn chair in our backyard and has me sit on a towel between her legs. She uses a nit-pick to ease out the bugs and eggs. *The worst occasion for Chinese hair,* she says. *We should be done with you by Christmas.* She soaks the comb in a bowl of rubbing alcohol. She kisses me on the shoulder. *I've got you,* she says. *If I see one more, I'll nuke 'em.*

Day Two: She buys a box of neon shower caps. *Wear these around the house,* she says, *and when you sleep.* I can't stop crying when I see myself looking like a Mario Kart Mushroom in the mirror. I feel like a dumb kid, like someone filthy. *Your dad and I will wear them, too,* she says, *so you won't be the only one looking like a stupid shit!* She snaps a yellow cap on her head. The elastic digs a red line into her forehead, and I feel like I have never loved anyone more.

Day Three: My mother tries to suffocate the bugs with mayonnaise. She spoons it out with her hands, piles it on my hair. She twists the black and white mound until it looks like ice cream, and snaps a new cap over it. I gag into the kitchen sink, dry heaving.

So there's a nymph, a nit, and a louse, she says, on day four. *We need to kill every one.* She's been reading about it, highlighting pages she's printed from the library. She tells me to sit in our bathtub, and I wear a ruffled bathing suit that fits too tight. She pours vinegar, vegetable oil, apple cider, then Listerine. My eyes prickle. She smothers my head in Vaseline before snapping on a new cap.

Day Five: We scald them. I sit in the bathtub again, knees to my chest, my bathing suit warm, just out of the dryer. My mother's cap is green today. She holds the shower head right to my scalp, turns the knob. *Bite me if you have to.*

Day Six: A straightening iron to every separated strip of hair. We listen to the bugs sizzle-pop inside the clamp.

Each morning, my mother takes me back into the yard. I sit on my towel; I yank off my cap. She combs through every section of hair, picking at movement. She tells me, for the first time, stories about growing up in Hawai'i. The old banyan trees in her backyard. The feeling of the Nu'uanu Pali winds on her shoulders. The places where she still misses her father, her 'ohana, makuakāne, *Here and here and here*, she says, touching every corner of her body. *Honey girl, there are so many people I've never quit missing.*

Each night, my mother boils the combs and tools in pots of water. She tumbles my clothes and blankets on high. She places my stuffed animals in the freezer. She drops my jewelry into tiny plastic bags, seals them tight. She stays at my bedside kissing every knuckle of my hands until I fall asleep.

They chose you because you're the sweetest, she says.

When I wake in the middle of the night, it's not because my mother and father are throwing ashtrays and glasses at each other. There are no crashing sounds. No cries. No smells of burning plastic or voices belonging to people who are neither my mother nor my father. Instead, this week, I wake to the hum of my mother's vacuum. She is covering every inch of the house—checking, cleaning, protecting every pillow—as if, by this simple act of cleaning, she is making the promise of a new life for me, a life in which two parents take care of a child. A life as simple as that.

By the following week, the bugs are gone. My mother checks the tender spots behind my ears. The warm places behind my neck.

Nothing, she says. *All good to go.*

Are you sure? I ask. *I still itch.*

You're good, she says. *Nothing.* She tears off her cap. Kisses me on the forehead.

I'm sure you're thrilled to go back to school. She winks.

Later that night, in the bathroom mirror, I move my palms back to my part. I press down on the hair again; again; I wait. This time, I don't see anything. I don't see anything moving at all. My hair is just my hair. My scabs have peeled. There's nothing alive on any inch of my head—no nymphs, no nits, no lice.

But they were right here, I say.

THE LIZARD

Here's another early memory: I'm chewing up a grilled cheese sandwich on the floor of my living room when I see it, the lizard, dashing out from behind the TV unit. It skitters across our white tiles on its lizard legs. Its head twitches around and around, looking for something in lizard motion, unpredictable in a way that makes me feel sick. I don't trust it.

My father is asleep on the couch, a sports game blaring, the remote still gripped in his hand. His chapped mouth hangs open; he's zonked but balanced, almost poised, on an elbow.

I pick up one of his empty glasses off the coffee table, a thick layer of extra crystal on the bottom of it. I'm clumsy with the glass; my hand can't even wrap the circumference. I sniff the inside. Gag, dramatically. I decide I must capture the lizard, show it who's boss. I decide that I must take control, for once, of a situation.

The lizard is unmoving beneath the kitchen counter. I take off crawling toward it, and it runs. I stand up, chase the lizard into the kitchen. I rush it up and down the wall, cupping my glass against the paint. My bare feet slap-slap the tile as I chase the lizard through the hallway, and down one step, until it slides beneath the mildewed crack of the garage door. This isn't enough. Now that I'm chasing it, now that my chest is pumping, now that the lizard is scared, I don't want to stop. I open the door and let my eyes adjust. Sunlight leaks around the garage door like a glowing picture frame. I look under paint buckets, around the oily car stains, I *will* find it, and then I do: the lizard, motionless, in the far right corner of the garage.

You can trust me, I say, *Shhhhhh.*

I move slowly, carefully. I make my voice sound high and coddling.

This time, when I approach it, the lizard does not run. It stares at me, breathing, its little red lizard balloon pumping at its throat.

I'm not going to hurt you, I say. I said that.

Once I am squatting right next to the lizard, I move the glass out from behind my back. I stare at the lizard, its darting eyes, the tiniest nails. I hold the base of the glass in my palm; I am perfectly still for two counts of Mississippi before I snap the empty side down, right on top of the lizard. The glass does not break, but the lizard does. The edge of the glass has severed the tail off, right in the center. It went down smooth, without resistance, as if the tail were made of lizard putty. The lizard tail begins waggling across the concrete garage floor while the rest of the body jumps inside the glass, pushing against it.

My scream cleaves the air as I run back into the house.

I never take the glass off the lizard. I never let the air in. Instead, I become afraid of the garage from that day forward, that awful rubbery smell, what it meant to be a grown-up.

For years, the lizard came to me each time I began falling asleep. I couldn't push it out from behind my eyes—all those lizard movements—the way it had finally trusted me. I thought of the way I had chased it, the blood rush of that. I thought of not much else. A body, severed, does not die right away. It fights, thrashes. Every part of it remembers.

CHICKEN & STARS

My mother is late, later than usual. I'm waiting outside the middle school building under the palms, alone, and I wonder if she's fallen asleep somewhere. I wonder if she remembers it's a school day.

My mother and father have been in their Other Place lately—the place they go when the sweating glasses come out, the pipes and powders and smokes that smell like acrylic nail drills. I've been calling them *Magic Sticks*, because it is only a matter of minutes between the blaze of those glass sticks and that Other Place, where my mother's voice changes pitch and her throat bobs differently and suddenly there's danger outside every window—bandits or elephants or the FBI or my dead grandfather—and we all play along with the same fantasies and fears.

I've been learning about some of this stuff from Whitney Houston on the news. I ask my mother about this, but she says it's not the same thing. Sometimes she buys a white powdered ibuprofen from the pharmacy and mixes it into her iced tea. She says, *See? Look. Read the package, it's harmless. This is what you saw*, she says.

My mother's black truck grumbles up around the corner. Her truck is not fancy. It has dents all over; a few of my horse ribbons,

sun-bleached, hang from the rearview mirror. My mother likes to call
her car *Big Beau*, petting the dashboard affectionately.

I roll my suitcase over, yank the handle of it when the wheels snag
on the sidewalk cracks. I open the backdoor of the car, chuck the suitcase in—*It's about time*—and slam the door. I open the passenger door
and scoot in.

My mother's face is battered, blue. Her bottom lip drags down as
if an invisible hanger were hung from it. Both eyes are almost entirely
sealed shut. Dark marks the size of boxed chocolates cover her arms.
She reaches for my hand and holds it.

There was a fight, she says.

He's asleep on the couch when we arrive home. My father has
never been a bedroom father, a kitchen father, a backyard father, an
office father, a roof father; he is a father of the living room couch.
I wonder if he was always this way, with his other family, that other
life none of us are supposed to mention. He keeps a worn photo of two
boys in the slip of his wallet, boys in the sun, playing ball. Even though
their faces are crinkled as petals, I can see that they have his nose
and eyes.

Now my father is facedown on the pink leather cushions, and I sit
down next to him. His left arm dangles. I lift it and let it drop. He
feels dead to me. Even like this, I love him.

Beneath his arm, on the floor, is his crown-sized ashtray over-
flowing with orange filters. It's almost beautiful this way, like an
exotic flower, or a Bloomin' Onion from Outback. When my father is
too drunk to walk or drive for more cigarettes, he lights each and

every butt in the ashtray, one at a time. He sucks at them between his fingers like he's drinking a milkshake through a cocktail straw. Around the couch are several empty vodka bottles, a cracked cobalt glass, rolled-up hundred-dollar bills, a smashed mirror. My father doesn't move no matter how much I touch him.

I watch my mother fill a cup with water from the kitchen sink, holding steady to the counter. We're rich—at least I think we are—but everything in our home has begun to smell. Our sulfurous well-water smells like cheese gunk, the kind that collects in the refrigerator drawers, so we plug our noses to drink. My mother points to our pantry, and I walk over to it. The wooden door hangs off its hinges. The shelves inside are split perfectly in half—*that's where my face went*—all the screws yanked from the walls. I lift a can of Campbell's soup from the pile of them on the floor, *Chicken & Stars*, twist it around and around in my hand. It is easier to look at your favorite soup than it is at blood. Campbell's soup, my every meal, the first thing I learned how to make for myself—that thermos necklace I always keep at my chest—*mine*. A large can of Campbell's is exactly 1 lb., it says so on the label, and this is the measurement by which I weigh everything else in the world. I weigh 81 soup cans. My pony Nicky weighs 705 soup cans.

My mother stares into the pantry, shaking her head. She sips slow and gently from her glass, careful not to spill. There are noises now— words coming out: *Money, investment, snapped, pushed*, and then, *the soup cans, the money*. I ask her to slow down. She says my father has been binging on his special stuff and hasn't slept in over three days. *The Other Place*, she says. The fight started in the kitchen, simple at first, before he took her by the wrists and didn't know what to do with all his love. She says things like this all the time lately, words like *love* to describe our suffering. She doesn't know if I'm old enough to hold the truth in my hands, to measure that.

I know, I say, *you don't have to explain more.*

I wish you didn't have to know so much, she says.

I know.

I hug my mother at the kitchen sink and let her cry into my shoulder. She leaves black and red marks on my white, crisp uniform. I am only five foot two, but we're the same height by now. From a slight distance, people mistake us for sisters.

I tell my mother I'll heat up two cans of Campbell's for dinner. I pluck them from the top of the pile. Wipe the blood with a paper towel. I crank the can opener till the aluminum exhales. I smash the pots and pans around, bang them into one another like gongs. The stove coils throb red. The stars boil. I open and close the dishwasher in a crashing swing, like I'm bowling. I want my father to wake up so badly, to tell me his side of the story, to bury his head in his hands, apologizing, changed. He doesn't move.

What are we going to do? my mother says, in the bathtub. It's one in the morning, and my father is still asleep. The water's gone cold, and I turn the hot lever every few minutes. *What do we do now?*

I wash my mother's body with a sea sponge. I can see every vertebra of her spine like this, curled over, her head down. She holds her shins close to her chest as if to give the water more room. There are no more wounds to clean, nothing I missed, but I can tell the sponge is comforting to her. It's a quiet touch.

Please don't cry anymore, I say. *We don't have to do anything.*

Has he ever hurt you? she wants to know.

He hasn't. He has never touched either one of us before today. Not like this, exactly.

Once, when I was younger, he was in such a spell that he came after me and my mother with a wooden baseball bat. He said he would kill us. He thought that we were somebody else, some other person or people who had hurt him. I think he'd hoped we were.

The two of us ran into my parents' bedroom and locked the door. My mother screamed, rocking me to her chest. He beat the door with the bat until it splintered, and fell asleep on the tile floor outside the bedroom, the handle still in his hand. He woke up and yelled, *Who broke this bat? I paid for this!*

That night, I asked my mother why he even owned a bat—he doesn't play baseball.

He bought it to protect us, she said.

The next day, when I asked my father, he denied the incident.

I didn't break the bat, he said. *You did.*

When my mother gets out of the bath, I wrap a towel around her from behind. I dip cotton swabs into the mouths of ointment bottles and make her wounds look glossy. I pull a T-shirt over her head, lift rose-patterned pants up and over her skin. Her face is still, staring. I help her into bed, right foot, then the left, walk to the freezer, drop fistfuls of ice into a grocery bag. I spin the bag, knot it, pass my father's body on the way back to her room.

I press the cool to her cheeks, her eyes.

I say, *It's okay, MomMom.*

My mother holds my hands against the ice against her face. She says, *You want to get out of here?*

My mother packs her bag, and I go into my room, pack my own. I don't have much to take: my diary, a Wiccan spell book, Drew Barrymore's memoir *Little Girl Lost*, my stuffed tiger, Tia, my riding boots and spurs. I spill out a drawer full of underwear, silk pajamas. I snatch my strawberry-flavored gas mask from my nightstand—the mask used for anesthesia when I got surgery for my nosebleeds—a mask that still makes me feel sleepy, relaxed, cared for, when I press it into my face hard enough and breathe. I drop all my things into a black garbage bag. I have always wanted this rush, the swing of my arms around objects that I will pack to remind myself of the way things used to be. *This was my life, back then.* More than anything, though, I have always ached for the runaway's return home, like in the movies—parents with their outstretched hands, heavy blankets with which to wrap you, the home-cooked meal with plates warmed in the oven, the tired, grateful faces. I have always wanted the reunion.

My mother carries our bags to the car. She doesn't even look into the living room as she passes. I walk to the couch, scoot my father's body over. The back of his neck is hot to the touch. I run my fingers through his sandy hair. I say, *You made a really big mess this time, Daddy.* My mother honks Big Beau three times. I kiss my father on the back of his skull, set the alarm, and run.

My mother says little in the car. She looks strong, her jaw clenched, her chin up. She gets like this when things are at their worst: upturned, dignified. She hands me a map and a new highlighter from the dash, says, *Find the best route out of here.* She is strong in ways I won't comprehend until I am much older.

An hour later, she calls up my half brothers, those other two boys, leaves a message: *You're on your own for the intervention. I'm gone.* I have never heard this word—*intervention*—and I ask her what she means. It's something that could save your father, she says, something they were planning for this week. My brothers were going to fly all the way to Boca Raton for this. They wrote parting speeches about missed T-ball games, flute recitals. They have what she calls *Bottom Lines* to offer. She repeats herself, over and over, like she's trying to believe it herself—*This will save his life, it will save him, it will,* and this explanation shocks me because I never knew he was dying.

We make one stop on our drive to Seven Devils, North Carolina, where we will hide out on a mountain for one month. Somewhere around Jacksonville, my mother feels too tired to go on, but I am awake. She pulls into a motel. She tells me to hush. She finds a metal gate to the swimming pool, lifts the peg from its hole. My mother says, *Go ahead, jump in. You have more clothes in the car. Tire yourself out,* she says.

Even though I don't know how to swim, I have always loved the water. I like it here in the shallow end with my T-shirt bubbling up in a tie-dye dome. In the water, I can be a dancer, a gymnast, an astronaut, anybody else. I can do things like balance on my toes. I swish around and flick the surface until my mother falls asleep on a lawn chair. She looks like she's sunbathing even though it's still dark out. Ripples of aqua light flick across her bare legs, her bruises.

I wonder if my father has woken up. If he has checked the bedrooms, the car.

I kick my legs as hard as I can in the water. Take a breath. There is nothing I love more than to sink to the bottom of a pool. See how long my body can keep itself from rising.

REWIRED

In rehab, my father has a heart attack playing water polo with dope addicts. His body was in too much shock coming down from all that. His heart too excited; rewired. So the doctors say.

My father calls us from rehab, after this incident. His addiction therapist is on the line to listen in on our call. My father asks about our day, my horses, what am I going to do for school? His words are clear and precise. No sleepy drag. He asks me questions and waits patiently for answers, and this makes him sound like somebody else's father.

Are you somebody else's father? I say. *Because I don't look like you, and I'm not cruel like you, and we have such different voices and hands, and I don't even feel that Jewish, and no father of mine has a heart attack in a goddamn swimming pool, and I am really starting to question.*

But what are you doing about school? he says. *How will you do well in school from North Carolina?* Some things are important, according to my father.

My teachers send homework in the mail. Yellow paper packets. Fat clips. Periodic tables. I tell each and every one of them somebody died.

Somebody died, I say on the phone, because my mother is too super-stitious to say it.

My teachers have always called me a liar. *You play sick*, they've said. *Nobody skips like you. Nobody is sick so much. Sick in your head, maybe. What do you do all day at home?*

Absent again, Queera? Clarissa will ask me on AOL. *Cheater.*

What I do all day when I'm at home: I watch Bob Ross flutter his paint strokes on the television in my room. I listen to him describe the world—the cockeyed birds, the fuzzed-over face of a rock. I want to shape my own planet this way, color it the way I want. I boil soup; I practice making coins disappear between my fingers; I call psychic hotlines; I wait for my parents to wake up.

Somebody died out here, I tell my teachers, *so we're burying them all up.*

Them?

Nobody ever believes me.

Plural?

What I do all day here in North Carolina: More soup. More magic tricks. I practice levitating playing cards, spinning them between my outstretched hands. I breathe into my gas mask and pretend that I'm dying. I ask my mother to drive us past the local orphanage so I can be dropped off and live like Little Orphan Annie. This always hurts her feelings. *Do you know what I've gone through to keep you?* she says. My mother is drying out here, too, but she doesn't have help like my father. Mostly, she sleeps. We listen to Tammy Wynette and watch a movie about Tina Turner having her face smashed in by Ike Turner. There is so much we're both trying to understand.

You're exactly like me, my father says into the phone. *Carbon copy.*

I am not.

My mother stands in the corner of the living room. She stands stiff and blank-faced as if in a crowded elevator. She's always in this elevator lately—arms by her side, waiting—and I wonder where she goes in her mind. Which floor. Which new view.

She looks at me on the phone, the curls of the cord warping my fingers bloodless. She says, *You have his canker sores. His bad hip. His receding hairline. You are both sharp when it comes to giving directions, but neither one of you can stand being left alone.*

My father says, *You're wrong, you have my hands.*

THE FEELS OF LOVE

A senior thinks you're cute, Beth Diaz whispers in your ear. These are the most amazing words you've ever heard come out of her mouth. There is you, and then there are high school *seniors*— seventeen-, eighteen-year-olds, with cars and sound systems, no uniforms on Fridays because they're now exempt. You ask, *Who? Who?*, your abdomen burning up with this news, and she whispers again, *Shhhh, it's Chad—that's who*, because her friend's brother's cousin's babysitter said so. Something like that, but it doesn't matter to you. A senior thinks you're cute.

And who are you? You are still a middle schooler, twelve years old, almost thirteen. You have two friends, four horses, a new splatter of acne across your forehead; you don't even wear a bra yet. Lately, you are known as *Queera* or *Twinky Chinky*. But now, everything is different—everything will change, you're sure—a senior thinks you're cute.

Here's what you do when you come home from school: Find Chad in last year's yearbook. Call Clarissa and Beth on three-way to tell them you found him: *Look, page forty-nine. Those lips!* they both say, and you agree. You have never seen anyone more beautiful than Chad. His eyes are squinty and green, like the deep end of a lake, his black hair spiked. The yearbook shows him laughing with a group of friends, sprawled out on a school picnic table in the sun. They look so much like adults you can't even believe it.

He's going to instant message you tonight, says Beth. *I gave my friend's brother's cousin's babysitter your screen name to give to him.* You all scream into the phone. You scream a scream that brings your father into the room, soggy from a nap, yelling. *The fuck is happening? You jacking up my phone bill?* He closes the door before you can answer.

Here's the thing about America Online, about the instant messaging: you can be anyone—Dominique Moceanu, Britney Spears's cousin, a milkmaid from Mississippi, a criminal—anyone but yourself. Recently, the jealous ex-boyfriend of a popular girl from school—*such a creeper*—uploaded some photos of her onto an AOL homepage. They show the girl lying on her stomach, on a bed, her pink thong blooming. Slats of light curve over her body from the bent window blinds. She wears dark-blue eye shadow; her hair is in a white-blonde ponytail; her pointer finger is in her mouth. You and Clarissa have been sending these photos to the anonymous men you meet online, in chatrooms, and they're all crazy about this so-called Ashley Flowers, a tenth grader in downtown Miami. They send erotic poems, photos of the stirring bulges in their pants, hyphen roses that blossom into @ symbols. One man named Richard sends a blurry photo of his cock next to a Coke can, for scale. In the dark, with your face inches from the screen, you feel like each one of these men might love you.

On the news, JonBenét Ramsey does a dance. Her case is still open, years later, and everyone still cares. You watch her stamped-on face, clickety-clack cowboy boots, the tulle, her curls of shredded heaven. You strap on your headgear, hook the elastic behind your big ears. One has to be so beautiful to be chosen like that, you think. Only beautiful girls are taken. Angelic, white girls. Adored and obsessed over. Too good for this Earth. Your parents sip their seltzers, hold hands, and say, *Such a damn shame. So cute, she was.*

It is important to this story to know that Beth is beautiful. Beth is Latina, whip-smart, a salsa dancer, the first poet you've ever met. But most important, she is beautiful. She is almost one full year older, the oldest of the seventh graders, while you are the youngest. She has always been kind to you and Clarissa, and you're both as jealous as you are grateful. Beth has friends, admiring teachers, and parents. Most of all, she has boys. You and Clarissa watch it happen in the hallways at school—a boy's arms wrapped around her, his little metal mouth going in for a kiss. *I put lotion on as soon as I get out of the shower,* Beth says. *In every place. The best way in is smelling good.* The next day, you and Clarissa go to the mall and buy the same Juniper Breeze lotion as Beth. You smudge it on your wrists, rub it through your hair to grease down the flyaways; you slick it between your legs even though it stings there. One weekend, Beth offers to do your makeup like her own. You and Clarissa sit still as figurines while Beth paints on the glitter powders, the goopy gloss. She traces black lines around your eyes and inside the rims of your eyelids. You can tell she cares, that she wants you to feel more sophisticated, older. When she is this close to your face, you almost kiss her.

Chad does instant message you. Every night, in fact, like clockwork.

Hey Cherry Top, he says, because seventh grade is the grade you dyed your hair Mars red, to offset the braces.

Hey you is what you always say. *You* sounds adult, closer than friends.

I think ur so cute, he says. *The first thing I noticed about you was ur red hair. Very punk! I luv it.*

Cute? ROFLMAO. Look who's talking lol, you say.

You gnaw at your cuticles and wait for him to respond, for the *bloop* sound of his messages.

You have abandoned all your other chat-room boyfriends. *Ashley Flowers is DEAD*, you tell the men. *This is her mother speaking and she is gone! My sadness is uncontrollable! I can't bear it!*

She was murdered, she had leukemia but didn't want to tell you, she slipped on a ski slope in Lake Tahoe—such a tragic vacation! It changes every day. You and Clarissa receive wonderful e-mails from Ashley's suitors—how much she meant to them, how she was the bright light of their days, how they've written ballads in her honor, how they would each marry her, they would. Clarissa takes on the role of Ashley's grieving best friend so she can continue chatting with those who show the most sensitivity.

But you don't need any of them anymore. All you need is Chad, a person in the real world, a real man who drives a real car. Chad, who knows what you look like, who noticed *you*, who even knows your school schedule and where you take your study hall. You and Chad chat all night about your favorite movies and Bill Clinton and the science teacher you've both had. *I think she might be an actual LESBO*, you say, and he agrees, *SUCH a dyke LOL.*

I think U might be the only person to understand me, you say.

Same here! says Chad.

Why aren't we real friends @ school then? U dun even say hi.

People would judge lol. They wouldn't understand us.

I guess.

Baby just consider us special friends, he says. *Our own little secret.*

Baby. You repeat the word aloud to yourself, read and reread it on your screen to be sure. Your heart thumps between your legs. *Baby.*

Secrets can b the most fun, he says.

Fifteen years later, you are twenty-seven years old, and your father has just died. You're in an isolated artist colony in New Hampshire in the frozen snap of winter, here to finish another project you have failed to finish, and you sob yourself to sleep every night thinking about how much you miss your father—his big sweeping arms, your smallness. You go so long without talking to other people that you begin having conversations with a rocking chair, convinced the chair is haunted by your father. He rocks it sometimes, on his own, and you try to decipher the code. While browsing through old e-mails one night, you find a message in your spam box.

It's Chad.

It's dated one year ago, almost to the day.

It says, *I need you to forgive me for the things that have happened. It is my one wish.*

You recognize this message. You have received similar messages from him over the years—delete, block, vomit, repeat. Each time you block one, Chad creates a new account and name, sends another.

You have never once considered responding to his pleas. The few people you have ever told have said, *Don't. Don't you dare. Forget you ever saw that.* It is satisfying to delete his words, to watch them disappear, but here's the thing: you can't forget you ever saw that.

Now, though, you are the saddest you have ever been in your life. Your father is dead. Your mother is off the wagon again. You can't finish anything. Just last week, your childhood house burned down with everything in it. You wonder when the world will stop hurting you.

You respond.

Chad is my boyfriend, Beth tells you on the phone. *I didn't want to tell you, because I didn't want your hopes and dreams to be, like, totally crushed. I liked that you liked that he liked you*, she says. *It was cute.*

But Chad is my secret boyfriend, and it's serious, she says. *Maybe even love*, she says.

She says, *You need to move on.*

Clarissa can't believe it. You're sitting in the school locker room, straddling a bench, snapping Bubblicious gum. Yesterday, you decided to dye your hair back to black, your natural color. You want to look sad all the time, and you think this will help. Your ears are stained gray from the dripping chemicals.

That bitch! says Clarissa. *Who does she think she is? She's probably making it up because she's crazy jealous of you.*

You both allow the lie to sit between you, to swell there.

But Chad doesn't stop messaging. In fact, he messages you more. He is sorry, just so sorry, that he never told you about Beth. He didn't want to break up your best friendship.

Do u have a private line? he asks you. *2 talk like adults?*

If I get off AOL I can free up the line, yah, you say.

It's the first time you've ever heard his voice. At school, he has only ever looked at you—through the classroom windows, from inside his car, across a swarm of students moving through the bells. He has never once even waved. His voice on the phone does not match what you'd imagined. It's high-pitched, ragged as puberty. *His laugh sounds like Pee-wee Herman crying,* you later tell Clarissa.

Are you in bed? asks Chad. *I wanna talk you to sleep like I'm tucking you in.*

Chad wants to know what you're wearing under the covers, if you know what sex is, if you've ever given a blow job, and if so, to whom.

Aren't these questions you should be asking your GIRLFRIEND, you say.

What I have with Beth doesn't change the way I feel about you, says Chad.

I can't even talk to her anymore, you say. *It's too painful for me.*

I have another friend who thinks you're cute. We both beat off to you, he says. *Maybe if you like him we could go on double dates. The four of us could always be together in secret. That way I can still be close to you, because I think I might love you,* he says.

I love you, too, you say. You like the gravity of that word. You feel sure inside of it.

Instead of calling Beth every night, you start calling Chad. Beth thinks she's too good for you and Clarissa. She's becoming a real snob, a bitch, you tell yourself.

That friend I told you about, says Chad. *I really think you would like him. I'll be so jealous but I really hope you can go out, so I can be around you in real life without getting in trouble.*

I don't even know who he is! you say. *He could be a creep!*

He's my best friend, Cherry Top.

I'm not even a Cherry Top anymore, thanks for NOTICING.

Talk to him . . . for me.

It doesn't take long for Gil to message you. Gil is another senior, and he seems nice enough, but maybe a little boring. You have similar interests. He sends you song lyrics from emo bands: *Your taste still lingers on my lips like I just placed them upon yours and I starve, I starve for you!,* and you tell him about your obsession with Chris Carrabba of Dashboard Confessional—*He just gets me!*—how you recently had him autograph your Charlie Brown T-shirt at a concert while your mom waited in the car.

Do you ever feel SO alone? asks Gil.

All the time, you say. *I want to kill myself almost every day. My mom is SO embarrassing and my dad's been drunk my whole life and I have NOBODY who gets what it's like.*

That was before me lol.

Gil is a good listener. Sensitive, sweet. You think he might be a long-term friend or maybe *husband material* one day. You plan to meet him the next day between C and D periods, just a wave in the hall, so you can find out who he is. You don't look him up in the yearbook because the suspense gets your blood pumping.

The next day, you wear your mom's bra under your school uniform. You stuff it with cloudy silicone pads shaped like chicken cutlets. You and Clarissa bought a whole pack at the mall last month, felt each other's double push-up bra padding as if you were lovers, *Oh yeah, baby, that feels soooo good.* The cutlets feel most like the real thing.

After C period, you stand by the door of your history class. Middle and high schoolers rush by, *Eat shit, Queera. Go kill yourself already.* You respond by holding up your pentacle necklace; you've recently promised that you are casting hair-loss spells.

You look for somebody cute, somebody you must have missed all this time. And then somebody approaches you and says, *Hey, I'm Gil*, and everything inside your body crumples. This man looks *old old*, like, thirty. He's over six feet tall and wears a ponytail—tinted, square, transition glasses, purpled by the sun. He breathes through his mouth, and it hangs open, underbitten, the smell of clogged dishwater. Most striking are his teeth, narrow and long as piano keys, the gumline black.

He leans in to hug you and you scrunch your face into a walnut—*disgusting*.

You ignore all messages from Gil after that.

Chad looks older now in his online picture. His face is bloated, hairy. The whites of his eyes have gone red. The picture is one he took of himself on a phone in a splattered bathroom mirror.

You respond to his message.

You say, *Why do you want my forgiveness?*

I dunno, I guess I just feel bad, he says. *About the way things happened.*

Why? you say again.

I didn't know if I should act on the feels of love for you, he says, *and I chose wrong. Anyway, I can't believe you would still be that mad about it now, after all this time. Beth didn't care.*

He's lonely, you think. Or maybe desperate. He only wants a way back in. You've heard rumors about his life after high school. Everyone has.

I was twelve, you say. *Those things don't go away.*

In my defense, he says, *I thought you were thirteen.*

* ✳ *

Let's put all this bullshit behind us, Chad says in an instant message. It's a Friday night, and you're alone, as usual. Clarissa is always babysitting. You refuse to speak to Beth, even though she tries.

I feel bad we've never actually hung out. Not very nice of me, says Chad. *Why don't we go 2 the mall this wknd? Buy sum presents?*

Just us? you ask. *Really 4 real?*

Just us, he says.

Why don't u pick me up tom morn round 10?

U shitting me? he says. *Not lookin 2 get arrested. Get dropped off @ the mall. Noon.*

You call Clarissa. *You will NEVER guess what I'm doing tomorrow.* Clarissa screams. You both scream. You father opens your door again. *When did it become always scream, scream, scream?* he says. You shuffle through your drawers, try to find the perfect outfit. Your school uniform consists of sweater vests, long khaki skirts, starched collars that cut. This is your chance, you think, to look like a sultry island princess, to embrace where you came from, to show off the exotic woman you could one day be.

You go through every outfit with Clarissa on the phone and decide on the perfect one: shredded bellbottoms, purple satin flip-flops with beaded flowers, a matching purple T-shirt that says HAWAIIAN GURL in silver glitter across the chest. You use your new Sapphire flat iron to press your hair straight. You light incense under your vanity mirror and practice applying your makeup through the snaking smoke. You blast Boyz II Men and sway your hips in the mirror like a woman. You decide to wear a bra, one that fits. Your mother bought it for you recently, a training piece. It's pink with red flowers, a little embarrassing, too *cute*, but the T-shirt covers the straps. You like the way it feels, tight across your chest.

You don't sleep that night. In bed, you read *Little Girl Lost* for the one hundredth time, trying to distract yourself. On the cover, Drew's hair is frizzed and lit from behind. Her lipstick is dark. Drew's life was so hard, you think. You used to relate to this book. Fucked-up parents; a choking loneliness. Her only friend was the robot of *E.T.* and your only friend was this book version of Drew. But that was the old you. That was before men. Look at you now.

* ✳ *

It is difficult to find the twenty-eight-year-old Beth. Years ago, you looked her up online. You had exchanged a few words, casual niceties, but now that account and address are gone. Vanished. Her old number is disconnected; it's as if she doesn't exist. Your remaining high school friends haven't thought of her in years.

There is one person who knows where she is. The friend whose friend's brother's cousin's babysitter helped make it all happen. You still don't know the story. She hands over Beth's e-mail address, wishes you well.

You write an e-mail with the subject line: *Difficult.* You divide this e-mail into two parts. Part one explains that you miss her. Part two explains that you're sorry.

You were such a huge part of my life, you write, *through those achey, formative years. But we are also connected in a way we never fully addressed.*

✳ ✴ ✳

Your mother drives you to the mall before a hair appointment. When she asks who you are meeting, you tell her it's Beth. She's too close with Clarissa's mom for the lie.

That's good, sweetie. I thought you had a falling out or something. I haven't seen her around lately. I've always liked Beth. A good best friend to have.

I'm sure you did, you say, rolling your eyes.

Daddy and I will pick you up at four. We'll go to Sushi Ray.

Whatever, you say.

Pick me out something good! she says.

Chad told you to meet him in the department store Burdines. Of course, you are early. You stand near the top of the escalator, knotting and unknotting your puka-shell choker. You want to look busy when he shows up, so you pretend the cord is broken, bothering you. You feel like *annoyed* is your most mature look.

Hey, he says, from behind you. You had expected to see him on the escalator, but he must have been here all this time, waiting.

Hey you, you say.

You hug an awkward hug. A few hard pats on the back. You wonder if, by the end of the day, you will kiss good-bye. If the hug will be tighter by four o'clock. If he might even slip you some tongue. If, by then, it would feel natural.

So I, ummm, I left something in my car, he says, and it almost sounds like a question. He smiles at you as he says it. His teeth are so wet and perfect. They glow under the fluorescent lights. He repeats himself, *Left something in my car?*, and looks at you as if you should know what this means, as if you should have expected this.

And shopping? you say.

It won't take long, he says. *Will you walk with me to the car?*

You could stop here. You could ask, *What exactly did you leave?* You could say, *No thanks, but meet me back here when you're done—I'll wait.* You know the kinds of things he has told you about—the kinds of things that happen in cars, in *his* car—the words that make him breathe so heavily into the phone you can feel the heat of each syllable in your ear. You could walk away right now and buy your presents. You could change the story.

But *Yes* is what you say. *Sure.*

Chad holds your hand as you walk out the exit, over to the covered parking lot. Nobody has ever held your hand before, not in *this* way, and it feels damp, uncomfortable. You feel self-conscious that he'll see your fingers in the daylight—the wet open wounds around your nails where you gnaw the skin off, where you've been cutting with safety pins at night. You always carry yourself with fists, your thumbs tucked in. Sometimes, when it's worse, you wrap each fingertip in bandages for school. Your mother says you look like a serial killer that way, and this only makes you do it more.

This is me, he says, motioning to the blue car you already know is his.

He opens the rear-left door and asks you to slide in. He slides in after you. It's dark in the car in this covered lot, but right away you see a figure in the driver's seat, the side of a face—it's Gil. *Hey princess,* he says, but he doesn't turn his head around. He doesn't even look at you. He smacks a button that locks all the doors in a quick *thwack.*

He moves his right hand around the seat, toward Chad. Chad gives him five.

You say nothing.

Chad leans in with his eyes open, staring at you. You can't believe a man is this close to your face. He tells you to open your mouth. You do. You feel his tongue on your tongue, and you feel like you might choke. You like this feeling. So this is a kiss. You don't know what to do with your hands, so you sit on them. Chad moans as he circles his tongue— it's that same laugh-cry sound from the phone. He pulls away. *Show me*, he says, as he lifts your T-shirt to your neck. *Flowers, how cute*, he says, as he yanks down the cup of your bra. In this moment, you are humiliated. Your bra has shape, but your breasts do not. Your breasts are nothing but swollen, sore nipples—puffed and pink as erasers. There is nothing else but that. Still, he takes them into his mouth, the left and then the right, and calls you *so sweet*, *sexy*, and says, *Is that what you've been keeping from me?*

You say nothing.

Chad pulls your shaking hand out from under your jeans. For a moment, you consider reaching for the handle of the door, but he catches your hand in his, wraps your raw fingers around his cock. You don't know when he unzipped his pants, when it appeared, but it's there, twitching. You have never seen anything like it before, this strange organ, the palest skin. He moves his hand and your hand with it. You are surprised that the skin moves, that it's not a solid thing. With his other hand, he takes your hair in his fist, pushes your head down, tells you to *be good*. You have no idea what you're doing, but you do your best to breathe. He says, *Cut that shit with the teeth. Open up.* You do your best to be good. He pushes your head all the way down to finish, and tears splash from your eyes onto his boxers. He opens the car door, says, *I'm going shopping*, and Gil gets out of the front seat, comes to meet you in the back. You had forgotten he was even there all this time; you had forgotten the world. His cock is already out, there is no kissing or touching; there are no words. It is larger than Chad's, the size of your forearm. It smells like chlorine. He is more forceful with you, squeezing your wrists in his big hands, clearing your pulse. He pushes and pulls your hair like a fast, violent knock on a door until the rot of him glugs down your throat, until you are coughing, crying, until you have bitten your lip so hard it's bleeding.

He calls Chad on his flip phone. *Come back to the car*, he says, and snaps it shut.

Chad opens the driver seat door. He turns the music up. Chris Carrabba.

They high-five again.

You can't just get out of the car like this, Princess, says Chad. *It'll look weird.*

They drive you around the loop of the mall, drop you off on the side of the road. *Thanks, Cherry Top!* says Chad.

You say nothing.

You don't for years.

✳ ✳ ✳

In the fifteen years since high school, Chad has been arrested for petit theft, grand theft, drug possession, assault, simple battery, battery of a law enforcement officer, burglary with assault, battery with prior offenses, multiple violations of parole, and has been declared a "Habitual Felony Offender" by Broward County. He has attempted suicide three times, overdosed twice, and spent three and a half years in state prison. He spent years in a homeless shelter. Once, in prison, he was strapped naked to a steel bunk and shit himself. The correctional officers dragged his soiled body around the grounds of the prison, hosing him off, humiliating him, scraping his body pink as a gumdrop.

Gil is an attorney in Boca Raton. He represents victims of sexual violence and harassment. He married his high school sweetheart—the eighteen-year-old classmate and girlfriend, you learn, that he'd had the whole time.

These are some of the things Chad is telling you now, on the Internet. They all check out. With a simple Google search, you're able to scroll through Chad's mug shots over the years. You find his Twitter, his dating profile, the racial slurs and flat-Earth conspiracy theories he has posted online. Still, it is difficult to think about him as more than a ghost, as a real person in the present world.

He has two injunctions of protection against him—one for stalking, one for repeated violence—but you don't know that yet. Just last year, after he was released from prison, Beth filed the first restraining order against him. He reached out to her for forgiveness, she will later confirm, and things got ugly from there. Another girl, a minor, filed an injunction soon after. When this essay is published one year after you write it in that New Hampshire artist colony, you will file the third.

✳

You walk along the side of the road, back toward the mall. Maybe, you think, this is what adults do when they feel the feels of love. Maybe they share their girls; maybe it's quick, forceful; maybe it happens just like that.

It's not even one o'clock. Winter in Florida. You push open the mall door and feel the suck of the air conditioner. You are nervous to be seen—you are absolutely *not* allowed to be inside a mall, or anywhere, alone.

You walk in and out of cosmetic stores. In the track-lit mirror, you look different. Your eye makeup is smudged like a bruise; your cheeks are flushed; your hair is no longer straight or smooth. Worst of all, your lips. Your lips are at least three times their regular size, raw and shiny, purple and inflamed from the teeth. Whose teeth? Whose bite marks? You can't be sure now.

In the mirror you think: I don't look like a girl anymore.

And then: I look like such a pathetic little girl.

And then: maybe this is what a woman looks like.

And then: I look sexy like this. Beaten. Theirs.

And then: I wish I were a boy.

And then: I look like every other girl there ever was.

You do your best with the sample powders, rub the beige cream under your eyes. Your mom will notice the mess of you, you're sure. You are nothing like your mother. Since drying out, your mother is clean and smooth as a candlewick. Pressed creases. Adored.

You buy each of your parents a present with their own money. A teacup for your mother. A baseball cap for your father. You buy a large bottle of orange soda from the food court—your favorite. You want the fizzy orange chemicals to dye your mouth, to blame the bloom of your lips on this simple thing.

Your parents pick you up from the entrance of Burdines at four o'clock. *Those lips!* they say, and you agree. You lift the empty bottle of soda, *Sorry, I must've drunk too much.*

You look like you're bleeding, says your father.

I tripped on the escalator, you say.

You sure about that? asks your father.

I'm super sure.

Something happen in there with Beth? he says.

Your father was never a great father, but, when sober, he was always a great man. He was the person who loved you most, and, fifteen years later when he dies, when you're talking to that rocking chair in New Hampshire hoping it is he who has possessed it, you consider this moment in the car—how the trajectory of your life and your relationship to him could have changed had you told him the truth. If there was no mother in the driver's seat, no fear of getting in trouble; if there was no escalator in that mall. *It's a father's job to protect his daughter,* he told you, more than once, but your story never got there. That story is not yours.

Just shut up about it, you say.

The only person you ever tell is Clarissa, sitting on her bed under her painted-on clouds. You tell the story calmly, sucking on your fingertips, no big deal. You tell her they both wanted you, they both *had* to have you, and you were very good at it. Their cocks were big, and you took the whole thing like a goddamn champ.

You are such a slut! she screams.

Jealous, you think. You want so badly for her to be jealous.

You gonna do it again? she asks.

Nah, you say. *They're graduating soon. I don't want them to get too attached to me.*

The truth: you never heard from Gil again. You heard from Chad only once, online. He asked if you might be willing to meet up with him the following weekend at the mall again, if next time you would let him fuck you in the backseat. He promises it will feel good, after it hurts. He warns you not to tell Beth. You block his screen name, unhook your private line. You begin sleeping in your parents' bed every night, a habit you were never able to fully break.

It was just so romantic, you say. You believe these words. That's how it works.

✳ ✳ ✳

Gil's e-mail address is listed on his law firm's website.

It's late at night in the New Hampshire library, your bracelets clattering against the desk. Another colonist named James watches your hands shake, says, *Are you sure you want to do that? Are you sure you want to open up all of that?*

You are.

Do you remember me? you type. *I have some questions. I would be grateful if you might be willing to answer them.*

Why did you hurt me? is the only question, the only one that matters, but you do not write this.

Of course I remember you! he replies, almost immediately. *I will give it my best to answer any questions you have. I hope you are doing good!*

You ask if he might be willing to share his memory of that day at the mall. *Your point of view would be helpful for my own closure*, you say, *no matter what that may be.* You ask if he has ever thought of it again, if the experience ever held any weight for him. You tell him there are no right answers. You believe this is true.

Gil responds from a different e-mail address. His personal one.

Let me really think about it, he says, *so I can give you my best recollection.*

I want to help you, he says, *in any way that I can.*

You never hear from Gil again.

On Skype, the twenty-eight-year-old Beth looks exactly the same. *There is a reason I am so difficult to find*, she says, *but I'm so glad you found me.*

She is still so beautiful, Beth. You cry as soon as you see her face on the screen.

I'm doing well, she says.

I love living somewhere with seasons, she says.

I heard about your dad, she says. *No one could ever forget him.*

Thank you.

Beth tells you that she still works every day to forget her experiences with Chad. She says she doesn't blame him, that blaming him would give him power. Beth believes that blame would add fuel to a dangerous situation, and anyways, it's a chapter she's closed. She is religious these days, at peace with her thirteen-year-old self and the decisions she knows she was not prepared to make. She says, *If I can wish him well, I feel that I have won.*

Do you feel that he assaulted you? you ask.

No, she says. *I think he only ever wanted love.*

You talk for an hour, maybe two, but these are the only details you can share here, right now. Remember, there is a reason she's so difficult to find. By now, you both are.

✳ ✳ ✳

One day, in the spring, Beth hands you a diamond-shaped note, not looking at you: *Meet me at the flagpole after class.*

At the bell, she swings on her backpack and almost hits you in the face with it.

Outside, in the sun, Beth's hair whips around her face like she's pulsing with electricity. Her eyes twitch so the tears won't fall. You know what is about to happen, and you miss her already.

Was it worth it? she asks.

Was what?

You cover your ears with your hands. You say, *No, No, No, No.* You cry. You take it. You deserve every last insult. You beg. You fall on your knees and stain your uniform in the wet grass. Your classmates walk by, shaking their heads. You almost throw up into the dirt. You say, *Please, Beth. No, please.*

Beth picks you up off the ground by your armpits. She hugs you like she means it, like she's the first person who has ever wanted to take care of you. You do not understand why, not yet, but no one has ever been more kind to you than Beth.

Beth tries to be your friend for the rest of high school, but it's not the same. You are a slut and you know it. You can't be trusted and you know it. Soon, you only occasionally wave to each other from across the halls.

No one ever speaks of Chad again, not once he graduates. Clarissa told Beth what you had done—*It was the right thing to do*—and, entering high school, the two of them become best friends.

You deface both of their pictures in your yearbook.

You sleep with the book in your arms.

* ✳ *

You tell Chad, Clarissa, and Beth that you're writing an essay about them. They all give you permission, tell you to rename them however you'd like.

I am so deeply honored that you would write about me, Chad says. *Although I'm sure your portrayal of me will not be glorious.* He has had a spiritual awakening, and he sends you a YouTube video about it. He asks if you are religious. He feels bad for you that you're not. He compares you to a plant growing in the shade. He wants to know if you're single.

You are not sure why you are even talking to Chad, what you think he can tell you.

Was there anyone else? you ask him. *Other girls our age—besides me and Beth?*

One name, and then another. And another. He lists four right then, though there will be more later (*That car*, one will say. *I can still feel the air-conditioning inside of that car*). These are girls you knew, liked. A girl from the school play. A girl who once made you a friend-ship bracelet out of telephone wire. Other girls everyone wanted to be.

Chad says, *My life up to this point has been . . . not so much fun. You could say I was paid back one hundred times over for what I did to you or anyone else. Does that make you feel better?*

Does it? I still don't know.

All of us in the same car, outside the same mall. All of us girls, now women. All of our hands reaching for a door.

PART II

THE GREETER

COUSIN CINDY

There goes Cousin Cindy again. She looks like Betty Boop, with the same red lips and hair. She's a tween but looks older—strapped up in all the right places—beloved. Men pay attention.

Here, in the Disney park, grown men in animal suits take their heads off to whisper animal things into Cousin Cindy's ear. They want to take care of her, bite the skin behind her knees. They want to make like Aladdin and show her the world. They call her princess and duchess, and she leans in to hear them better, a Firecracker popsicle rounded out in her mouth—*What's that, Mister Nice?*—her sweating, budding chest against their fur. She pulls her shorts up by the belt loops, lets the perfect moon-curve of her ass hang below the frayed denim and bounce there.

My Grandma Sitchie always says Cousin Cindy got the looks and I got the brains, the sweetness. I'm the sensitive one, she always says. A yolk to my heart. *If I could combine the two of you, I'd have the perfect granddaughter.* Grandma Sitchie is my father's mother. She's Jewish; she gets her hair set at the salon twice a week; she hates my mother; she's the reason we're in Boca Raton.

She's a bitch, that Cindy, dumb as a gnat, but prettier than Hepburn, Grandma explains one day while eating a Bundt-mold of savory Jell-O. She points the wet spoon at me for emphasis. Lucille Ball's laugh crackles through the kitchen.

I want to be Cousin Cindy when I grow up. I tell my Grandma Sitchie I'd trade in all my brains and sweetness to be a little more like her.

It's true, she says, nodding, *that life gets on much easier, much better, if you're pretty.*

Cousin Cindy, babysitting me in North Carolina. It's the summer I turn eight. Yesterday the whole family went white-water rafting down the Watauga River. We played Red-Neck-Bingo with homemade score cards—checking off satellite dishes, yard art, tires and couches on roofs—as we shot past the country homes.

Our rafting guide's name was Alphonso, and he joked that he could sink our very raft with the weight of himself, depending on which way he leaned. He kept biscuits under his armpits and between the rolls of his skin to keep them warm and dry. Cousin Cindy loved this, sat on his lap, ate the biscuits from his big, meaty hands, laughing. When Alphonso threw my sandal into the river, Cousin Cindy snatched it up between her acrylic nails, slapped him across the face with it, said, *Don't mess with my baby, you bad boy, you.*

Now she is babysitting me in my family's cabin, turning off my bedroom lights, telling me to *nod off already, go to fucking bed, Jesus Christ, I take it back, I didn't mean it or anything, but for real can you go the fuck to sleep, aren't you tired? No? Seriously? Not even after all that rafting, the food I made you, Jesus I never want a kid, and what kind of kid eats so much even? How many boxes of Velveeta can you chow? Is that your Chinese side? Why's your nose always bleeding, it honestly freaks me the fuck out, do I need to do something about it?*

Cousin Cindy presses her hands together like she's praying. She says, *I'm sorry, but when you're seventeen you'll understand.* She closes my door.

I've been reading *Harriet the Spy* and keeping my very own spy journal. I decide there is no better time to write, to report, than tonight with Cousin Cindy. I crawl to my bedroom door, lower the brass handle. I push it open and breathe into the triangle of light. Cousin Cindy is standing at the dresser mirror, next to the front door. She paints on black lipstick with a tiny brush, teases her curls with a pick. She clasps a big silver cross around her neck so Jesus hangs squeezed between her breasts. She sprays perfume from a diamond-shaped bottle into the air and walks right into it, spins three times.

There's a knock on the door. It's Alphonso, in real clothes. No life vest, no biscuits. In our house, he's just a college boy—an Appalachian State University sweatshirt, tattered camouflage pants, a beeper clamped to his pocket. Cousin Cindy kisses him long and hard, like they've been waiting for this moment all their lives. She walks backward and pulls him by the sweatshirt until they reach the plaid couch. She pushes him onto it, kneels down, unzips. Alphonso doesn't know what to do with his hands, so he holds them up by his face. I think, this is what Alphonso must have looked like as a child—this face widened with shock and awe—a boy who tripped over his sandcastle, who peeled open the eyes of a newborn kitten, a boy who just destroyed something for the first time.

I write down what I see. Their limbs tangle, and the two of them fall asleep like this. I am jealous of Alphonso, seeing my cousin this way, this other view of her body. I want to be closer. I want this image of a woman all for myself.

My parents walk in soon after. *What the / from the raft? / our daughter, where? / the biscuit boy?*

I never see Alphonso again.

✱ ✱ ✱

Cousin Cindy, taking me to my second concert in the world. I'm eleven. It's Britney Spears, and Britney is wearing white leather pants with pink patches on her knees. We're in the first row—my mother bought us the tickets—and Cousin Cindy is sneaking drags from her Newports, blowing the smoke beneath our seats. The bouncer wraps his hand around her neck, tells her it's okay—*I won't tell if you won't, sweetheart*—and she gives him a wink.

I am standing, dancing, my belly showing like Britney, but Cousin Cindy stays knees-up in her folding seat. She acts annoyed, but every once in a while I catch her mouthing the words—*My loneliness is killing me*—smiling. I can tell there is something inside her that is burning to be here. The lights, the glamour, Britney's long, plastic ponytail, the bubblegum beat. I think, Cousin Cindy should have been a star. She has never talked about a life she wants, but maybe this is it. Maybe she was right to drop out of beauty school. Maybe she's meant to be the glittering girl on this stage, uglier girls at her feet, their hands cupped around their mouths screaming *Cindy! Cindy!* as she pauses before the last word of everyone's favorite song, closing her eyes, making the whole world beg for it.

Cousin Cindy is sad on the car ride home. She chain-smokes, pops the car lighter, bites the side of her lip till the scarlet drags off. She says it's a good thing I have her to take me to these concerts, to show me a good time. It's a good thing she's around to take care of me, since my parents are so fucked. *Fucked how?* I ask. I've never heard the words used in quite this way. *Cracked out*, she says. *Coke, rocks, all that shit. Your parents are the reason I'll never get high, swear to God, that shit ain't for me. You're so goddamn lucky you got your Cousin Cindy.*

✻ ✱ ✻

Cousin Cindy, calling my first cell phone. I'm thirteen.

Your mom can't hear, right?

No way.

I've got a new job in Hollywood. It's rad; the people are nice. I'm tired all the time but most of all, I miss you. Come out, she says, *I miss my baby.*

Hollywood, Florida, is nothing like the Hollywood on television. There are no movie stars, no hills. Instead, there's a trash mountain big enough to block out the sunset, where men in jumpsuits torch diapers under the buzzards. My mother says I'm not allowed to go to this Hollywood, this particular block Cousin Cindy is describing, where sex shops line the streets in mean yellows.

I can't come, I tell Cousin Cindy. *You know I can't. Everybody knows about your job and what it is.*

Jesus Christ, it's not like I'm a stripper, she says. *I'm a waitress at a strip club. I serve drinks, chicken wings. I don't take my shit off.*

I know. I didn't say—

Tell your mother I don't take my shit off.

We know.

I need my baby, she says. *I'm lonely. Just come down for lunch, will you? The wings are so good here. You'd like them. Extra hot.*

✳ ✳ ✳

A weekend with Cousin Cindy. It's been a while since the Julia Roberts movies and the matching manicures and the *Tell me, how's it like in real school? So goddamn rich the kids have diamonds on their cell phones, no? You still have those spy laptops? Those yacht parties?*

Tonight we're on a cruise ship because I am this winter season's Grand Champion Equestrian. It's the end-of-the-year awards banquet, and the Wellington Horse Show Association wants to hand off ribbons taller than I am, little statues and trophies with golden ponies on top. My parents haven't left their bedroom in almost a week, so Cousin Cindy volunteered.

Free steak? A reason for my party dress? Duh.

She wears crimped hair teased and fastened in a circle by glittering pins. The mound of bright blonde curls is bigger than a cantaloupe. Cousin Cindy never liked the natural ash of her hair, and has been painting on boxes of dye since she was old enough to ride a bike.

During the award ceremony, a shipmate dressed in all denim approaches Cousin Cindy at our table. He whispers in her ear, presses a folded piece of paper into her palm. When the trophies are gone, she takes me below deck to meet him. She holds my prizes in her arms.

The denim man is waiting in a room full of humming machinery. His name, he says, is Sean Connery. *Oh my God, like the movie star?* Cousin Cindy asks. *Any relation?*

A different spelling, he says. I'm S-H-A-W-N. I'm bigger, you see. He flexes a bicep and stares at it, points at the bulge, as if surprised. I don't know who the real Sean Connery is, but I hate this one.

Why don't you girlies let Shawn Connery take you on a tour of the underbelly?

Can I drive this ship? asks Cousin Cindy.

If you're good. Shawn Connery slaps her ass.

It only takes three rooms, three explanations of the rudders, the hull, before Shawn Connery starts eying me differently, closing a metal door before I can step into the room. *Don't you have pony stuff to do?* he says, giving Cousin Cindy a smile, an emphasis on that question mark in a tone they both believe to be *Grown-Up Talk*—a language all children, anywhere, understand. I step outside the room and wait a few minutes. I wait until I hear Cousin Cindy whispering Shawn Connery's name before I get it, feel relieved, before I ask if they can at least hand over my trophies.

* ✳ *

Cousin Cindy takes me to the state fair, her favorite day of the year. She wants the wind in her hair, the rickety coasters. She wants to suck on cotton candy and ride the Gravitron until we crawl across the wall to each other, in slow motion, puking. I say, *Sure, Cousin Cindy. I'll go with you, sure.*

Outside the Fun House, Cousin Cindy meets a man named Costas. He works the kabob stand, but says he owns an island somewhere in Greece. His white T-shirt is tight, dirty, grease stains blooming over the muscles of his chest. He looks like a movie star playing the role of Greek Kabob Man.

Is this your child? he asks Cousin Cindy, pointing a kabob at my face. *She no look anything like you?*

Baby cousin, she says. *Ain't she cute?*

Too bad, I love kids, he says.

Costas gives us free meat all night. Kabobs piled on Styrofoam plates, lamb shawarma. We gnaw at the chunks of salty meat until our faces glow turmeric orange. When Costas's shift is over, he leads us to the front of every line, wins us bags of fighting fish, Chinese finger traps. We tell Costas we're ready for him to take us away to his island. We will eat all of his food and we'll be good wives. Costas kisses Cousin Cindy goodnight with a gentleness I have never seen from a man. Cousin Cindy smiles the whole way home and, for once, doesn't want to talk about it.

One week later, our family sits down to eat dinner at Stir Crazy, a restaurant in the Boca Raton Town Center mall. Grandma Sitchie informs me that I'm a *very rude girl* for reading *Go Ask Alice* under the table, and tells me it's time I learn to hold knives and forks properly, instead of chopsticks.

Costas shows up with Cousin Cindy, hand in hand. He's holding a bouquet of daisies wrapped in brown paper, and his shoes are flawless, shining. I think he must have bought them this very day, for us.

Good-looking fella, says my Grandma, nodding. *Why Cindy?*

I find her fascinating, he says. *And obviously, quite beautiful.*

Fascinating. She pauses on the word, sips her merlot. *Do you know what your fascinating girl does for a living?*

Cousin Cindy hates all fairs, all amusement parks, after this night. She says they're for kids.

* ✳ *

Cousin Cindy doesn't call much anymore. She's working the Cheetah Club at night, and Diamond Dolls during the afternoon. Tonight, in that year before my father checks into rehab, there's too much noise in the living room to sleep. My mother is gone—she's visiting her own mother in Texas—and my father has invited his friends over. I can picture each one of them on the other side of the wall as they yell, the scene building as I listen: Voss, with hair so gelled it looks like a swim cap; Harvey, with his old eyes and young girl-friends; Brad, shaking his baby bags of pills and powders; Nikhil, who once swallowed a live goldfish. I hear their voices boom, a wild clattering of glass. Something is funny, just so funny, but I can't make out what it is.

I want to tell them to keep it down. I want to tell them I have school tomorrow, remember, there's a kid here. There's a kid who never makes it to school because of whatever you're always doing in my living room, which is mine, with my horse pictures hanging on the walls, my ribbons, my shoes kicked muddy across the carpet, my hermit crab loose somewhere in the couch upon which you are sitting.

I open my door and walk down the hallway toward the living room. This is against the rules and I know it—*Do not leave your room past ten P.M., do not interrupt when friends are over, do NOT.* The light in the living room is an adjustment, the smoke; I have to blink hard and fast to see. The friends are all sprawled on the couch, the carpet, burning cherries of Marlboros in their mouths, some with their belt buckles hanging. My father is passed out on the floor with an ashtray next to his head. Between two of the men on the couch, the back of a woman. She's wearing nothing but a cheetah-patterned bra, a thong. She's snorting powder off a flat, metal end of a lobster fork that another man is holding up for her. Her hair extension is loose, swinging by a platinum thread.

Hi, Cousin Cindy, I say, but she can't place exactly who I am to her, where she knows me from, why I'm even here.

* ✳ *

When I'm in high school, Cousin Cindy tells me and Grandma Sitchie she's a cam girl these days. She keeps her toddler son in the other room while she talks sweet to men around the world, crawling toward the blinking light on her computer, pulling her straps down, waiting for the money. This is how she explains the new job over dinner. She enjoys telling our grandma the details.

That's a whore thing to do, says Grandma. *You should be more like your cousin,* she says, *just look at her.* She looks at me. Cousin Cindy looks, too. *Homely as a toad but not a whorish thing about her.*

Thank you, is what I say.

If only I could combine the two of you—

We know, says Cousin Cindy.

Who's the father of this kid of yours anyway? Where's the fella? Isn't he brown?

He's Italian.

He looks like a terrorist.

I make bank with my cam work; I even bought a new body.

And what about your son, Cindy? Your SON.

Pass the butter? I say.

✳ ✳ ✳

There goes Cousin Cindy again. She's on her cam, eyes black and clouded over as frozen grapes. Tonight, she gives her shoes a plug over the cam, *They're comfy, and on sale!*, spreading her legs into a V, holding her boots by the ankles.

Her name on this site is *Beach Miztress*. There are two columns beside the cam box, "Will Do" and "Won't Do" (*Pussy, Anal, Toys, Lesbian, Group, Dom, Sub, Dance, Private*), and a scrolling chat box of usernames and cartoon coins.

Cousin Cindy turns her back to the camera so the chatroom men can watch as she unhooks her bra. She's got a large cactus tattoo with neon colors above her ass, *Desert Dream* etched in cursive on the cactus's arm because Cousin Cindy was born out there, in Arizona. She had a life, other than this one. A childhood on red sand; a stepfather who— it's been said—hurt her for years in the dark. She was once just a girl who played with action figures. A girl with scabbed knees and teen idols sticky-tacked her wall, a kid who just wanted to get out.

Mr. Big, are you there? she says.

I'm here, I type.

You want to see me put this tentacle in my ass? She holds up a rubber Octopus toy with suction cups. She sucks on it for us.

No, I type. *I want to talk to you about politics. Who was your favorite president?*

That's a whacky fetish you got there, Mr. Big. She stares right into the camera, pinching her nipples, looking confused.

Shut it with the politics, Mr. Big. Are you a fucking fag? The other men in the chatroom type furiously, one after the next.

List one favorite president, I type. *One policy. Anything.*

I'm t-t-t-thinking, Cousin Cindy stutters a bit—her nervous habit.

Can you not list a single president? You fucking moron?

I want her to be humiliated. I want her to pull a sweatshirt over her head, focus her pupils, snap her laptop closed. In this moment, more than anything, I want to see Cousin Cindy cry.

I don't see why you care, she says, forcing a giggle. *We're not here for that!*

She's right! the men type. *On with the tentacle, please!*

Prove me wrong, I type. *Just one.*

Can't it be enough, she says, looking straight through my screen, *to be quiet and love you?*

CAN I PET YOUR BACK?

Something happened when I got to high school: I found pretty. I found pretty in my slick of teeth, the metal brackets popped off with pliers, the sticky strips of bleach in my mouth. I found pretty in emerald contact lenses, and the squares of tinfoil that sucked the dark right out of my hair. I found pretty in the tanning salon; Playboy bunny stickers arranged on my hips; that blue scream of light baking my naked body. I found pretty in thick foundations that smeared away my freckles, and in inch-long tubes of Styrofoam secured to my eyes for a lash perm. Pretty in the leather seats of high schoolers' cars and in the back rows of movie theaters and on MTV; I found pretty on the Internet. I found pretty in a stranger named Lennox Price, queen of Fort Lauderdale, in the way she'd document her life on Myspace, her lonely car rides, her breast augmentation, her fishnet tops, the way she drizzled liquor down the mouths of men in the club scene. I found pretty in the plastic clamshell cases of pills—*for regulation, not for sex*—that bloomed my chest to a size C. I found pretty in acrylic nails and Abercrombie & Fitch and scratch and sniff G-strings on plastic hangers, pretty when I threw my riding clothes away—the breeches, then the boots—because I had been looking *too fat* to be a jockey *too fat* for show jumping *too fat* for the Olympics *too fat too curvy too woman too soft* (how many more times can a body betray you?). I found pretty in a homecoming Duchess crown, in the wave of my hand from the convertible car creeping around the football field because I was *Most Changed*—I was that kind of pretty. I found pretty in boys calling me hot. I found pretty in calling girls hot. I found pretty in calling girls fat. I found pretty in calling girls sluts. Girls. I found pretty when the same boy who once asked, *Are you a goat? Can I pet your back?* didn't recognize this new version of me, and asked to jerk off into my eyes. I found pretty in the feeling of a razor nicking the hair off my calves, my arms, my back, my pussy, my stomach, my nipples, my sideburns, my armpits, my big toes, my fingers, my neck, my chin, until my skin buzzed with a smooth purity. I found pretty when I dreamed of being raped under bridges and being raped (while drowned) in a Jacuzzi and being raped in Temple and being raped in the gym locker room because I should feel lucky, I guess, being pretty enough for that. I found pretty in Skylar Fingerhut and her summer nose job and chin job and cheek job and all those oozing bandages, like nebulas on gauze, how she invited me over for the first time, let me lift a straw of chicken broth to her mouth as she healed, saying, *Symmetry, that's the key to all this pretty*, and I felt as if I were fanning Cleopatra herself. I found pretty in telling my mom to stay in the car at the pickup line, and in the way neighborhood boys beat her hummingbird mailbox with golf clubs, slowly, so that one wing dangled, then both, then the beak; now, only the body is left. I found pretty in the swirl of my lunch from my mouth into toilet bowls, and in the spots of light I'd see when I'd blink away hunger. I found pretty in clavicles, in the nose ring I'd get while I watched a new friend have a needle shoved through the hood of her cunt. I found pretty in the cast of the *Real World* and in Carmen Electra, pretty on Chinese New Year, my family dressed in red, picking at the cheeks of a snapper, the way I could shift the food around my plate and go somewhere else behind my eyes and say, *I'm not like you, I'm prettier than this.* I found pretty in my C grades, then Ds, in new classes with no Honors, in the word *expulsion.* I found pretty in stupid. I found pretty when my father began referring to me as *daughter* instead of *son* when he got a call to move to New York, get out of town. The way he said, *You'll be fine staying here, growing up this way. You're already such a good woman.*

LONG LIVE THE TRIBE OF

FATHERLESS GIRLS

Your name is *Kinky Chinky*, they say to me, these girls, as they drag on their Parliament Lights. Harley and Nelle—all ass and stomach and lip gloss and tongue rings—they don't belong here at this party, though all of us want them.

This is the first time I've been invited, and I came here alone. This is the beginning of a story, a new one. This is me without a father or a mother or a best friend, a boat parade bash in a mansion overlooking the Intracoastal, 2003. I'm a sophomore, fifteen years old, my knees cratered and red from sucking off a boy named Brandon in somebody else's closet.

Kinky Chinky, it suits you.

Another sophomore named Craig hosts this party every year around Christmas, where the richest kids in our class watch America's finest yachts split black water like a zipper. Nobody misses Craig's parties because they have the best drugs and shelves full of blue-colored booze. At least a handful of our class always ends up fucking in a closet, or in Craig's hot tub, or on the floor of a bedroom, but usually I only hear about it.

Harley and Nelle corner me in the billiard room of Craig's house. The lights are dim, Ginuwine's "In Those Jeans" playing from somewhere downstairs. This is where they stand, smoking, staring at my knees.

Brandon Friedman? Really? He's got the body of a fridge.

Harley Pelletier and Nelle Roman don't go to our school. They're childhood friends of Craig's—their parents have done *business* with his parents. I knew Harley once before; she went to our middle school for one year before moving south to Davie. She was sweet then, with hair like fondue chocolate down to her waist, light oval eyes— *just like Adriana Lima*—clear braces that somehow never yellowed. She and I spilled chemicals into the mouths of beakers in our sixth-grade science class. *I've never met a Chink before*, she said to me once, lovingly, holding a scalpel in her gloved hand, a formaldehyde-softened frog between us.

Harley and Nelle don't look like any other girls at our school, and the boys at this party can tell. Harley has a short, bob haircut now, body of a blade, with nose freckles and a silver tongue stud that glints when she speaks to you. Everybody calls her "Lips," and she seems embarrassed by the nickname—*These fish lips? Gross!*—but we can all tell that she knows their DSL appeal. It's the way she puckers them when she's thinking, the way she wraps them around a bottle between every sip.

Nelle is more understated. She barely wears makeup—she doesn't need it—and her tan skin glows as if lit up from the inside. She has deep auburn hair, hips and breasts, a tongue ring with prickly neon strings sprouting out of it like a sea creature. She calls this her *Kushy-ball. Better blowies with this*, she says. *Drives men crazy.* Tonight, she wears a neon-green Von Dutch trucker hat, which she turns backward and forward depending on which boy is flirting with her and how much she likes it.

You're so cute, Nelle tells me. *Is your hair really that thick or do you have extensions?*

No, she's really Chinese, says Harley. *It was the same in middle school.*

You don't even look that Asian, says Nelle.

You're actually really pretty, says Harley.

The two of them have a way of picking up each other's sentences in quick succession.

You look, like, really sad though, says Nelle. *Why Brandon? You're hotter than that.*

Because he asked me to, I shrug.

The truth: Clarissa recently spent the night with the first boy I ever thought could be a *real boyfriend*, the first boy I thought I loved. Eric was his name. He had big, friendly ears that he pinned back with cosmetic surgery a couple of years ago for his thirteenth birthday—bar and bat mitzvah year—the same year everybody but me gets their face and body fixed. I met him at Jewish summer camp, and he wrote me a love ballad called "Jazzy Girl," which he sang as he dipped me across a keyboard for a kiss in the camp computer lab. Next thing I heard, Clarissa lost her V-card to Eric. The two of them tell me they only dry humped, but still I cry into my mattress, I cry on the phone to my father, I cry to Ashanti, I cry off fifteen pounds. I swear I will never speak to Eric or Clarissa again—*I hope you two get AIDS*—but many years later, when Eric takes his life in a motel room in upstate New York, Clarissa will be the first person I call.

I correct myself: *I'm on the rebound. My best friend fucked my boyfriend. Once a fat bitch, always a fat bitch I guess.*

BURN! They both scream. *Let's get you shwasted!*

Harley and Nelle bring me a large glass of Red Bull and vodka. It's weird to swish the vodka in my mouth, something as familiar to me as water, but somehow new, like this, when it's mine. The three of us drink this combination all night, their fingers clinking the ice around in the glass. We cuddle up in Craig's bed as the boats drag by. The later it gets, the more I feel understood by these girls. They both stroke my hair, my thighs. They move their hands up my shirt and slowly tickle my stomach—*Such a sick bod! / Thanks, it's the mono*—and I don't mind this. For the first time in years, I don't mind being touched. The caffeine from the Red Bull has my heart feeling huge and my lips are numb and wet and I'm biting them and pinching them to feel more like Harley and I have never been drunk before, I have never seen yacht lights flashing through windows, I have never seen girls' faces this close up to mine, talking.

Craig takes out a disposable camera and tells the three of us to pose. He flashes the camera while we smile together in bed, on the floor, in the baby crib of his guestroom. Our faces are flushed, and we're holding hands in every picture. Nelle's green hat—we all took turns wearing it. I find the photos twelve years later, each photo scissored out in the shape of a heart. On the back of one are words, though I cannot remember who wrote them, or when. They read, *Best Friends Forever.*

* ✳ *

I am a new person after our school's holiday break. I don't care about any kids in my grade; I continue ignoring Clarissa; I start lining my lips with dark lip pencils to make them look bigger. Harley and Nelle have decided to adopt me—*File the paperwork, it's official*—and they pick me up from school at three thirty on the days I show.

Harley is sixteen now, older than me and Nelle, and she drives like a maniac. She weaves around other cars on I-95, plays chicken in the wrong lanes, uses turbo. She's been driving crazy since years before she got a license, Nelle tells me, but none of this matters to us. The way we see it, Harley is beautiful, and she can legally drive, and that's the end of it.

From my school, we go straight to Harley's house. Her mother usually stays at her boyfriend's apartment, but sometimes she's passed out on the couch with a half-drunk glass and a bottle of nasal spray. Her father lives somewhere out west. Harley's room feels so grown-up with navy-blue walls, clicking beaded streamers at her doorway, an open shower in the middle of her room, a mattress on the floor. My room at home is still pink with porcelain dolls and twinkle lights lining the perimeter, but I don't tell them this.

Tonight, we're going to a bonfire party off Dixie Highway called The Circus. Public school kids. Bass music. Nelle stands at the bathroom mirror smudging on charcoal eyeliner, a cigarette bit between her teeth. In my memories of Nelle, there's never a moment that she is not smoking. *Fuck, it's making me water!* she says, fanning the smoke from her eyes.

You ever smoke before, Chinky? Harley asks me. The two of us are sitting on the love seat in her room. *Why you always staring at her?*

I haven't.

Ugh, you are such a Martian.

I'll try, I say. *I mean, I love the way they smell.*

It's nice out—let's go outside.

The three of us sit on the wood planks of Harley's deck, palm trees whistling. A streetlight glows close and our eyes are gold with it.

We like cloves, says Nelle. *Bali Hai's. They taste like doped-out candy.*

Harley puts one between my lips. *Suck*, she says, lighting it.

I hold the thick flavor in my mouth. I switch between trying to breathe through my mouth and my nose. I don't know how to inhale, but it's true, I do taste the bright sugar. Nelle and Harley exhale the smoke from their nostrils in teapot streams.

Let it out of your nose, that's how you know you're doing it right.

I listen to the paper crackle between my teeth. The sound is amplified in my head, and I pretend that each crackle is a strand of my brain dying out.

Do you have parents? I ask Nelle. *I mean, how do you come here every night?*

My mom's always up my ass, she says, *but Harley's mom covers for me on the phone. Says we're watching movies or doing math problems or something. My sister's in college.*

And your parents let you—

Her dad's dead, says Harley, *if that's what you're trying to ask.*

Nelle doesn't look at either one of us when Harley says this. She takes a longer drag, snap-cracks her knuckles against her knees.

Well, I've always wanted a sister, I say. *So that's cool.*

And what about you, shoe princess? Nelle says. *Don't you spend a lot of money on prep to be skipping every day?*

My dad moved to New York last year, I say. *For the business. And my mom doesn't give a shit about school.*

Isn't your whole family in prison or something? Chillin' with Martha Stewart?

Harley jabs Nelle with an elbow—*Rude.*

What! Nelle says. *I mean, it's on the frickin' news.*

It's cool, I say. *The prison thing.*

What'd they do again?

Different stuff. Mostly money.

Do you miss them?

Nah.

Well, we're your sisters now, says Harley. Nelle nods. *Like blood.*

At the bonfire, the three of us sip Coronas and sway our hips to Biggie Smalls—*bitches I like 'em brainless, guns I like 'em stainless*—thumping out of a boom box. We're in the middle of a parking lot behind a block of abandoned warehouses near a great stretch of trees, and the fire is piled high with tires and cardboard boxes fluttering inside a metal trash can. Groups of older kids laugh around the orange sparks, sucking on cigarettes, kissing. A senior from Nelle's public school walks over to us and wraps his arms around her waist. *Hey, Pimpstress, you smoking tonight?*

His name's Monty, Harley whispers to me. *He's in love with Nelle and he's always got green.*

Monty plucks a cigarette out from behind his ear. It looks like it's been wrapped with a brown paper bag.

That a joint? I ask. I don't recognize this. The only joints I have ever seen are my mother's, and those are always wrapped white.

A blunt, says Monty. He chuckles at me. *Where'd you find this girl?*

She's our prep school tropical princess, says Harley. *Ain't she cute?*

Monty lights the blunt and takes it in, passing it over to Nelle, who passes it over to Harley.

I'm assuming you're a weed virgin, too? she asks.

I nod.

Open your mouth, she says. Harley sucks the blunt until the burning worm almost reaches her nails. Before I know what's happening, she presses her mouth to mine, exhaling the smoke down my throat. I hold her by the back of her head—I hold her right there—I don't want our faces to part.

Relax, lez, she says, pulling away. *Suck it in.*

We circle this blunt, and then another, several more times. My tongue feels like a pinecone. Everything I say ticks around my head like a film projector, and I can't tell if the words are coming out now or if they came out fifteen minutes ago, or if I haven't even said them yet.

Look at Chinky's eyes, says Nelle. *Now you can actually tell she's Asian!*

Why do you both say white girl shit like that? I say, surprising myself.

Excuse me, I'm one-eighth Bolivian, says Harley.

I laugh so hard at this that a long string of drool drips down to the gravel. The drool looks bedazzled to me with the bonfire behind it. Slow motion.

I wonder if my mother feels like this all the time. If my father did, before rehab. In this moment, I think I understand drugs and booze and the big deal about them. I feel infinite here, with these girls, strong, like either one of them could choke me or yank out fistfuls of my hair and I would love it. It'd be the feel-good burn of a loose tooth you can't stop tonguing, a thoroughbred pounding beneath you on a track, those flashes of life when your own body surprises you with no more ache, no more tenderness.

I think, *This is why they like it. Mom and Dad. This is why they don't come back to themselves*, and I feel connected to them in places I've never felt before. *I'm their daughter.*

In what feels like seconds, or maybe hours, another man approaches us. He is tall, with high-spiked hair. For a moment, I wonder if he's a talking tree.

Go away, Paul, Nelle says, and the words tunnel out.

And then another man. Short, bald. Granite eyes. His name, someone says, is Tonka.

I hear more words in no particular order: *Paul / No / My girl / Fucking kill you / Tonka / Jump him / Nelle / My girl / Paul / Fucked her / Chicken-head / When*, before Monty and Paul and Tonka begin swinging their arms and smashing their glass bottles and Monty's face is pressed against the asphalt, beneath a sneaker. I think, *This is sexy.*

In what feels like seconds, or maybe minutes, the blue of sirens whirls in my eyes, and Nelle says *Run, run*, and the trees turn to coral, we're all underwater, and my body is pulled into Harley's sinking car before we speed off, looking for Monty. He limps out of the woods to the street, bloodied pulp of a body in Harley's headlights. Nelle and I let him lie across our laps as we drive him to a hospital, Nelle kissing his forehead, smoothing his hair back with the wet black of his blood. Smashed ruby of a boy, all those cut-open places—it was the most beautiful thing I had ever seen.

* ✳ *

I have this problem, Harley screams from her bathroom toilet. *I hate wiping my own ass.*

It's true, Nelle says. Nelle's flipping through a beauty magazine on Harley's bed, peeling open the pockets of sample lipsticks and perfumes between the pages. She sniffs the spine.

Are you shitting me? I ask, reaching for the joke.

I just can't, Harley says.

I don't understand.

Chinky, can you come and wipe my ass for me? Please?

I look at Nelle. *Is she serious?*

She shrugs. *The Lips beckon.*

In the bathroom, Harley extends her arm with a wad of toilet paper pinched between her nails, her toes pointed inward like a toddler on the aquamarine tiles.

Be my best best best friend, will you?

There's a glittering viciousness to Harley Pelletier when she wants something. The slight cock of her face to the left, the bend of her pupils as they gaze up at you at just the right angle. A look that says, *Love me? Even when I'm fucking with you? Even when I'm not? Prove it.*

But I'd do anything. That's the problem with me. It still is.

I never even pretend to hesitate.

✳ ✳ ✳

There are nights without parties sometimes. On these nights, we pull on sweatshirts and yank off the top of my father's navy convertible, which we've decided to take as our own—*Just until he comes back*. We drive around until the sun bulges out of the sea, back and forth along A1A, Usher or Juvenile or Bubba Sparxxx on the speakers. The heat blasts in streams against the thick wet cool of the Florida winter, and we call it hot-fudge-sundae-driving.

I haven't seen my father in several months. He flies down to northern Florida every weekend to visit my uncle in prison, but he does not make the full trip to see me. He says it's because my mother is using, and seeing her high is triggering to him and his sobriety. When my father does not visit, my mother uses more. She says his not loving us is triggering to her and her sobriety.

In my father's car—that corrugated edge of fear and desire that I can't stop touching. *What if we all get found out? What if I get sent away to live in the system? Could the girls come with me? Would they?*

The music thumps in our stomachs and we never talk much, we just smoke and smoke until our throats burn our voices out. When this happens, Nelle and I plug one nostril with a finger and put the filter into the other nostril. We snort the cigarettes as hard as we can, until our vision curls and collapses like a wave.

Long live our tribe of fatherless girls, Nelle says, wind-whip of hair stinging our faces, daybreak warbling from bird-blackened trees.

* ✳ *

Both girls like to kiss me with their tongue rings. They like the way guys look at us when they do this. When they take the new girl's face in their hands and kiss me hard and sloppy, running their fingers through my hair, letting me tug at their barbells with my teeth.

Have you met our Kinky Chinky?

Fucking freaks, men say, in the best way possible.

I love it when they kiss me, too. Especially Nelle. I position my face next to her face as often as possible, as close as I can, but none of this has to do with the men around us, or what they think.

Pervs, we say, once we get home to Harley's house in the mornings, peeling off our plaid miniskirts, our studded belts. *Disgusting needle-dicked pervs.* But we like pervs. We're good with them. Pervs get us whatever we want if we wear the right clothes, if we act stupid enough. We pick up pervs in downtown Fort Lauderdale, on the strip, on the beach, outside the Primanti Brothers pizza shop, at lot-parties. The pervs must be old enough to buy us alcohol, and scary enough to make the whole experience worth it.

One night, we meet a drug-dealer perv named Josh outside a downtown tattoo shop. He looks about thirty-five, with a chin-strap goatee and barely any hair on top. We decide that Josh will do anything for us, so long as we love up on one another. So long as we let him tell us what to do and follow his instructions. Josh likes me most because I'm the shy one, and because I'm a virgin. He wears a gold ring with his name on it, a little diamond inside the *O*. He cradles my face in his giant, jeweled hand and puts his tongue in my mouth. *I'll let you wear this ring as long as I own you*, he says. *As long as I can call you my little bitch*.

I wear his ring on my thumb with great pride, knowing that I belong to someone. At school, everybody stares at the ring, the glittering *JOSH*. There are several Joshes at school, but no one can place where this one came from—not a Goldberg or a Greenberg or a Rothblatt—this other kind of Josh.

Josh likes to take us drag racing at night. The three of us are so drunk in the backseat, we barely ever look at his speedometer the way he would like us to. We are never impressed with Josh or his car, we just sit on each other's laps, kissing, making jokes about dying together in a crash, till death do us part.

How 'bout I get you girls some Incredible Hulk? he says one night, when he's tired of this. We usually drink Malibu with orange soda, and the sound of a new drink with a muscular name has us intrigued.

Josh stops at a liquor store, picks up a bottle of Hennessy, and a mystical-looking bottle of milky-blue liquor. *Rub it and a genie will come out*, he says.

The next stop we make is at a 7-Eleven. Josh brings us three Big Gulp cups full of ice. He pours and mixes the two liquor bottles in the cups until we each have our own full bucket-sized cups of liquid. It's a dirty swimming pool color; muddy. *Careful, the Hulk's vicious.*

Do you even have a job? we ask. *Do you go to college or something?*

I go to the college of Hard Knocks, U.S.A., he says.

We drink the bitter-sweet through our straws. Harley and Nelle stick their monster-colored tongues out for Josh above the center console of the car—*Please?*—and he drops white pills of Xanax on them. *Good girls.*

I love bars, Harley says. *You're missing out, Kinky Chinky. Pills give you wings.*

Josh drives us down to Miami. We have never seen it before, at night, lit up and strobing. We ask to stop in a pizza parlor to pee. Inside my stall, the walls begin to drip down around me. I've finished my Incredible Hulk, and my feet feel like they're on a treadmill, rolling away. My hands reach for anything to hold on to so that I can stand up, or sit down, or keep my balance somewhere in between.

The green starts bursting out of me. I vomit on my bare legs, the floor, the toilet seat. I hear somebody else doing the same. A gagging chorus. The heels of our shoes slip through it, leaving squiggled trails of tile white. The three of us walk out of the parlor, onto the strip, goopy liquid running from our eyes, our mouths, down our chins. Josh is gone. I crawl down the sidewalk, spewing more green into the gutters. We stumble over one another and grip our shoes by the straps. The girls hold my hair.

I love you. I love you. I love you, too.

None of us can remember how we ever got home.

It was suicide, Nelle tells me. Nelle's father committed suicide two years ago. She was at a friend's house watching a movie when it happened. Her mother was out shopping, buying Nelle's older sister a prom dress. Her dad called the friend's house line.

Can I pick you up? he said to Nelle. *Are you ready? I'll come.*

I'm busy right now—we just got to the good part. Can't you wait until later?

He was found swinging in the garage—a strappy piece of workout equipment squeezed around his neck. His deep plum skin on a hospital gurney. Nelle knew it before it was declared.

She talks about this only once, and then tells me to forget it.

Doesn't matter anymore, she says. *That was then.*

But he was her father.

We go back to Craig's house for another party. Harley and I are lying belly down on Craig's bed as a room full of people look at my new tat. Today I went to a tattoo parlor in East Boca and asked for a Hawaiian beach scene on my lower back. *Something scenic*, I said, *or maybe Bob Marley lyrics—artist's choice.* What I got was a cartoon palm tree right above my crack, with some sway marks around it. Neon waves and a plumeria flower float around the tree, a few red clouds, the whole scene beaded with hardened blood.

Did it hurt? they say. *Did it tickle?*

Looks like a flaming meatball, says Craig.

Wasn't so bad, I say, even though I cried the whole hour that warm, vibrating needle thrummed through my skin, until the man with plugs in his face said, *Check it out in the mirror, hula hula girl.*

Harley is kicking her legs, annoyed.

It's just a tat, she says. *Big fucking whoop.*

Efraim shows up in his new Phantom Rolls-Royce—a birthday present. He stands in the doorway of Craig's bedroom and spins the keys around his pointer finger. *Anyone wanna go for a ride? Mink interior.*

How big's your exhaust pipe? Or stick shift? Harley asks him.

Big.

Harley squeezes my hand, presses her lips to my ear—*Watch this.*

That stick, she says. *Want to watch us pull our skirts up and fuck it?*

My father doesn't live out west, Harley tells me one day. *He lives in Miami.*

The Bolivian? I ask. *He's fifteen minutes away?*

Yeah, she says. *But that doesn't mean I see any of him.*

What's his name?

Doesn't matter.

This confession comes the same week Harley's mom and boyfriend argue in her living room all night. Harley's mom began lighting matches, flicking them onto furniture, cushions, trying to burn the house down—*fry, motherfucker*—before the boyfriend dragged the hose inside. The fight was over which television show they would watch.

We called the police and left in our pajamas before anybody got there.

* ** *

The girls don't typically come to my house, but today, after school, I need to stop by and pick up more clothes. It's my turn to contribute to our shared collection. We've all dropped down a couple of sizes since we met, since we don't eat, and what I do eat are clenbuterol hydrochloride horse respiratory pills, the kind Calorie Valerie, a girl at my school, gets from her mother. We order the pills on the Internet using my parents' credit cards.

Inside, my own mother is sitting at the dining room table with all the lights off. She's spilling candle wax onto a sheet of paper, and onto the surface of the table, and onto her hands.

Look, she says, holding her palms out to us.

She did dry out in North Carolina, years ago. She shook it out, let the fever take over. On the worst days, her body let out a slime that I wiped from her skin in a circular motion. I changed the sheets. Massaged her limbs. After that, we had a good span of time together, the three of us—Mom, Dad, and Child.

But last summer, before school one morning, my mother slipped in the shower and shattered her teeth, her jaw. The doctor prescribed pills for the pain, for the surgeries and wires and caps. Soon after, more doctors. More scripts. When I think about my parents, these are still the days that ache most: Internet prescription mills calling our house. My father screaming into the phone, *One more pill and I'll fucking end you*, slamming the receiver into the wall. Just last year, there had been so much hope. But then the scripts, the phone calls. The clicks of those locked bathroom doors.

My uncle got caught soon after—that Wolf of Wall Street business. So did my father's friends. My father didn't go to prison—he went to New York instead. My mother stayed here, with me.

Let's go, I say.

I collect my clothes in a plastic Walgreens bag and slam the door on our way out.

In the driver's seat, I pull the top down. Harley has taught me enough about driving to get us around, though she still has to help me with directions sometimes. There's no greater thrill than taking I-95 in my father's car, speeding, hoping for the scream of sirens.

Before I pull out of the horseshoe driveway, another car pulls in behind us. A black, cubic car. Spinning rims of chrome on the tires— tinted windows.

A man in a gray suit gets out of the car and begins walking toward us. He walks with a slight limp. I recognize him immediately, from years ago; he was in my living room with Cousin Cindy. She always called him Boca Brad, the richest dealer in the south. Nelle is sitting behind me in the car and lowers her sunglasses down her nose.

What's up, hot stuff?

Don't, I say.

Boca Brad smacks his gum between his teeth. His cologne carries on the humidity and nips in my throat. He bends down to see Nelle a little bit closer.

Here to see her mom, he says, pointing at me. *But maybe I'm really here to see you.*

He reaches out his hand and cups her under the chin, his fingers digging into her cheeks. I have seen men touch Nelle for all the months I have known her, and I will see them do it again, and again, in the months after this moment, but I have never seen Nelle truly scared or frightened of anything like she is right now, still as an animal in crosshairs, like she's just seen something too grown-up for us to understand yet. Was it his smell? The dig of his nails? The way he held her gaze? Later, she'll tell me she couldn't be sure, but there was *something,* she said, that kind of woman-intuition one hears about. It came ringing in.

Drive, she says, swatting the man's hand away.

✳ ✴ ✳

My father is flying my mother up to New York for a visit.

I begged him on the phone—*Daddy, she needs you. She needs this. She needs help.* I want my mother back, I want her grilled ham and cheese sandwiches and her watercolor paints and her half-remembered, half-imagined stories. I want the smell of her, like gardenias. I want everything about her. I want her to live. But I also know that sobriety will mean I'll have to go to school again; I'll have to give the credit cards back. I'll have to stay home and put my dishes away, and I won't get to drive my father's car. I won't wake up under a highway overpass anymore, or beside a motel pool, or on the beach with horseshoe crab shells in my hair and men I don't know. Most of all, I know if I have a mother, I can't keep the girls.

We are curled up in Harley's bed like cats when I get the call.

She's leaving, I say. *My dad says she's going to New York.*

How long?

Who ever knows, I shrug.

What should we do with your crib to ourselves? Harley wants to know.

We could throw a party, I say.

A themed party? Nelle asks. *Please, I love themes! I slay at themes!*

It takes us three hours to drive to the Aventura Mall and find the perfect sets of coordinating lingerie. In Hollywood, we pick up handcuffs, whips, paddles, and various colors and sizes of dildos. We drive to my house and get dressed. Harley is playing the role of Jenna Jameson tonight, a cloud of blonde wig, a white-and-blue garter belt, silver glitter, *like an angel.* Nelle is playing Briana Banks, with a black lace-up corset and smolder eyes. I'm playing the only Asian porn star we know, Kobe Tai. I wear fishnets, a lavender bustier, and several sets of handcuffs attached to my garter belt. Because Harley and Nelle have tits and I do not, the girls help me triple up bras beneath my bustier, pulling my skin up and over it. We paste on thick rows of eyelashes, and press on several inches of acrylic nails. We decorate my house with the dildos. We suction them onto the pool table, the mantelpiece; we leave the small ones on the bar to be used as drink stirrers.

By nine P.M., almost a hundred people arrive at our Porn Star Party. Public and private school kids, a couple dealers we know, the older boyfriends of girls in my grade. Clarissa shows up in a white-and-pink number, and Nelle calls her a troll, tells her to leave me alone. Beth shows up fully clothed, *What are you, a pilgrim?* before Harley convinces her to change in my room. Several Ron Jeremys appear shirtless, with plungers—*Got a leak?*—and other girls arrive in thongs, nipple tassels, capes, and extra-padded push-ups.

Harley, Nelle, and I take every shot we're given. Red Bull and Jägermeister, Lemon Drops, Cocksucking Cowboys with cream. We lie down on my pool table and begin to kiss one another while the boys and men cheer us on.

Cousin Cindy once asked me, *What do you think love really is?*

I think it's being able to kiss someone whenever you want, I said.

I can kiss Nelle whenever I want. And I do.

The other girls at the party roll their eyes, move to the corners of the room—*Sluts*, they say. A few of the boys kick off their Air Force 1s and stand on top of the pool table. They begin Crip Walking around our bodies, a dance some of them like to do when the hip-hop hits come on. Tonight, Nelle is wearing her door-knocker tongue ring—my favorite—a heavy hoop of metal that I lift with my tongue. The music gets louder before it turns off.

Somebody's ringing. Somebody's here.

Go get it, Kinky Chinky.

When I open the door, two cops seesaw their flashlights in my eyes.

Party? they ask.

What's it to you? My vision bloats their bodies. I try to snap into focus.

You look pretty young, young lady, says one of the cop-heads. Interested, I think.

If you think you're going to arrest me, I say, *I'm going to have to arrest you first.* I take the handcuffs off my garter belt and move toward them, trying to clink the metal rings around one of their wrists. The cops back up. I fall on the pavement and my knee begins to bleed through my fishnets. *Look what you did to my outfit,* I say.

Rather than evict anyone from the party, the cops declare a lockdown. This means they check all the exits, move us to the center of the room, and take a head count. They write down names and schools. They want us all to call our parents and explain what we've done, but we're all slurring, laughing, calling Pizza Hut delivery instead. They call my parents—*We've got about a hundred kids here in their underwear*—before shaking their heads, *Well you better fly back from New York because we need a guardian.*

I've got a guardian, I say, twisting a strand of bubble gum around my nail. I call my Aunt Trista, Uncle Kai's wife, who's new to the family, in the neighborhood.

I'm in a jam, Auntie Trista.

Fifteen minutes later, Aunt Trista comes dressed for the theme. A black glittering corset. A leather miniskirt with two slits up the thighs.

I'm the guardian angel, she says, shooing the cops out the door. When she locks it behind them, she turns to the rest of us, sitting in a circle like we're playing Duck Duck Goose.

Now, she says, *who wants to get your guardian a goddamn drink?*

* ✳ *

They left.

Harley moved to New York that spring to make it in acting, to find the right light for her face. She gave herself a show name, and we spoke on the phone a couple of times a year until we didn't. I wish I could say our good-bye was difficult, but something inside me, that gnarled knot of ass-wiping girl-love, was relieved. These days, I watch her on a television drama in which she plays the lifesaving teacher inspiring inner-city students to read books and dream big. She's a stranger now, a married woman—older, slighter, that upward gaze.

Nelle was picked up in the middle of the night by a Catholic couple in matching blue polo shirts. Her mother waited in a neighbor's apartment while they took her daughter, kicking and squalling. The couple handcuffed Nelle in her pajamas and carried her into a PT Cruiser, drove her to live in a reform school for girls in rural North Carolina. Nelle would find a job in a ski lodge up there in the mountains and meet a gang of cowboys to buy her cigarettes, send and receive her letters.

This is what she tells me now, anyway. We never wrote to each other.

I got my driver's license that summer. I was left with my mother, with those piles and piles of clothes, the empty wrappers of horse pills. Left with a dull hammering at my temples when I ran out of cigarettes and didn't know how to get them. At night, I drove along Deerfield Beach and waited for that fullness in my ears, those voices deep and melodic as a gospel as we crawled through the streets of Miami looking for somebody, anybody—*I love you. I love you. I love you, too*—alone in my father's convertible.

He bought me a new car—fancier—the month before he died. I want the old one back.

Dear Tribes of Fatherless Girls: I'm still here.

HOW TO SURVIVE IN

BOCA RATON

Some days, in the corner of the school cafeteria, Calorie Valerie feeds dollar bills into the vending machine. She looks over her shoulder to make sure no one is looking, then packs each crinkling bag of chips, each box of cookies, neatly into her backpack. She pushes each package down like she's trying to drown it, fits more than what seems possible into her little pink bag. Nobody pays attention to druggie freak Valerie anymore, except for me. I watch dollar after dollar after dollar after dollar.

THE GREETER

They call me The Greeter. I sell shoes at the Boca Raton Town Center mall—bedazzled stilettos and platforms, neon-strapped pumps saved for special occasions. I stand by the entrance of the store, heels dug into the carpet, tummy tucked in, and I greet people. *Hi, How are you, sunshine? Have you seen our shoes today?* I wear sparkling eyeshadow for the job. I smooth out the inky shine of my hair with coconut-scented spray. I bend at just the right angle as I crawl on the floor, my legs spread like a dumb secretary in the movies, the perfect C-curve of my waist. I pull the shoes out of their boxes, the tissue paper out of the shoes. I slip them on one foot, then the other, and secure them just right.

That's a perfect fit, I say, propped up on my knees. *Take a walk in them.* No heel grips necessary, no insoles, no pads. I know how to fit a shoe.

You're adorable, the customers say. *How old are you?*

Sixteen, I say. *Too young to work this hard, but my name's inside the shoe.* I point to the label. I wink. They love this part.

The customers hand over their credit cards, and I make my dimples show. *Would you like to wear them out? You can't return them if you do, but I'm sure you won't want that!*

I clean up the wads of tissue paper, use a metal wand to lift and store the boxes back in their proper places in the stock room—*thwack thwack*—I bang the boxes until the wall of cardboard looks smooth.

I move to the front of the store again, after each sale. I suck in until my ribs show, try to catch the gaze of anyone walking by, *Hello, there. Have you seen these shoes?*

On my break, I spend all thirty minutes smoking cigarettes in the mall alleyway, next to the dumpster. I close my eyes and lean against the wall, blowing smoke into the wet heat. When I finish, I chew out the final Parliament with my heel, clean the heel with a tissue, squirt antibacterial gel on my hands, neck, and face, rub cucumber-melon lotion on these places, smooth my hair again with coconut oil, and smack on a piece of gum. I am The Greeter. The Greeter must smell good. The Greeter must smile.

I count down the hours until my boss, Eliza, will drive me home in her black Pontiac, where we'll chain-smoke, talk shit about our rudest Snowbird customers. I'll do my purification process all over again before walking through the front door of my home.

Nothing smells good here. Inside, my mother has begun writing pages and pages of words by candlelight. The title reads "Story of My Life," but the black inky words are all illegible. They slant off the loose-leaf pages in drooping angles; they continue onto the dining room table.

Inside, my mother tries to cook food, but she forgets what she's cooking in the middle of it. I find SpaghettiOs mashed up with scrambled eggs, coffee grounds on top. I find crumbling sheets of seaweed inside our containers of mint chocolate chip ice cream.

Want dinner? she'll always offer, spooning out the mixture she made.

No thanks.

This is not a problem for me, because when I do eat, it's a cold cut slice of turkey that I roll up with a single slice of provolone cheese. I give myself up to fifteen minutes after eating the roll before excusing myself to the stockroom or school bathroom, where I jam three fingers at my tonsils until it gives. Sometimes, I eat a handful of hard-boiled eggs. I hate them so much that the gagging turns on without effort, and I'll take anything that comes this easily.

The Senior said he would give me a lift whenever I needed, so long as I let him move two fingers, sometimes three, up between my legs before my shift. I let him do this in the mall parking garage, bored, lifting up my school uniform skirt, staring out the car window. Sometimes he jerks off in the driver's seat with his other hand. He cleans up with a Papa John's napkin.

Tonight, my mother calls me on the store line, when business is slow.

Hey Greeter! says Eliza, *It's your ma!*

What's up? I whisper into the phone. I cup my hand around my mouth. *What's wrong?*

Can I pick you up tonight? Need to talk to you about something.

Eliza's taking me home, I say. *Eliza always takes me home.*

I'll be okay driving, I promise, she says.

I can tell from her voice that she is, indeed, okay. It's my mother on the other end; I haven't heard her in a while. My mother, who gave me language, who grew up in a house of Chinese and Hawaiian and Pidgin but still found her own vocabulary, her own exquisite hand-writing, who used to spell words like *Hello* and *You Are Mine* in frosting on my breakfast toaster strudels until I learned how to read.

Hi, Mommy, I say. *Sure.*

At nine thirty P.M., my mother is waiting outside the back exit of the mall. She's punctual, and I am impressed by this. As I walk over to the car, I pull a fistful of my hair beneath my nose to make sure it doesn't still smell like tobacco.

Hi, MomMom, I say, as I climb into Big Beau. I snap the seatbelt.

Hi, Baby, she says, really looking at me, rubbing my knee. *How was work?*

Slow, I say. *Didn't hit our numbers.*

I hate the idea of you and Eliza walking to your cars this late at night, she says. *It gets so dark here. Is there even any security?*

This is the Boca Raton mall, I say. *Safest place in the world. What'll they do, hold us up with Botox needles?*

After I graduate high school, in December, the same month it is now, a serial killer will hit the Boca Raton Town Center mall. The killer will ask mothers to withdraw money from a nearby ATM before duct-taping their wrists and snapping black-out swimming goggles around their faces. The first victims will be found alive, but the killer will shoot two of the victims—a mother and her daughter—point-blank, the car still running, and never be caught.

But we don't know that yet.

Ten minutes into our drive, at a red light, my mother opens the car door and pukes on the street. We're on Glades Road, and the head-lights behind us are a blinding spotlight on her face, on the stream of yellow liquid spilling from her throat. When the light ticks GO, cars begin to honk. I rub my mother's back. *You okay?*

I'm fine, she says. *Something I ate.*

My mother pulls over and pukes four more times before she asks me to drive.

Do you need to go to the hospital? I ask.

She's all shakes; her lips greening. Her teeth clatter so loud I can hear them from the driver's seat. *Something I ate*, she says.

What'd you want to talk to me about? I ask her. *Why'd you pick me up?*

I just wanted to see you, she said. *That's all. Just wanted to see my baby girl.* She squeezes my hand.

My mother will later tell me that this was the day she made a decision—this was the morning she flushed the bottles of pills down the toilet in a colorful clicking stream, changed her bedsheets, got dressed, sprayed perfume. She wanted to pick me up from work and tell me about it—this new life that would unfold for us, this new chapter, how sorry she was for losing herself again, how she was done this time, she really was.

She'll tell me she wanted to make me proud. She wanted to live.

Instead, she's sick all week. She kicks the new sheets off her bed. She sweats, sleeps, gags herself with the corner of her pillow when she can't stop crying. She mumbles words to herself—sentences I can't make out. She stares at the ceiling with eyes like seeds. *Something I ate*, she says over and over again, as I press cold washcloths to her forehead.

On the seventh day, she is not sick anymore, but she is also no longer my mother.

The piercing parlor is just off the train tracks and you don't need an ID to get poked. Instead, you offer to pay cash, keep a secret, and wear the shortest skirt you can find. This is what I'm told, anyway, by some of the girls at school. Addison Katz got her nipples pierced here, and she shows off the wink of silver by pulling her white uniform shirts tight against her chest. *Can't wear a bra till it heals!*

I have the night off work, so I've decided to go to the train tracks after school and do my best. Jenny, who is still DJ Banana, wants to get poked, too, and we decide that we'll hold hands. I want my tongue pierced, because it reminds me of Harley and Nelle, and because it's the one thing my mother has said she would break my neck over. *Tattoo your eyeballs for all I care*, she has said, *but you'll have a tramp-ring over my dead body. Or yours.* Jenny says she'll decide what to pierce once she gets there. She's spontaneous like that. A few girls from school decide they want to tag along and watch. Even Beth shows up.

On the way to the tracks, I call my mother. *I'm going to a movie with Jenny*, I say. *So don't try to call me tonight.*

Well then maybe I'll go to the movies, too, she says. *I could use a laugh, a self-date.*

In the parking lot of the parlor, I roll my khaki uniform skirt four times and pull off the Soffes I wear beneath it. I roll the skirt high enough so that the slight curves of my butt show below the pleats. I goop on lip glass. Tie my shirt into a neat side-knot to expose my stomach, my tanning bed tattoos.

Seventeen? Eighteen? I ask Jenny.

You're not fooling anyone.

Jenny has always looked older than me, and she's wiser, too. She knew how to rim her lids with liner when I still used Milky Pens on my own eyes, and she was the first person to tell me what a Brazilian wax is. Most important, she's got the nicest, roundest ass at our school. I know she won't have any trouble convincing the men inside.

The shop is quiet when we open the doors. Two men stand behind the counter, under a wreath of mistletoe, looking at something on their computer.

We're here for tongue rings, says Jenny. *And we'll pay cash.*

Four girls stand behind us in their school uniforms, waiting.

You old enough? says the bigger man, with butter-colored sweat stains mooning under his armpits.

Yes, says Jenny.

How 'bout little China?

Yes, I say. *We've got cash.*

All right then, says the thinner man. The holes of his ears dangle like stalactites of skin. *Give us five, we'll get set up.*

I need a cigarette first, I tell the men. I'm trying to sound confident, mature. *So I'll come back in five.*

Jenny joins me outside. She doesn't smoke, but she likes the smell of it.

Can you believe it? she says. *That was so easy! We didn't need to suck a dick to make that happen.*

We both laugh at this. I take a long drag and try to steady my hands. I am terrified of needles. We're quiet as we watch the cars pass over the train tracks in hard thumps. This other part of town. Garbage blowing all over—plastic bags, McDonald's cups—the smell of seaweed. Apartments nearby that we visit for public school parties, the bad ones.

Shit, is that your mom? says Jenny.

It is. I hide the cigarette behind my skirt, instinctively, though I know she does not see me. My mother is driving Big Beau over the tracks. I watch her through the window. Sweet, pale moon-sliver of a woman, a sad face. Her black hair is cut jagged, framing her chin. My mother. From this view, she could be going to the grocery store to buy wonton wraps, going to Blockbuster to pick out just the right movie, meeting our family for dinner on the pier. But I know where she's going in this part of town. Cousin Cindy has told me where Boca Brad lives, and I watch my mom's car take exactly the turns I expect. Here we are on the same block, Mother, neither one of us near a movie theater, so far from where we ought to be.

Inside, I swish my mouth with so much Listerine it makes my eyes water. I lean back on the chair as the dangling-ear man adjusts his light, moving it along my whole body, taking his time. I open my mouth and the man pinches my tongue with a metal claw. Drool pools around the corners of my mouth. I look him right in the eyes as he brings a needle the size of a soda straw to the underside of my tongue, jabs it up, delivers me the sharpest pain I have ever felt and a high I've never matched since.

My mother is no longer fighting the sick. She's in her Other Place again, writing in her secret language across the pages, the table. Today, she has conspiracy theories about how my father spends his time in New York. He has a secret wife up there, she says. A white woman. Tall, in a pink dress. Nothing like her.

Not true, I say. *He's working hard in the city. Probably freezing right about now.*

Go to school, she says, *and maybe he'll come home when you're out.*

I don't think so, I say, kissing her on the head. I wonder if she knows who I am. *Glad you're feeling better.*

The rage—it's never toward my mother or father. It's their dealers: Boca Brad, Uncle Nacho, Nurse Harmony, Karate Kurt. I fantasize about slitting them with paper cuts between the webs of their fingers, their eyelids. Karate Kurt has kids push the drugs for him, kids in his karate class. He gets them hooked. In two years, he'll wrap his lips around a handgun—later, Boca Brad will do the same—and I'll smile both times I hear the news.

Addison picks me up and drives me to school, popping her gum and chomping on about The Senior and how I should stop putting out for free rides to the mall. *You've got quite a name for yourself these days*, she says. *Kinky Chinky. Remember when you were Queera? When you only hung out with the fat girl?*

You gave The Senior a hand job last week, I say.

I didn't do it for a ride.

Fuck off, I say. I hate Addison, but we're friends because people expect us to be.

The day goes on like any other day. I cheat on my history exam using an answer sheet rolled up under my pen cap; I get another talking to from my English professor, who says she knows I'm not an idiot but I sure act like one. *"Gregor Samsa can blow me"? Really?*

The Senior drives me to work after school. He reaches between my legs, but I tell him no; I'm on my period. Instead, we talk about some holiday rager coming up. *You going? What'll you wear?* And, *You think you'll apply to college?*

Nah, I say. *I'm not smart like that.*

I change out of my uniform and into my work clothes in his backseat. I spray the coconut.

My mother calls again, in the middle of my shift. She sounds worse than she did this morning. She's crying by now—I can't make out her words.

Chicken, is what I understand. *Made chicken. Need sleep.*

So go to sleep, I say. *Eliza will drop me off soon.*

But I don't want Eliza to drop me off soon. I want Eliza to drive me all around town, and I tell Eliza this. I want her to buy me as many packs of cigarettes as I can afford, and a bottle of anything, and I want us to talk, the two of us, in her car, on the beach, anywhere. I want her emo music turned down low on the radio as I tell her what my life's been like; I want to tell her about Nelle and Harley, about The Senior; I want to tell her that once, I could have been an Olympic athlete, or a jockey. Once, I even liked writing stories. I want to talk to her until my mother wakes up. I want my father. Most of all, I don't want to go home.

Instead, we drive around until ten thirty P.M. talking about guys, before Eliza says, *I do have to go home, you know. I'm tired. You good?*

Sure, I say. *Of course.*

Tell your mom I say hi, she says. *Your mom's the bomb.*

She'll like that, I say.

I look at my house: the fountain trickling near the entrance, the ginger plants that ooze fragrant juices when you squeeze them, the royal palms, the white stones and smooth wooden fence. It looks beautiful like this, peaceful even. Like my mother brought a small piece of Hawai'i here with her. My home.

Inside, all the lights are off. I flip on the kitchen switch and watch cockroaches skitter across the counters, into the spaces between the crusty stove coils. *Shoo shoo*, I say, ignoring them, making my way to the fridge for a drink.

Usually my mother's food combinations are contained in a bowl or a Tupperware, but this is different. There are chunks of chicken everywhere—smeared in peanut butter, most of the pieces raw. The chicken is on the shelves, in the drawers, slugging down a bottle of orange juice.

I go to my mother's room. The lights are on, the TV blaring a special on country music. She's lying sideways across the bed; her fingers are playing an invisible piano.

Mom? You okay?

Okay, she says. *Need sleep.*

You need some water?

My eyes sting. I am used to this by now, used to knowing that I will never be used to this—that this part of her will never not break me, that this may be the rest of our lives. The two of us here, in this house, waiting for my father. The chicken.

Goodnight, I say, and close the door.

I pick up my portable landline and call Beth.

What's up? she says. *It's sure been a while. How's that tongue ring?*

Got caught, I say. *But I'm sadly still alive.* I am shimmying my pants off, kicking out of my heels. I count the cigarettes in my purse. I keep the pack inside a dirty sock, in case my mother ever looks. Six left. I've changed into pajama pants and a sweatshirt when I say, *I miss you, Beth. We used to do so much stupid stuff together.*

We sure did, she says.

Tell me a story, I say. *What's new with you?*

Beth is telling me about her family and the Tradewinds Christmas light show, her father and his new house, a new dance move she learned from her cousin when I hear the crash. The crash sounds like wood splitting. Furniture, I think, but there is also a nauseating, thick-sounding thump. The sound feels like it takes forever. It breaks into its own syllables. By the time Beth says *What the hell was that?* I realize that I'm already opening my mother's door. Next to her bed, my mother's body is ragdoll twisted on the tile floor. The nightstand came down with her—she must have tried to hold on to it. A pool of syrupy black blood begins to inch out around her hair like a halo, until it finds thin, straight paths on the grit between the tiles. Red foam swells out from between her teeth.

I hang up the phone. I am on my knees, bending over, staring at the eggshells of her eyes, afraid to touch her. There are no pupils, no screams. Her body convulses like it's being shocked, or like it's the trout my mother once helped me catch when I was a child. I caught it in a pond in North Carolina with a single kernel of corn. The way it flopped in my hands as I pinched the hook from its mouth—the way I just wanted to throw it back into the water where it could breathe,

survive. *Please, please, Mom, make it stop shaking like this.* All that hurt
for a kernel of corn.

It doesn't even feel this, my mother had said to me. *Animals are resil-
ient like that.*

The paramedics will not let me ride in the back of the ambulance
with my mother. *You sit in front*, they say. *Ride shotgun like a big
girl.*

The way they're treating me, like a child, is comforting. I want to
stay curled up like this, in this dark seat, for the rest of my life.

So brave, the driver says. *Not even crying.*

Is she going to die? I ask. I don't hear the sirens. The traffic lights
whip by. Blowing the reds is not as exciting as I imagined it could be.

I don't know, he says. *I can't tell you that.*

I want to crawl into his lap. This man. I want him to take me home
and feed me.

I have my own waiting room in the hospital. It's a tiny room with a
closed door, with bars of light so brilliant they ache behind my eyes.

Do you have another guardian? somebody says.

I have a grandmother, I say. *My mother's stepmom. She lives nearby.*
They call her.

After my grandmother arrives—*She fell, grandmother. She was
sleepwalking*—a group of men ask to speak to me alone. My grandmother leaves the room.

Unnatural, is what I hear first. *She fell unnaturally. The way she fell. Your mother. Twisted. Backward. Unnaturally, the way the nightstand was. The way her arm was. Her neck. Does your mother speak English? Your mother's not responding. Does your mother speak Chinese? Who is your mother? Did you want to hurt your mother? Do you love your mother? Were you mad at your mother? Are you in trouble at school? Where is your father? Did you strike your mother? Your feet*, they say, *your feet are covered in blood. Why didn't you call sooner? We'll get you some shoes. How long had she been like that? Skull fracture*, they say. *Are you sure you love your mother? Who were you on the phone with? When did you hang up? Unnatural*, they say. *Is she taking anything? On any medication?*

No, I say.

Are you sure? This could be life or death, sweetheart.

I imagine police tape around my house, twitching in the wind. A stranger's gloved hands finding the bottles of pills, the potions, opening the lids, photographing my mother's clothes. I imagine them handcuffing my mother in her hospital bed, the way she would wake up, confused, bandaged, screaming for me. I imagine them sending me to live with a family that is not my own. I have protected my parents for as long as I've been alive. If someone comes after them, I have teeth.

Is she going to die? I ask.

Depends.

My mother, I say. *She just fell.*

After my grandmother tells the doctors the truth—*opiates, drug addict, overdose*—words I had never before associated with my parents because none of us had ever said them aloud, because there was never a name for exactly what this was, after my family in Texas drives through the night to clean out my house, after my father arrives two days later (something I will never—even after he dies—forgive), after the doctors pump her stomach and stitch up her scalp, after intubation, my mother wakes up from an induced coma. My family lets me see her in the intensive care unit, but they ask that I do not speak to her. *We need to discuss next steps first*, they say.

My mother holds my hand in the hospital bed. This is not a private hospital room fragrant with roses. Rows of bodies are being resuscitated all around us—thin sheets hanging between each one. We look at each other, knowing. There is no coming back from this. This time is different.

Back home, my Auntie T offers to adopt me. She shows me a website for Wylie High, in Abilene, Texas. *You'll have me and your cousins there*, she says. *You'll make friends. You just have a year and a half left of high school. Think about it*, she says. *We have a nice church, and great hamburgers.*

I'm not leaving her, I say.

I tell my father about this offer, hoping he'll take me to live with him in New York.

You could like Texas, he says. *Jesus people can be nice. Maybe you could use some nice.*

The doctors send my mother home with pamphlets for treatment centers. They all look like hospitals to me—hospitals with palm trees, and yellow doors, and smiling people on lawn chairs. *Be the best that you can be!* one pamphlet reads.

Back at home, my family preps me on the speech I am supposed to give. *You're the only one who can do it.* They will stand behind me while I speak, they say, and I am supposed to lie. I open my mother's door and approach the bed. The room is dark, but I still walk around The Spot, as I will call it for the next twelve years, until this house burns down.

MomMom, I say. *I need to tell you something.*

She nods. She doesn't speak. She knows what's coming—we've been through this before. I can barely see her in the dark like this, just the shine of her pupils. I can hear her jade ting against her Hawaiian name bracelet.

I'm moving to Texas. I'm enrolling in Wylie High. I'm going to go to church, I say.

She nods.

I need to leave you, I say. *I can't be alone anymore.*

She nods. I wonder if she believes me.

It hurts, I say. I tap a finger at my heart.

I know, she nods. *When you hurt I hurt.*

No one can hurt you the way a mother can. No one can love you the way a mother can.

My father and I drop her off at a treatment center later the same day. We walk through the yellow doors and say our good-byes as doctors take her vitals, ask her to open her mouth for a fat popsicle stick. This is the first time I check my mother into rehab, though it won't be the last. The next time will be just after my father dies, and I'll be wearing his monogrammed shirt; I'll sit in the seat he takes right now as he sandwiches my mother's hand in both of his, saying, *You've got this, baby.*

When the doctors ask her to announce her drugs of choice, my mother lists them off, quietly. Embarrassed, I think. She rubs her arms like she's freezing, rocking back and forth. It is a long list. I feel guilty being in this room. This part of her life is both mine and not mine.

My father doesn't say much on the way home. I watch his steady hand on the wheel, the gold recovery bracelet he wears now—a new ruby on the triangle for each year he is clean. Three by now. *I'm sorry I left you with this,* he says. *I didn't know what to do.*

It's okay, I say.

I'm not solid yet, he says. *Not well enough to see it. To be around it.* He begins to cry, and shakes his head in a quick thrust, like a horse shooing off a fly. I can tell this hurts, and I know he's been struggling. I know it by the way he picks up the phone when I call him sometimes. The drag of his voice when he says, *I'm just tired, really,* and his anger when I don't believe him. *I'm working so hard, but it's so much fucking harder than you could ever know,* he says, once he confesses to one drink, maybe two. *And I hope you'll never have to know it.* He always hangs up on me.

In the car, I say, *I think you're solid,* and *I'm so proud of you.*

Proud? Well—

It's okay, I say.

I've got to head back to New York, he says, *but I'll be back for Christmas.*

That night, after my father takes off, I call The Senior. I ask him to score the best drugs he can find. After I smoke and swallow everything he gives me, I leave his house and drive into a ditch off a road in Weston, Florida. I fall asleep like that, behind the wheel, in this U-shaped ditch, the rain patting my windshield. By morning, nobody has found me.

Where's your mom? my half brothers want to know. They flew in to meet our father in Florida for the holidays.

With her family, in Texas, I say. *She's been gone two weeks.*

We're sitting on the gray couches in my Grandma Sitchie's living room, smearing liver on crackers. Cousin Cindy is on the back patio, screaming into her phone, smoking. I would strangle her for a cigarette.

And she just dumped you on Christmas? the older one says.

Sucks, says the younger one.

I don't like Texas, I say.

My father and brothers watch television all day long in Grandma's living room. They exchange Hanukkah and Christmas gifts. A new phone with a twenty-four-hour sports radio, a wooden backscratcher—*So you can stop using the spaghetti spoon, Pops.* My father gives all three of us wads of cash.

I miss my mother. The hand-pressed paper over her presents, origami wrapped. The bows that shed glitter in a purple mist. She writes cards for every gift, writes cards for every person she's ever met. Her writing, those loops and crosses—*I love you to the moon and back*—I miss her.

Here, says my older brother. *My girlfriend gave me this to give to you.* It's a bag of Sour Patch Kids. *Merry Christmas.*

I drive to my mother's treatment center. She's made it through detox, and Christmas is my first allowed visiting day. A nurse leads me through a long hall to the backyard. The people inside stare at me. They must know I am my mother's, I think. We look the same. There's no mistaking it.

Outside, a fountain spits into the sky. The sun is beating down, and I'm sweating in my chair. I peel off my sweater. Pills of cashmere stick to my forearms like fly tape.

I hear her before I see her—*Merry Christmas, baby*—behind me. I stand up and turn around as she opens her arms. We hold each other so close her hair is in my mouth. I crumple into her. *I miss you*, I say. It's all I can seem to say. The tears come down my face, and, for once, I let it happen.

My mother speaks to me slowly, measured. I can tell she's medicated so she won't fever again. We talk about other things: the weather, the news, other patients inside the center. *Good, good people. You'd like them. Some of them are around your age.* I tell her about Grandma Sitchie's house, the liver, the Sour Patch Kids. Before I get to ask any more questions, our time is up.

Take care of yourself, baby, she says. She picks up a glass of water from a lawn table and sips it. She holds my hand a moment longer. *You doing okay?* She is earnest in her question.

Of course, I say. I sit up straighter. I smile.

Make your numbers tomorrow, she says. *One of the biggest shopping days of the year.*

That trout. I wrestled with the hook to free it; I was in a hurry. *Easy, like this*, said my mother, and she did it in one motion, a popping sound. The hook had pierced my finger, and I sucked the blood so hard my fingertip went white. I tossed the fish back into the mud of the pond, and the two of us watched it shoot off like a single strand of tinsel in the sun before it disappeared.

What I mean to say is, it lived.

PEOPLE LIKE THEM

I have a famous uncle in prison in northern Florida, a second uncle locked up in the middle of Texas, and a third who will join this club in a year or two. It doesn't matter why.

Today, I'm visiting the Texas uncle, Uncle Kai, the one with the *habits*, the one without God, and my Auntie T says, *Careful now, you won't be let in with an underwire bra.*

Why not? I ask.

Because a bra could be used as a weapon.

It's all I have in my suitcase—this bra with the wire in it. I am thirteen and my padded, white, diaper of a bra has a wire running all the way through it. I'm too embarrassed to tell my family this, to show it to them, so I decide to visit prison for the first time braless.

I walk through security with my arms crossed over my chest. I walk like this all the way through a building that smells like microwavable burritos and bleach, until we're directed outside, to an enormous barren yard, where my uncle sits, smoking a Newport, at a picnic table.

I don't want him to hug me, because of my chest.

I say, *Hello.*

He tells me about the latest visitors. How a group of wives shat balloons full of black tar heroin into the toilets. How he was going to get his very own guitar string tattoos, or learn how to give them. How lately, people have been smuggling juices from the kitchen in order to make alcohol.

That sounds nice, I say. *Complicated.*

This is the last memory I have with my Uncle Kai. Here, he is still mellow, himself. Soon, he'll be released, take up new chemical drugs, ride a stone horse monument in the middle of Parkland, and beat my mother up on the side of the road. Soon, he will threaten to take out his whole family with explosives and black magic. Us, I mean.

It's not so bad here, he says.

The blank Texas sky reminds me of a green screen, like I could cut out his body and move him anywhere else, drop him into any other world.

We share a hamburger from a security-monitored vending machine. I break mine into little pieces. The meat is a grayish purple with pockmarks, and he chews like an animal given a treat. We look alike, my uncle and I. Gummy smiles, deep eyes, the ragged edge around our nails where neither one of us can ever stop picking.

At twenty-two years old, I begin teaching inmates in a county jail.

I prepare notebooks with no staples, no paper clips. Rubber golf pencils. I walk through the metal detectors with ease, wired bra and all, drop my belongings into little plastic crates and clear baggies and wait for an officer's eyes to magnify behind them.

One night, as I'm leaving, a correctional officer corners me in the elevator. He is standing too close to me. His breath on my neck. I hold the papers to my chest.

Why do you teach these losers, he says, *when they are so fucking stupid?*

They're not, I tell him. *They write brilliant.*

I go through their mail sometimes, he says, *and laugh at their stupidity.*

They're brilliant, I say.

And anyway, he says, *What's someone like you doing with people like them?*

BROTHERS

There are two boys in my life. The older boy, Shawn, is very serious, his eyebrows thick and expressive like a tract of cables running straight to his heart. The younger boy, Blake, likes to perch on top of cushions, or steps, or countertops, with his knees to his chest. He's always kicking something, needing something, digging at something. Scabbed and ready. I don't know who these two boys are, not yet, only that we pose in pictures together from time to time, and that, somehow, in some places, I love them.

There are two boys in my apartment. That's what my mother tells me, anyway, when we have to pack up for the weekends and stay with my Auntie T. When we leave, my father locks up the room with my Breyer horses spread across the carpet, my mother's lipstick-smacked tissues piled up in a garbage can—a door locked in front of any lingering silhouette of a woman or child. My father plays catch with the boys on the weekends, buffed leather to ball, a square of sun behind the building. I wonder, still, how he explained our locked room. If it supposedly served any purpose.

There are three children on a beach. The two boys, now teens, and me. I'm chubby-legged, wearing a flopping sunhat, shoveling my feet into the sand. My mother is reclined in a chair, darkening beneath the sun like a soft, worn saddle. My father is speaking to the boys, the boys in their neon swimsuits, white smears of lotion circling their shoulders, their backs. They all look at me, sitting on my stupid towel. Their faces are exquisitely serious. Waves crash over in fangs. The two boys remember this day, this moment, more than I do. They remember every second of it.

A boiler room. An extra closet. A secret Narnia. A reclusive roommate. A door to nowhere. Just a door, long stuck. Another liquor cabinet. Storage for cleaning supplies. A grown-up room. A room of hidden pets.

My father was an excellent liar. His lies were like laminated sheets of paper—the facts were the facts—shining, reflective, unable to be torn even when a corner peeled.

I don't actually remember their neon swimsuits. Of course I don't. What I remember is a photograph taken on the beach that day. Two boys squinting into a camera, me in the middle—*look at them, together!*—none of our faces are ready. The two boys, now teens, looking at me on the edge of my towel. Round, Asian child, a face nothing like theirs, kneading hopelessly into colder sand.

You see her? said my father. *That girl?*

Yes, say the boys.

She's not just that woman's daughter, he says. *She's your sister.*

There are two boys in need of a home. Hurricane Andrew chewed up their land, spat it out in splinters. My mother, father, and I drive down to Coconut Grove, where we bring the two boys canned foods and bags of chips. A woman pearled with sweat opens the door to an apartment. It's dark inside, damp; there's no power for miles. The woman looks at me more carefully than anyone has ever looked at me—*his other child*—*Hello*, she says. The two boys at her side, guarding her like soldiers.

Are you old? I ask her. My words have no malice, no motive. I am just a kid, carrying cans in my arms as if they are baby dolls.

One of the boys says *Mom*, and I can barely breathe.

This mother is nothing like my mother. This mother is not my father's. How many mothers can exist in the same world? And do they all live in locked, dark rooms?

There are two teenage boys visiting from South Africa, where they now live. My mother, father, and I now live in the big white house with the indoor pool. My brothers stay in the guesthouse with black-and-white Berber carpet, a lofted bedroom area, a drum set. The older boy keeps to himself, folded inside the pages of Hawthorne, Faulkner. The younger one has just dyed his hair electric blue, and he *body slams* me into the mattress each time I try to sneak into their house. I love it when he does this—when he raises my body above his head and throws me down into the springs. I try and try again to bother them, to get the slams, these stunning moments of rage. Somehow, even then, I already know we all need this.

If you asked me, I would have told you I was an only child. If you asked again, I would have said I have two brothers, somewhere. *Where somewhere?* Africa. *Why?* To be away from me. *And their mother?* I hate their mother.

My older brother doesn't speak, I tell my friends at school. *He's a real asshole*. At the time, I think my brother hoards all his thoughts and words and opinions for later, for the people he thinks deserve them more than I do. I never remember seeing him smile. Everything about him was in his eyebrows. One day, while visiting, he finds a box in our garage full of his high school photographs, love notes, yearbooks. He reads the scraps aloud on our living room floor, laughing, grafting together different pieces of paper, different memories. It's the first time it occurs to me that my brother has a life outside the few days a year in which I see him. He has jokes.

He's been in love. I don't even know him. I feel at once both enamored and deceived.

I never hated their mother with any purpose—I never even knew her. I hated her because there were two mothers and only one father.

If you asked the two boys, they might tell you they had a sister, somewhere. *Where somewhere?* Boca Raton. *Why?* Because she got a life better than ours. *And her mother?* Well, they hated her, too.

Imagine that locked room in the weekend apartment, imagine a father around less and less, a man moved from one home to another—my mother's lipstick on his collars, her scent everywhere—my father's new habits, a new ring, his new life. Would you blame them?

After she dies, I will wonder about the two boys' mother. I will study the African seed pods she collected, floating in a glass shadow frame on my older brother's wall. I will consider the dimensions of her urn on the mantelpiece, next to my father's urn. I will touch the art she collected over the years, each paint stroke, the frames, and wonder at the value she placed on each one, the ways in which they may have moved her. She was an artist. She made two beautiful men. Once, she loved my father. Sometimes it feels like too big a wonder.

I keep things from my brothers. I don't tell them about the baseball bats or the women and men who've appeared in our house in puffs of smoke; I don't tell them about the pantry incident; I don't tell them about the burning stink or the *stuff* or the way our father turns off in the middle of speaking sometimes, his face bloodshot, his eyes gone. Instead, I ask the younger brother to teach me how to play the drums. In the guesthouse, he lets John Coltrane spool around a cassette until the button clicks, and then we play him again, again, as he shows me how to wrap my fingers around drumsticks, how to keep time, snap the hi-hat, stuff the bass drum with a snail-rolled towel. We beat the snare until it silvers, until we can't hear anything outside the sound that it makes, until it needs a new skin.

If there are real men, I haven't met them yet. Not when my father moves to New York, not when my mother falls. So when my brothers and father come home for Christmas, when my brother hands me those Sour Patch candies, you must understand why I said nothing. I'm still trying to explain.

I'm visiting New York—a teenager—and there's a concert in Brooklyn. Blake is playing in the show, and Shawn wants us to come out and watch. Shawn takes me down into the subway for the first time, and I scream when I see a rat on the tracks. He laughs at me, covers my eyes with his hands. Perhaps, I think, this is the first thing he's learning about me as a person removed from a mother or father. I am a girl who is afraid of rats.

We make it to a dark Bushwick living room where my brother plugs at the bass. He's wearing a silver tie, and everyone in the room is screaming, cheering him on. Shawn nods his head to the music. He is mostly quiet, listening, sipping on a beer. Blake shreds the strings. He hooks his arm around my neck when he sees me. *This is my sister,* he says to his friends.

We all have our own languages.

As adults, in a hotel room, I tell the younger brother the truth about the pantry incident. The way my mother's skin tore like a piece of overripe fruit. The purple of it.

That's why we left town, I say. *We didn't mean to leave you two with the mess.*

Blake looks at me, blinks hard.

I didn't know, he says, *any of that.*

Sometimes it feels like we are only this: moments of knowing and unknowing one another. A sound that is foreign until it's familiar. A drill that's a scream until it's a drill. Sometimes it's nothing more than piecing together the ways in which our hearts have all broken over the same moments, but in different places. But that's romantic. Sometimes it's realer than that.

My older brother speculates that my father knew he would die before we did. Just days before, my father wanted a shave. He'd been in a coma for two weeks, and a beard scrabbled out of his face—unnatural, patchy—the color of his old cigarette ash. My father was obsessed with the shave, the right razor, a smooth finish.

The best sign! I said. *He cares about the way he looks—he must be coming back.*

But my brothers had seen this before—their mother wanted lipstick, a compact, the day before she died. A dazzling exit. My older brother's face became a gray wedge in his hands as Blake and I shaved my father's cheeks. Nobody said a word as we moved the blade above and below every last tube, humming a song. Children being dutiful children. All that brutal love.

We were so careful not to cut.

When I file that restraining order against Chad, Shawn takes me to Whidbey Island, to a residency, where I will feel safer. My brother rides the Mukilteo ferry with me, buys me swirled cones of ice cream, takes me out on the deck to look at the sea. *I'm proud of you*, he says. After the court hearing, I arrive back to his house in Seattle, where he blends smoothies for me, makes my bed, picks up my favorite kind of crab for dinner. *Remember how Dad made them?* I ask. We don't, but we make up a new recipe of our own.

There are three of us in a photograph. One of us, me, does not look like the others. I am always in the middle of these two men, who are tall, handsome, protective in their postures. We do not fit, but I can tell you that we have the same fat toes, the same predisposition to

canker sores, the same ability to mimic accents; we land imper-
sonations. We drink when we are lonely, sometimes when we're
together, but mostly alone in our separate cities. We chew the same.
We laugh with our eyes closed. *There are thousands of ways to love
men*, Lidia Yuknavitch once wrote, and when I watch my brothers
button their shirts, or body slam my niece, or dance with their lips
puckered, I think I know all of them.

There are two men in my life. Their names are Shawn and Blake.
The older, more serious one, pushes his daughter on her bicycle as she
lifts her feet from the pedals. The younger one has three different
colors of hair—dark on top, graying at the hairline, red in the sideburns. Every word from him sounds like jazz. They are beautiful,
good men.

The three of us take a walk through a park in Seattle. It's spring;
we are all still grieving the same father; I am twenty-nine. The leaves
of a tree glow bright and then darken as the clouds pass, as if the tree
has a pulse. *When will we see you again?* my brothers want to know,
and I believe them. I believe that they miss me for every year we didn't
have, the way I miss them, too. Sometimes I miss them most when
we're all together, when we're already looking back at the moment,
wondering how it will ossify with time, how much more we will know
and unknow about each other.

That little girl on the beach. I was yours.

BIG HAIR, BIG HEARTS

Daphne Beauregard can smoke an entire pack of Parliaments and drink a liter of vodka in one night, just watch. She does lines of cocaine like they're pixie sticks, huffs keyboard cleaner spray into her nose, gulps pills, sucks the bong, and still, she is beautiful, regal even, a Dixie queen from Kansas with the best rack you ever saw. Daphne Beauregard lives with me. At least until my mother comes back.

Daphne doesn't have parents, either. Not really. Her father's back in Kansas and her mother's usually traveling for work, reviewing hotels across America. She's got no siblings, and calls me her sister—*The bumpkin and the Chink*, she says. *Perfect match for this place.* Her drawl is thicker when she drinks. I ask her to read receipts aloud to me sometimes, pages from my books, magazines, alien romances from the *National Enquirer. Talk, just talk,* I say, in bed at night. When I close my eyes, I pretend we live in the country, just the two of us, back in Kansas where a lightning storm has just cracked the sky open.

Daphne has a grandma in the Florida panhandle, and one weekend we decide to drive up and visit. We drink vodka sodas and puff on joints the whole way, bare feet out the window. Her grandma isn't home when we arrive, but we're thrilled to find a tanning bed in the middle of her living room. We strip naked; I climb inside the glass bed and pull the hood down. I light a cigarette and let the buzz drill through me. I ask Daphne to take my picture like this on her disposable camera, the filter slanted out of my mouth, ribbons of smoke glowing under the light, my nipples purpled in UV. I tell her this portrait will be my masterpiece, the photo I want blown up and framed when I die. I will call it *Human Cancer on Cancer on Cancer.*

Daphne is too mature for boys. *They don't make 'em like they do back home*, she says. *To hell with these polo and sweater vest chumps.* She wants a real cowboy and she tells me so. A man who will spit dip into a plastic bottle. A man who can two-step. *I come from big hair and big hearts*, she says, *not this rah-rah money crap.* One night, during a party at my house, I smoke weed laced with angel dust. I hallucinate beetles are digging into my skin; I need to be held down to keep from scratching. A boy named Stratton from math class puts my head in his lap and smooths back my hair. *You're too good for this*, he says. Stratton believes in God and I don't. *You're too smart for this; you could go to college, get straight.* Daphne does not approve of this boy, though he'll be the one to save my life, the first boy to ever love me.

Daphne and I start drinking first thing in the morning, to dull out the throbs. We skip school and sit on my back patio and smoke—tell stories about her first boyfriend (Glenn), my first drum set (a red Pearl), her first road trip (Kalamazoo), my favorite nostalgic smells (strawberry gas mask, hotel sheets, Vegas casinos, pine). We only sit down with the past.

I think before I was born, before this life, I was an artist, she says.

I dab out my cigarette.

Once, I was a horse.

I'M STILL HERE

It took my mother ten minutes with a chain saw to get us out of the house. Now she, my Grandma Sitchie, and I are sitting in the lobby of a Marriott, playing cards on the carpet.

Who are you? my grandma says, *and what have you done with my curlers?*

The hotel rooms surround us in a circle going up and up. Families have set up lawn chairs, mattresses, radios on every floor; they read magazines, leaning into the light. One TV works down here in the lobby, and swarms of people fight over which channel, which star. Right now, it's disaster coverage—Katrina, Ophelia, Rita, Wilma—the reason we're all here.

I'm your granddaughter, I say.

My granddaughter's sweet, she says, *seven years old with a bad haircut. I could show you a picture.*

I'm still here, I say, shuffling the cards.

Did you know Katharine Hepburn was a dyke? says grandma.

I need some quiet, says my mother. She stands up, moves to the other side of the lobby with a paperback and her mug of tea.

Want to see a magic trick? I say.

Want to get some wine, she says. *No magic tricks*.

My grandma stands up and walks fifteen feet to the bar in the center of the lobby. It's crowded over there. She orders a glass of merlot, looks at me, *Whaddya want? What's her face?*

I'm okay, I say.

When I became official with Stratton, I swore I'd get clean. I haven't touched a bottle; I haven't rolled a joint; I threw away my cigarettes, every last stash. Last week, I lost my virginity to him. We were in his dorm room at the University of Miami, his roommate gone for the weekend, a single candle lit. Usher's "Nice and Slow" played on repeat, and we kept most of our clothes on. As soon as he pushed his way inside me, I flipped over onto my stomach; I wanted to feel like an animal. I can wear pastel polo shirts and chew Winterfresh gum and learn bedtime prayers and bring his mother tulips, but in that moment I could not put myself away, not once I felt that kind of pain. Blood dripped onto the sheets. *Pull my fucking hair*, I said.

Stratton kept rocking, gently. He pressed his hands over my back tattoo to cover it, *I'm sorry*, he said, *I can't with the old you*.

My grandma sits back down in her floral, upholstered chair. She has a glass of merlot in each hand. She crosses her ankles. *I'm gonna meet myself a fella tonight*, she says. *What's your face again?* There are so many ways to lose a person. Of all things, this is what I know best.

Every airport is closed. On the one lobby TV, we watch dots of people bobbing through the rushing waters of New Orleans. It's been the worst hurricane season in history—so many dead, an entire alphabet of storm names—and most of the south will remain without power. I stay up all night and sit by the glow of the TV, trying to find something else. I bite into Sour Punch Straws to keep myself from finding a smoke.

A girl from middle school is here, wrapped in a blanket. Her name is Morgan. The roof of her home caved in, and she's been here four days.

So what have you been doing since the Craptop years? she asks. *What's new?*

I flip through the channels. I make up lies.

Going to college on equestrian scholarship.

Where? she asks.

North, I say. I hadn't considered the question.

My grandma is curled up on a bench in the lobby with a homeless man. He told her he would get her out of this hotel, this town. He took one look at her earrings and held on.

What else? asks Morgan. She is braiding and rebraiding a piece of her hair, pulling at it, twisting it. Dogs bark through the shadows of the halls.

I have a boyfriend, I say. *He's gonna marry me.*

When do you think you'll get out of here? asks Morgan.

I told you, for college.

This lobby, she says. *Where's your home?*

ANOTHER WORD

FOR CREEP

Hey neighbor! she writes. *I hear you're from Boca! Me too! Small world, huh?*

I'm twenty years old, single with an Adderall addiction, a fashion design student in New York City. It's seven in the morning, October, and I'm drinking coffee out of a mug when Lennox Price's name shows up on my screen, in my inbox, calling me *Neighbor.* I read on.

Well, I recently moved here for a guy but we broke up, and then I met this dope chick named Leah who said she dormed with you or something and I told her where I was from and she was like, another Boca girl! Sweet! You two should be friends! So, what do you think, neighbor? Hang sometime?

I stare at the screen. I light a Camel. I look up recent pictures of Lennox Price. *When did she move to New York?* She looks the same as she used to on Myspace, though she's platinum blonde now, with a diamond Monroe piercing to look more like Marilyn. She poses with the boyfriend—a comedian, I recognize him from his late-night specials—the square jaw, a scar across his cheek. The two of them look happy, beautiful, symmetrical in their power. In some photos, Lennox uses a book to cover her face from photographers, but I can tell by her eyebrows that she's smiling. I call Clarissa, to whom I haven't spoken in years.

You won't believe this, I say to her voicemail. *Remember Lennox Price?*

* ✳ *

My mother picks me up from the Fort Lauderdale airport two days before Christmas. I feel more mature in my college clothes, *New York clothes*, wearing a black turtleneck and emerald, tweed pants.

Aren't you hot? my mother says. *Aren't you dying?*

I'd rather sweat to death than dress like Jimmy Buffett, I say.

How's my college girl? she says. *My Project Runway girl?*

Same old, I say. *Dog piss freezes up there.*

My mother's spray tan is wet; she looks like she's been smeared all over with syrup. She and my father, who now split their time between Florida and New York, recently employed a woman named Elna to come over to the house and assemble a pop-up tanning tent in front of the living room TVs. My parents take turns standing in the structure, naked save for goggles, while Elna has them spread their fingers, their toes, spraying their bodies with bronze. The two of them have never been happier.

We drive straight from the airport to Best Buy. *We need to pick out some Christmas and Hanukkah gifts*, says my mother. *Choose some cool electronics—I don't know electronics—and we'll hand them out. Doesn't matter who gets what, just choose some nice shit.*

I pick up cameras, iPods, DVD players, USB drives. They clatter in my blue basket. I silently assign who will get what, based on how I currently rank everyone in my family, and who voted for John McCain.

On the way back to the car I say, *I think these gifts are good.*

Good, says my mother. *Good, I thought so. Expensive enough.*

Also, I think I'm in love, I say.

David? she says. *Still? He's no good for you, baby. He's really such a pussy. He's really a scumbag shit-mouthed mooch of whiney white garbage. And a liar face.*

Not David, I say.

Stratton again?

It's a girl, I say, as my mother pops open the trunk. *Girl,* the word shapes my mouth in a new way—tongue to teeth. I feel like I'm playing the role of a daughter testing her mother, a daughter grinding her way through a rebellious stage, pushing buttons—*Girl*—just to see how far it can go. *Her name's Lennox. We've been friends since high school. It's actually very sweet.*

My mother pulls the bags from my arms one by one, loads them into the trunk of our car. She lines them up in neat rows. Pats the plastic flat. She smooths her shirt. Takes her sunglasses off to wipe the steam, squints dramatically at the sun, places the glasses back on her face.

What do you want for dinner? she asks. *Anything you've missed?*

✷ ✸ ✷

It's true—I'm from Boca! I type back. *Parkland, really. I try so hard to forget. How funny that we don't know each other!* I include my phone number. I hit Send before I can change my mind.

Hours later, Lennox responds. *How about tomorrow? Natural History Museum? I've never been.*

Great, I type. *There's a new show at the planetarium. And the whale—the whale is really something.*

* ✳ *

It's not that I never thought about it. Girls. Women. It's that I thought about it too much.

* ✳ *

I wait for Lennox in a café near the museum. I run my fingers through my hair to smooth it; I straighten my tie. Lately I've been going to an evening writing class in Midtown, where a woman with a shaved head has been instructing us to keep a journal. In the café, I pretend to write in this journal to look busy, scholarly, like I have something important on my mind, but I am only writing Lennox's name in rows.

I'm so focused on the loop of my *L*'s that I miss Lennox walking through the door. She just appears, across from me, every detail of her, breathing. She's twenty minutes late. *I'm sorry,* she says. Those are the first words she ever says to me. *But I think I just saw James Franco outside. He winked!*

I laugh, covering my teeth. I say, *It's nice to meet you,* and, *tell me more about James Franco!* because I want to be this friend; I want to be the kind of person who is there for Lennox Price. Her cheeks are a deeper pink in person. Her teeth, sharper. She's wearing the same leather belt she wore in 2005 in photos from her BFF Kelly's graduation party. I wonder where Kelly is now.

So talk to me, I say. *What's your story?*

An hour later, Lennox Price and I recline our chairs and stare up and into the galaxy. Meteors corkscrew overhead; they look like giant cookies. We laugh as Whoopi Goldberg's voice booms through the auditorium, telling us how small we are, reminding us that we will all burn out into dust. At the end of the show, a child approaches Lennox—*You look like a fake! Like a doll! So pretty*—before the child's mother yanks her by the arm. Lennox smiles at me in the dark.

You get that a lot? The attention?

All the time, she says.

* ✳ *

We spend Christmas in the Florida Keys. My parents and I drive with the top down, wind blasting, a turquoise wall snaking us all the way down past trailer homes, roadside coolers of bleeding fish, rusting statues of dolphins. We stop at the Shell Man, where a fisherman tries to sell us hermit crabs, conch shells that will bring us straight to Jesus if we listen carefully enough. My parents squeeze each other's hands the whole drive, singing their favorite songs—*I believe in miracles. Where you from? You sexy thing*; they make out at every stop sign. They're like teenagers—this sober version of them, these final years of my father's life—as if they've just been reunited after a lame summer apart. As if that's all they had missed of each other.

My brothers and their partners meet us down there, at the resort. Shawn's wife, Maya, is a fitness instructor. She runs me up and down the beach, a stopwatch in her hand. She counts my pushups and puts money wagers on each set I complete. She promises extra food and alcohol if I finish another circuit. This has always been our bonding.

Maya wants me to practice wellness. When she tells me I could have a life full of sweat and centeredness and rippling ribbons of muscle, I believe her. She has always wanted what's best for me. She checks in, long distance. Reminds my brothers of my birthday. Before she ever met me, she sent those Sour Patch candies to Florida—*she's your sister. It's time you get to know each other.* Maya's kind like that.

That evening, we sit by the swimming pool. I jogged one mile today, and I've wrapped my ankles in ace bandages in order to feel more accomplished, like an athlete. Tiki torches blaze behind our heads. A man splays his fingers across a classical guitar while steel drums hammer behind him. He sings about margaritas and lost dogs. He sways and spins in slow circles as he sings, tangling and untangling the mic cord as he goes.

I have to tell you something, I say to Maya. *I don't know who else to tell.*

We're slurping down blue drinks. BINGO plates slick with other peoples' tanning oil rest on our laps.

What's up, buttercup?

I'm involved in something, I say. *I mean, with someone.*

David? That guy is such an asshole. Don't tell your brothers if you're back with him.

There's a girl. Her name is Lennox. She's so beautiful, Maya, you wouldn't believe. Her nails are these perfect little squares and she took care of me after the accident last month. She's also super in shape; you'd be impressed.

Involved?

I'm feeling a lot of things about it.

Well, it's okay, she says. *We all have experiences like this at some point. That's college.*

I think it's more.

Listen, she says. *I wouldn't go telling anyone about this just yet.*

How come?

Let's see if it sticks before we cross that bridge, okay?

It's sticking.

Let's just see before you say anything. You can't unsay something like that.

Or, perhaps, I never had the context to think about it—*girls*—in the right ways. I wanted to be them. I wanted them to like me. I wanted to smell like them and dress like them and know what girl tastes like, know how to walk pretty and line my eyes so they would look more open and shave the girl parts of my body and once, the first night I met that butch writing instructor, I wanted to run my hands all over the shaved parts of her neck. I wanted to tip the woman at a café more because she held that smile a beat too long. I wanted to have sleepovers with that middle school science teacher—*SUCH a dyke*—I wanted to try on her slacks, stand in front of her closet mirror while both of us fussed with the belt, the pleats; I wanted her to tell me I looked good, hot, handsome even, maybe wink at me, slyly, in the middle of class— *our secret*; but believe me—girls—I never knew how much more I wanted them.

Lennox Price eats junk food. Jars of peanut butter by the spoonful, chicken fries, bright, shiny taffies. She is also an online life coach. Other things that surprise me about Lennox Price: She does not speak to her family—*not even your brothers? / Never. They're all still in Sweden.* She likes to get high in the small, dank bathrooms of East Village bars. She has never been on a vacation that a man hasn't paid for, and her real name is Louisa—*but don't say that shit in public, okay?*

We're eating spaghetti on the Upper East Side. She uses a fork and spoon to twist the pasta in perfect form. I use the chopsticks I carry in my purse, and try so hard to be neat, tidy. No slips.

My last breakup was so bad, she says.

With the comedian?

Mmhmm. We had a cat together. Little bitty thing. She looked like a baby koala, so I changed her name to Koko. She was a koala or a moose, depending on the day.

I say, *Those are very different things.*

It was bad. I miss Koko. I miss living in the Village, rent-free. Stars are tough to date, all that ego—you know?

Oh, sure, I go. *Of course.*

We're trying joint custody with Koko, but I guess that doesn't matter. What matters is I think I might, maybe, sort of, be done with men for good, you know? On to the next.

She reaches to click her glass against mine.

I don't think I understand.

I mean I've marched in a Pride parade before, in Florida. I marched with bisexuals.

I stuff my mouth with pasta. I nod into my bowl.

Are you not . . . ? she says, leaning back.

No. No, I don't think.

No offense, she says, *but you seem really gay. Like really, really gay.*

I've thought of it before, I say. *I mean it's not like I've never—or anything.*

I could tell.

I mean I think I've even loved a girl before, maybe once. Paula. Back in Florida. She doesn't really know who I am, though.

I could tell.

* ✳ *

November. Lennox's face under the blue glow of a bar on Graham Avenue. She looks like a drawing of herself in this deep swell of light. Every waiter and bartender, every bad date, eyeing all of Lennox Price, the pale halo of electric blue hair, her high leather boots. She kicks them up and on the bar to show me the stitching, something Lennox Price can do without pause. Her bangs are growing out, caught up in her eyelashes, twitching as she blinks.

You should touch me more, she says. *What's the shy about?*

I'm just a very serious person, I say. *That's all.* I lean into my elbow, looking at her.

You always look like you're about to cry. Do you know that?

I usually am about to cry, I say.

Put your arm around me if you want.

Okay, I say. I sit up. I move the weight of my arm around her without letting it fully rest on Lennox's shoulder. I don't want to burden her with it. I strain to keep it there, in position, a slight hover on her skin. My hand there. There.

It's like I want to take a picture of you every second of every day.

You're drunk, she says.

So are you.

It's like you love me or something.

I just get you, I think. Maybe it's a Florida thing.

Why'd you leave? she says.

*My dad—I wanted to see him more. I had shit grades but design school
let me in. Wonder why,* I say, sipping my drink.

Does the shoe stuff get annoying?

You have no idea.

You like it here? I miss the sunshine.

I'll never go back, I say. *I can be alone here, surrounded by people.
Best combination.*

That's kind of sad.

Can I tell you a secret? I say.

Anything.

*I used to—I think I once saw you on the Internet. When I was some
dumb kid. You had a webpage, right? Pictures, diary entries?*

Yes, oh my god. Her face scrunches. *That is so embarrassing!*

Yeah, I saw you there. Maybe I did love you a little, yeah.

That's so cute, she says.

I scoot closer to her. I look at her, steady, really try to see her. I don't
laugh this moment off. I want her to see me, too.

And by cute, I mean creep, she says, pinching my nose.

Careful, I'm a bleeder.

The bartender says our last round is on the house. I can tell Lennox
is used to this. He pushes over a receipt on which he's drawn a sketch
of Lennox—square jaw, apostrophe eyes—a ballpoint pen masterpiece
in which she looks perfect, alone.

* ✳ *

Once, I did mention it. To Clarissa. My favorite specials on the black
box. Misty's dance teacher, Jaqueline. Ren Stevens on the Disney

Channel. Winnie Cooper in her cat-eye glasses. Every girl who's ever worked her hair into a pencil twist. Ms. Dyke Hoochie. Dr. Frank-N-Furter. Linda Perry. Leonardo DiCaprio just before he freezes to death; the way he looks like he's wearing lipstick.

That would change if you ever had sex with one, she said. *And, like, how do you even have sex with one?*

* ✳ *

It's a nickel-slapping kind of rain, a silver bounce to it. It is not cold enough to snow. Outside the bar, under the awning, we shiver. I rub my gloved hands up and down Lennox's arms.

Call me a cab? Can you call cabs in Brooklyn? she asks.

Would you come home with me? I say. Even five drinks in, I don't know how I possibly say it.

Okay, she says. *Sure.*

I'm close.

I start to run. Slowly at first, and then faster. A neck-throbbing run. We run from the sharp pings of freezing rain and we run to keep our blood from freezing. We run for Lennox's hair. I run to keep my hands from trembling. She runs to show me how well she can run in heels. I run because I don't want the time to talk, for her to take back what she's just said, or for me to do the same.

We run under the Brooklyn-Queens Expressway, a relief from the rain. We run beneath that hollow ribbon of orange light, the echo-swish sound of cars; we run around skateboard ramps made of milk crates, crookedly parked cars, browned, dimpled mattresses. We run past the people who live under here—*gimme some sugar!*—we run wet and dizzy until my breathing can't keep up, until I barely know where I live, until I round a corner and find the doorway of my gate and push in the key, lean into it, release. We run up the stairs, into my living room, where we shake our clothes off. They slop on the wooden floor—the garments pooling out with a steam to them. I push her onto my bed and run my fingers through the hair by her ear, and she's moaning before I even kiss her.

You know what you're doing? she asks.

I think so, I say.

You think so?

I think I can manage.

Have you fucked a woman before?

No. I regret the truth as soon as it comes.

Lennox is silent. She stares at my ceiling, covers her face with her hands. She laughs a little, the sound muffled.

Sweetheart, you're sweet. But I can't be with someone who's never fucked before. Are you for real?

I mean. I—

I've fucked at least four of my friends. You haven't?

No. I shake my head. *I don't have friends like that.*

Whatever's happening here, she says. *Let's pretend it's not happening.*

* ✳ *

In the Keys, my parents take me deep-sea fishing. I drug myself with Dramamine, because I know how this will go. I always get seasick, but my father is a fan of exposure therapy, excess of anything until the fear passes. I have used wristbands, medicines, oils, the horizon. Still, I am sick for days.

Back in the condo, my father watches the Sunday game. The rest of the family is back out on the boat, but I can't move.

I thought it'd be different by now, he says, shaking his head. *Sorry, Kira Kukamonga.* He calls his bookie, and I rest my head in his lap. The shoulder pads on television spiral in and out of my vision. The noise is too much for me. *This is MadMan46, let's go two-thou on the Steelers*, he says into the phone. He strokes my hair. Hangs up and slams the cellphone into the table.

I stare at the hammerhead shark mounted above the TV. The eyes are bulging; the mouth looks like it was painted with birthday cake frosting. It's the same shark David has mounted to the wall in his apartment, the shark he swore he once caught.

Daddy, I want to tell you something, I say.

This quarter's almost over, he says.

I'm dating a girl, I say.

What's that? he stares into the television. His knees bouncing under my head. He leans with the play. *Go baby, go!*

I'm dating a girl, I say. *She's coming to town for New Year's—she's from here. Maybe you could meet her.*

What's that? he says.

I want you to meet her, this girl I am dating. She's coming to town.

She hot? he asks.

She is.

She can come around then, he says, eyes still on the screen. *But I wouldn't mention this to your mother.*

* ❋ *

For my tenth birthday, my mother bought me a Barbie doll who could talk. All I had to do was type her dialogue into a computer program, plug Barbie in, and on she went. I typed and typed.

Leonardo, baby, take me to dinner?

Yes, anything, I said, stroking her ponytail with my thumb.

Leonardo, be my man?

It's because of that boy in Titanic, my mother explained to my father, smiling. *She loves him.*

Leonardo. Leonardo. Leonardo. Leonardo. Sometimes I didn't feed Barbie any questions. Sometimes I just wanted to look at her while she called me that.

I'm finally picking up the rest of my things from David's West Village home; it's been five months since our breakup. David is ten years older than me, but he has never used the kitchen of his studio apartment, he never learned to cook, so he uses this area for extra coat racks and shoe storage. I open his oven to look for my clothes. His sink is clogged, full of bong water.

On the counter, next to a sock, two wine glasses. Lipstick prints. I smudge the color with my finger and rub the waxy red on my own lips. My clothes are scattered around the apartment, and I'm surprised by how little I feel. I feel distant, like I'm observing the artifacts, the evidence, of somebody else's relationship, somebody else's life.

Downstairs, I wobble with the bags of clothing, my purse, a backpack full of toiletries. I drop everything into the snow and hail a cab. I tell the driver to take me to my parents' apartment on Mercer Street.

In the cab, I call Lennox. *I did it,* I say. *Finally. Nothing left.*

I hope they're happy together, she says.

I'm laughing about this. About the years I wasted on David and David's cocaine habit. David's bad spelling, and his job as a "Gentlemen's Club" director. David's secret JDate account and fetish chatrooms, the way he sang Bowie's *Oh, oh, my little China Girl* into my ear when he first picked me up, at eighteen, outside a nightclub in the Meatpacking District. I am laughing into the phone until there's a screaming of tires, a horn, then another, the driver's voice—*Please don't, I can't get in trouble, Here, Go, Stay*—a hospital, a nurse—*hit the glass divider, you're at St. Vincent's, you're okay*—and my father's voice and my mother's voice—*You didn't get his cab number?*—and my suede boots, freckled bloody, they look so filthy against the sheets, a wheelchair, a flashlight in the eyes—*The driver, he dropped her and fled*—Where are my bags? Where are my things?—*The driver—do you remember his name?*—my bags in the hospital trashcans. *What about my phone?* I just want Lennox there, on the other end.

My mother stays with me in the hospital. She wheels me around each floor. She takes me into the hospital cathedral because the lights aren't as bright in there. She massages my neck.

Daddy and I have that big trip to China, she says. *Do you want us to cancel?*

I'm okay, I say.

Can any of your friends come over, take care of you? Why were you leaving David's apartment?

I'm okay.

We'll see you for Christmas, she says. *That'll be nice, huh? Florida sun? David-free? No fishing?*

Lennox shows up to my parents' apartment with soup and cartons of juice. She calls herself my nurse. We spoon mint ice cream into each other's mouths in bed. We watch movies but face each other the whole time as the television light flicks the walls—*What did it feel like to almost die? / You are the most interesting person I've ever met*—I ask her to read pages of Frank O'Hara aloud; we take my painkillers with large bulbs of red wine. We clasp hands under the blankets. I rest my head on her bare stomach, kiss her rib cage, her belly button, but never her lips.

I always want to kiss you, I say.

Then kiss me. Anywhere.

The truth: when I'm around Lennox, when our noses come too close, I fear that she'll feel my weakness right through my shirt, the same weakness that makes me say good-bye early each night I see her, that brings me straight home or into a stall of the closest public bathroom where I will jerk my hand down the front of my pants, give in to that knot inside me that only loosens when I think of her long enough to make myself come, the knot that tightens back up as soon as it's finished, as soon as the tears come in hiccups. But what I say is, *Let's just take it slow, okay?* We don't leave bed for days.

✳ ✳ ✳

I tell my college roommate, Karolina, a Romanian ballerina with the personality of a nubbed crayon. This is later, the aftermath. It's been years since we've seen each other. *Gay* is the word that I use.

While you were with David?

Sometimes.

I thought that was a phase. That sad crush on your writing teacher.

It wasn't.

And then you had a—girlfriend?

I did. Her name was Lennox.

Karolina zipped her purse just then. She wiped nonexistent crumbs from her lipstick with a napkin. She cleared her throat once, twice, three times, tilted her small head as she looked at me. Her hair, gelled slick into a bun, shone under the lights like a chess pawn.

I lived with you, she says. This bitch, she started crying. *I changed my clothes in front of you.*

✳ ✺ ✳

So you eat pussy now, is that what you're saying? Addison Katz French inhales a Marlboro. It looks like gray tapeworms are winding from her mouth into her nostrils.

I guess you could say that.

Lennox Price. Really?

I nod.

Figured you would, you always had it in you, says Claudia.

We're having a small high school reunion at Dani's mom's mansion. We wear black paper top hats with gold, mirrored lettering, *NEW YEARS 2009*, cardboard noisemakers piled on the patio table like Chinese finger traps. Dani's mom bought us these accessories—*Let me take a picture, the girls back together again!*—before locking herself in her room with a romance novel, a glass of champagne, and their dachshund.

It's not like I was always—it just happened to me, I say. *But leave it, she'll be here soon.*

The four of us have nothing in common—we were barely friends in the first place—but we are the only people back home in Boca for the holidays. We reach for conversation from every corner of the room—Addison's new haircut, Dani's ailing dog, Claudia's new gig at a makeup stand in the mall—but the conversation always circles back to Lennox Price, the girl she once was in her pictures, the woman she is now.

So what're you lesbos doing tonight? asks Addison. *Besides eating pussy?*

Going to the beach, I say, because this is our plan: Lennox is picking me up after her family reunion, just before midnight. She wants to kiss me just then, she said, on the dot, as the ball plummets in Times Square, as people recite wishes and resolutions, as fireworks trail the sky like chalk. A new beginning—she and I. We'll go to the beach, whip open the bedsheet I packed, let champagne dribble down our chins and into our shirts. We could be the better, truer version of *us* going forward, now that we are telling people, now that we're ready.

Well what time's she coming? Because it's almost here, says Dani, lighting another smoke from one of the packs on the table. Her hair keeps sticking to her lip gloss, so she lumps it together at the top of her forehead, snaps a rubber band. There is a way in which Dani has always looked older, over it, ready to retire to Palm Beach.

Lennox hasn't called yet. Rumor has it that the cell towers are down. That's what I tell them, anyway, these girls. The lines are busy. Too much traffic. Too many calls.

* ✳ *

Once my head is healed from the accident, Lennox takes me out for dinner and drinks on St. Mark's Place. She wants me to meet an old friend of hers, a childhood neighbor. His name is Thomas, and he carves ice sculptures. Thomas does not acknowledge me; he does not shake my hand. The three of us sit. We sip Manhattans, poke at a limping salad.

I didn't know you were this way, Louisa, I didn't. What about your parents?

Thomas, she laughs. *Come on, stop.*

It's not right, he says.

It's nothing, she says.

So what's it like, I ask him. *To spend so much time making art that disappears?*

These drinks are strong, says Lennox.

You're a child of His, don't forget. Thomas excuses himself to the bathroom.

This is fun, I say.

I think he's always liked me, she says. *It's nothing personal.*

Everyone likes you. That's not an excuse.

Do you want to just, go? she asks.

While he's in there?

Yeah.

We don't say another word before standing up and shoving our chairs under the table. Before I have time to think about it, I take her face in my hands and kiss her.

I kiss Lennox every five feet of our walk. I kiss her on every corner. Against every building. I kiss her in front of every person we pass. If someone says something about it, I kiss her harder. If they say nothing, I kiss her harder. I kiss her for every girl I have ever not kissed.

I kiss her against the door of my parents' empty apartment, and against the kitchen sink, and then in bed. *Let me fuck you*, I say. *I want to love you.*

She takes her top off, nodding. I unhook her bra, easy. I'm relieved to manage this part. She unbuttons my shirt, unhooks me. We press chest to chest and I have never felt this naked in my life. Her breasts are large, shining, firm.

You ever feel these before?

I press my hands over them—up, down, left, right, like a Hail Mary—unsure of what to do. I lick. I suck. I crunch my hips against her, but I'm not sure what kind of contact I'm making, or where. I move my hands down between her legs, under the lace, fumbling for something familiar. *It must feel familiar right?* Nothing feels familiar. I am shaking and circling my hands, grinding my torso against her leg like a newly neutered dog. She is sucking on my neck, moaning, *Oh yeah, that's right*, but I know this is an act of kindness. Of mercy.

It is true, when I say that I am always about to cry.

* ✳ *

By two thirty A.M., Addison, Dani, and Claudia are packing bulbs of purple haze into a glass pipe shaped like an elephant.

Let's call this pipe Anne Bowl'leyn, I say, but nobody gets it.

The girls speak with flat, croaked voices as we swat smoke and mosquitos.

Sorry, dude. Maybe the lines really are tied up, says Dani.

Or maybe she drives really, really slow, says Addison, chuckling to herself until she forgets what it is she's chuckling about. We are high.

My phone is in the middle of the table, between the ashtrays. A dead, blank face to it. Nothing. Claudia's inside, shouting the contents of Dani's refrigerator as we scream yes or no. Addison pulls on a lace bodysuit she plans on wearing to a Lady Gaga concert. Her nipple rings glitter here, in the dark.

I don't smoke grass, I say, sucking from the trunk of the elephant.

Yeah, it doesn't look like it, says Dani.

Remember when you used to bug out? says Addison. *You always thought you were dying.*

We're all always dying, I say.

You're so full of shit, Addison goes on. *You don't smoke grass like you never drank, like you never sucked dudes off in the school parking lot. You always deny everything you want.* Addison, always a philosopher when high.

True, I say. *But that's not the same as not wanting it.*

What the fuck are we talking about? asks Dani. *Like, what?*

In middle school, Clarissa and I went to Disney with our friend Geri. In the Universal Studios bathroom, Geri leaned back on the stall door, Manic Panic green bangs sweat-smeared across her forehead, and she laced her fingers behind my neck, said, *Practice. Why don't we practice for the real thing?* She opened her mouth for me, just like that, the O of her choir face, and so I leaned into it. *Let me in on the practice*, Clarissa said, and the three of us kissed one another—*1-2-3, you go left, I go right*—tongues sloppy, braces clicking. Later that night, we met some boys near the hotel pool. Clarissa kissed someone in the dark as I watched the blue glow on Geri's bare stomach. Geri's pruned feet. One of the boys leading Geri away as she let go of my hand, laughing, saying, *I'll be right back.*

✴ ✸ ✴

We all take the stairs to Dani's bedroom. It's still pink, lacy as a table-cloth, unchanged since high school. The lavender sachets in her pajama drawers are brown by now. The sheets, too starched.

The girls fall asleep with their clothes on. I curl up on the carpeted floor, watch the lights of passing cars slash up and down the walls. My phone does not buzz in my hand. I check and recheck to make sure it's on, charged. Sometimes I feel like I've spent my whole life waiting.

Louisa. Lennox Price.

Her name drags me down the stairs, out the door, to my car, where I drive home along the beach. The sun lifts and bleeds out along the ocean. It's a new year, and the air is already warm. Louisa. I walk barefoot into my house, bury myself under my childhood covers, and sleep.

The next day there are pictures of her, partying in Fort Lauderdale with her old friends. In the days after that, more pictures of her appear on the Internet, with the comedian. She posted the photos herself, the two of them in a white, linen bed with Koko the cat. *Happy holidays! We love you!*

She does love him, I think. The look of her—she does. Whatever comes before or after men is a footnote; my life has taught me this by now. I nod my head at the computer, understanding, forcing a smile, as if this were our final conversation. Lennox Price went back to the boyfriend who would love her, need her, the simpler life, of course she did.

By spring, I do, too.

FOOTNOTE

This is how it goes for a while:

Jane's fingers are long and her knuckles are smooth and white as beach stones. She's a painter with a shaved head and a lip ring, and I don't know anything else about Jane except for the way she looks at me across the bar. Her hands when she pours a drink. The exact distance between the blue of her jeans when she walks. We scoot orange pills across the surface of her bar that keep us up all night, sipping bourbon, smoking when the lights dim, talking. I always come here alone.

Jane pulls down the bar shutters with an aluminum thwack. There's a blizzard outside. We share a cab—we do this sometimes—but tonight, her hand squeezes my knee.

Need a place to stay? she asks. *It's nasty out there*, she says, as we cross the Queensboro Bridge. This is no longer in the direction of my home.

I don't answer Jane's question, but I follow her out of the cab, I shut the cab door, I steady myself against her—*Careful now*—I don't want to slip. The snow is coming down in great creamsicle smears beneath the street lamps, and then I'm following Jane inside her apartment, into Jane's room, where I nudge off the lights and crawl on top of Jane and unbuckle the teeth of Jane's belt.

Easy, she says.

I pull her pants down to her knees and push my face into her and taste what I want to taste. I fuck her with my hand. *Relax*, she says. *I'm the one who tops here.*

Jane tries to flip me over, but I don't want her to touch me. As if by reaching inside me she will find the very pith of my fraudulence. *I have a UTI*, I lie, crushing my hips into her leg.

Sometimes I jerk off thinking of you, she says.

I come when she says this.

The next morning, Jane breathes on her window and traces my name in the steam. We do not kiss good-bye. I wash my face in her chipped sink, pull my hair back into a bun. I call a cab and travel back over the bridge, where I buzz open the door to David's apartment, crawl into our bed, and tell him it was bad out there, too dangerous to go so far.

COLLECTED DATES WITH

MY FATHER

I.

Every night, my father bends one arm under the crook behind my knees, the other around my waist, and carries my body to bed. He tucks my mermaid covers up to my chin, squeezes my feet over the sheets. Darkness is heavier when alone in it. My father moves the pads of his fingers down my nose, across my forehead, so slow and gentle, like he's offering me holy water. He calls this "fingertips" and tells me not to be so frightened, there is nothing that can hurt me, not as long as he lives.

I close my eyes and the stories come: *There once was a little girl with a flying horse. Everybody loved her. The fact that the horse could fly was a secret only the little girl knew. The girl wanted to live far, far away. Paris, maybe, or Kentucky. Somewhere with grass blue as twilight, where the wind would comb it flat and sweet. But the horse told her, No, no. You must stay where you are, in Boca Raton! The horse could speak, you see.*

But I hate Boca Raton! said the little girl. The Rat's Mouth is gross!

The horse says, Let's make a deal. You stay in the Rat's Mouth during the day, with your parents who love you, and at night I promise to take you away. I'll fly you to the moon and back, to every country in the world, I'll get you the hell away from here, as long as you're not so afraid.

The girl says, I'll take that deal.

The horse says, Hold on.

II.

My father is taking me to my first baseball game. I am seven years old and ready for it, with new Keds sneakers, a Hawaiian-print fanny pack buckled around my hips, a real grown-up baseball cap. My mother takes our picture before we leave the house. We stand against a palm tree in the front yard, beaming. My father's hand rests on top of my cap.

In the car, my father sips from a glass in the center console. He finishes it quick, makes clucking sounds with his lips at the taste. He tries to explain baseball to me—the plates, the diamonds, the way the dirt will spray majestic and red. He waves his hands around with each description, his gold rings glittering, a Merit hanging from his lips. I right the steering wheel.

Lately, when my parents' voices sound garbled and tired, when their eyes get sticky and small, I call them Sleepy Girl and Sleepy Boy. I open the driver's door of Sleepy Boy's Mercedes and pull him out by the pinky. We walk a funny walk to the big bleachers, wave hello to the people he knows. I am so proud to have Sleepy Boy as my date, to be at a real baseball game with real teams. The mosquitos curdle black around the stadium lights as I chew, open-mouthed, on a hotdog without the bun. Sleepy Boy screams, growls some, his arms golden and pumping when the right man runs. Two trophies on fire.

Our team wins. My father is my father again, awake, standing. He runs down to meet his friends at the bottom of the bleachers, screams, *Wait right there, son!* in his rasp. The tin bleachers thunder under me.

I watch my father with his friends for a long while. They smack each other on the backs, clap their meaty hands. They down drinks from plastic cups, crush them on their foreheads and beneath their sneakers. From here, they're the size of a postcard. If I sent this postcard to my mother, I would caption it *Happy Men.*

I kick my feet up and on the bleachers, press my cheek into the metallic cold. I feel safe here, watching him.

When the father knocks on the front door (he's lost his key), the mother asks, *Where is the daughter?* The father asks, *Who?*

The daughter is sitting on the bleachers, watching each and every light wink off. The daughter zips and unzips her fanny pack, crunches on the Cheerios kept inside. A woman named Heather finds the daughter in the dark, offers her a ride, pulls up a car. The daughter does not know her way home.

III.

I am four, and it's about time for me to begin school. This means the doctor's office. This means shots. My mother cannot calm me down for days. I know what's coming: the needles, the rubber ball, the snap of a band, the blood. I've seen it in movies; I've heard about it. I know it all before the knowing, and I am inconsolable. My father volunteers to take me to the doctor, gives my mother a break.

Pretend this is fun, he says, *like we're going on a date!*

In the waiting room, I scratch a blue flower from the wallpaper. I flip through magazines I cannot read. I move colored beads around on a wire—stack the beads, unstack them, *click click.* My nose begins to gush, because it is always doing that. My father pulls me onto his lap, rips the permanent stash of tissues from his pocket, presses hard into my face. *You know what to do,* he says. *Calm down, squeeze the spot. You know it's a nervous thing.*

Will life always be this nervous? I ask, beneath the tissues. My head is rocked back, and I stare at the ceiling until my eyes cross. The blood gurgles in my throat.

Yes, my father says. *Abso-fucking-lutely.*

In the doctor's office, a nurse sits me down on a thin sheet of paper. My father rolls two tissues into slug-sized wads, stuffs one into each of my nostrils. The nurse gives me a chalky-looking lollipop, and I begin to kick my legs, cry. She snaps her gloves into the garbage can, closes the door.

Listen, says my father. *When I was in the army, we had to get hundreds and hundreds of shots. Imagine? This is jack shit next to that.*

I cry harder. Nobody understands my pain.

Okay, okay, here's what I did, he says. *I had the docs stand in rows, facing one another, with their needles, the medicines. I walked down the line in between them, shimmied my shoulders, left, right, left, right, left, let them poke me all they wanted as I did this stupid dance.*

My father does the dance for me. He shimmies his shoulders, pretending to be pricked. He says, *Ow! Ow! Ow! Ow!*, walking toward me with exaggerated wobbles.

When the needles come, I'm still laughing. My father and I make the sound effects, the warped faces. The first two needles aren't so bad, but then they begin to pop through my biceps. They hurt. When I stop laughing, my father takes my baby toe and pinches it.

Ouch! Why! I scream.

Focus, he says. *Move it. Put the hurt somewhere else.*

IV.

Billy Joel is my favorite singer. I'm eleven, and my father is driving us to his concert. He's been Sleepy Boy all night, sipping juice from little cobalt glasses, driving the rumble strip all the way down to Plantation.

At the stadium, my father speeds past the parking spaces and pulls up on the sidewalk. He drives right over it, honks his horn at a chain of Snowbirds in our way. An attendant in a glow-in-the-dark vest motions for my father to roll down his window. He does.

You can't park here, sir, says the attendant. His face in the sliver of window seems so small compared to my father's. His nose is crooked, his cheeks are pimpled and rosy, and I decide that he is kind.

My daughter, she's retarded, says my father. *I forgot our handi-pass, but she can't walk right.*

My father pats my knee with his hand, looks into his lap with his head shaking.

There's nothing I can do about that, sir, says the kind attendant.

Give her this night, says my father. *Billy's her man.* My father palms him a small wad of cash. The attendant looks at me with his eyes all squinty, as if to check. I smile at him—the metal braces, clamps, rubber lip bumper, turquoise bands connecting my buck teeth to the bottom. I am ugly-cute, I know, like a too-deep sea creature, but I embrace it. I work it. My father is so handsome that everybody thinks I was adopted—a charity case—a mutt from China, or Cuba, or Mexico, or Samoa. Nobody can be sure.

The kind boy closes his eyes for a few seconds. I feel sorry for him—nobody can ever look at me for long. He says, *Fine. Go 'head.*

Outside the car, my father wraps his arms around me. He whispers, *Limp, you've got to limp. Hang your mouth all dumb.* He rubs my shoulders as if I'm cold, like he's protecting me. I do what he says. I want to be a good daughter. I drag my feet across the sparkling sidewalk and tuck my elbows into my waist. I let my tongue roll out of my mouth as I stare up and into the ashy, polluted sky.

In the stadium, my father passes out in his seat. His bottom lip gleams wet, and I wipe it for him with the bell sleeve of my shirt. Billy sings about love, and I swear he's singing directly to me. My father wakes up to "Piano Man," says, *We have to go, let's skip the traffic out of here.*

But "Piano Man" is my favorite song in the whole world.

We leave anyway. I listen to Billy sing about bread in his jar over the speakers that line the parking lot. In the car, my father begins to cry. Hard, hiccuping sobs.

What's wrong, Daddy? I rub his back.

The song, he says. *It's just so true.*

V.

I'm five, and my father is taking me to see Siegfried and Roy in Las Vegas. I've been practicing my own magic tricks at home with balloons and straws, blowing on my fists, squeezing foamy trick bunnies.

Tonight, I wear a big fluffy coat with a Dalmatian pattern on it. My front tooth is loose, and I can't stop tonguing the sharp edges, the dangling thread of flesh. My father is dressed beautifully, a pressed jacket and pants that smell like big city. He holds my hand as I watch the show, my eyebrows tight and high as the Siberian tigers jump through hoops, appear and get gone.

I decide, I want to marry my father. I want us to go on these dates for as long as I live.

When the show ends, we take a walk on the Las Vegas strip. We walk to the monorail, so we can shoot back down to the Luxor. The whole sky coruscates with lights, a real city, like nothing I've seen.

One more thing before we go back, he says.

My father swings his arms in a wild, big way. He makes a Froot Loop with his mouth, his eyes wide, rimmed white. From behind his back, he pulls out a stuffed tiger—just like Siegfried's. I am so amazed I scream.

I sit on his shoulders for the rest of the walk home. I squeeze the tiger to my chest. I bob and sway with his steps and turns, forget to be afraid.

If my mother gave me language, my father gave me magic.

VI.

I'm twenty-seven, and my mother has the flu. *We'll spend the day together!* says my father. *I'm bored with your mom in bed, come over, let's have a date.*

I drive to their house in Atlantic Beach, New York.

It's Sunday morning, and we watch television in the living room. My father rocks his knobby knees back and forth on the couch, smiling at Charles Osgood, his favorite anchor. He says, *This ought to be good.* It's a special on Houdini. On the show, a voice-over explains Houdini's escape methods. A man holds up the straitjackets between his fingers, shows us some of Houdini's old water tanks. The voice-over explains that when Houdini's mother died, he went around debunking mystics and mediums all over the world.

Why'd he do that? says my father. *Nothing better to do?*

I think he just missed her, I say. *I think he wanted somebody to prove him wrong.*

Before I die, he says, *should I give you a code word? So you can test it with the mystics?*

We decide it might be *Fuck.*

I'll definitely know it's you then, I laugh.

After the show, my father and I take a drive. We cruise along the pale beach, and he shows me the Sands Club, where he had his senior prom, where he saw the Ronettes, the Shirelles. *But that was once upon a time,* he says, *early days.* A few blocks away, he waits in the car with the top down as I pick up his dry cleaning, piled above my eyes, the plastic wrap sticking to my arms.

This is not a very good date! I scream.

He drives me to the groomers so we can pick up our dogs. In the car, he talks about love. He likes my new girlfriend, Hannah, warns me not to get too drunk and sloppy at a wedding we will attend. *They don't like lesbos in Mexico,* he says, winking. *No tongue kissing.* This is the first time he brings up my girlfriend on his own. I squeeze his hand. The conversation circles back to Houdini.

You don't believe in life after death? Not even a little? I ask.

No, he says. *But I do know this: I'll know when I'm going to die. I'll feel it. The doctors say I'm not doing so hot but I'll know it, I swear.*

He pats me on the back.

I'll know it, okay?

I nod.

At home, my father eats a bean stew I slow-cooked for him. He says it tastes too healthy, but he'll take the health. The recipe is ancient, Mayan; legend says that eating a bowl of it every day will make you immortal.

You saved me today, he says. *You cooked, you cleaned, you kept me company. So good,* he says, *you're always so good to me.*

Stay over, he says. *Call into work. I need you longer.*

Please, stay, he says.

I tell him I can't, I have a date tonight. I tell him to call me if he feels worse, to call whenever he wants. I promise to come back if he needs me.

You know you can call anytime, you know that.

You fixed for dough? he asks. He hands me a wad of cash. *Be good, Kukes.*

I kiss him on the forehead. I say, *I love you, Dad.* I say, *I'll come by next weekend.*

This is the last day I ever spend with my father.

VII.

I am eight, and my mother has decided that enough is enough, that Sundays will now be *Father-Daughter Sundays* and we must have fun, we must have laughs, we must have quality time, no bullshit, no drinking, no drugging, enough.

This week, my father has quit drinking again. On Sunday, he drove another man's car home from a bar because the valet gave him the wrong key. The cops surrounded our home at four in the morning, and my father answered the door with his fists in the air, naked, screaming, *I want to see MY car in MY driveway before I let you take this one.*

My father promises my mother that we will have a nice, sober day. He's going to take me to Sam Ash Music Store, he says. Let me bang the snares off the Pearl drum set I want so badly. Then he'll take me to La Bamba, he says, the little Mexican restaurant nearby. We'll share arroz con pollo and Cherry Cokes. If we have time, we'll even take a drive to the beach.

My mother hugs us both good-bye, smiles with watery eyes. She says, *I am proud of you,* to my father, as if he is her other child.

My father keeps his word. He drives me to Sam Ash in the strip mall, pulls up right in front of it. He says, *First, can we check out the scores? Then we'll play those toms.*

Next door to Sam Ash is a sports bar called Gatsby's. It's a horseshoe-shaped bar, with fly tape twirling from the ceiling. A jukebox pulsates with rainbow lights in the corner of the room like a giant jellyfish. My father helps me onto a stool at the bar. He sits next to me, gazes up at the football game, lights a smoke. He's placed his bets, he tells me, enough money to pay my college tuition. This is another thing he was supposed to quit. He taps his gold pinky ring against the bar in triplets.

A woman named Irene brings my father a glass of orange juice, but I know there's more to it than that. Irene doesn't even need his order, she just says, *Hi, Boss, I got you, Mad Man.* She squeezes my cheeks between her long, sharp nails. *What is she, boss? A Oriental?*

I ask her for a Shirley Temple, please.

My father takes down his juice. He makes a sound of relief, the same one he makes sometimes when he takes a leak on the side of the road. A second glass arrives before he even asks for it. *You're not supposed to be doing that anymore*, I say.

Doing what? says my father. He doesn't look at me. He doesn't shift his eyes from the game. The little men running.

The bad stuff, I say. *Sleepy Boy stuff.*

It's OJ, says my father. *Made of oranges, pulpy, sweet, full of vitamin C.* He dips his fingers in his glass, flicks some of the juice in my face. *See?*

I know better. I know we won't make it to the music store or share our chicken and rice. I know we will never walk along the shoreline; we won't bring home shells.

My father screams at the television. Irene screams with him. *Go, Go, Go, Baby, Go!*

I take the half-drunk glass out of his hand and chug the bitter down. It stings my throat, makes my eyes well. I take it down like it's medicine. I cough.

My father finally looks at me, forgets the screen. He stabs his Merit into the amber ashtray. He says, *What'd you do that for?*, shaking me by the shoulders.

Shirley Temple didn't come, I say. *I was thirsty.*

We look directly into each other's eyes, and I think, for the first time, we understand one another. My face is on fire, but I try to keep my mouth steady, stern.

Let's go, he says, pulling me off the stool by my armpits.

At home, he locks himself in the bathroom. He doesn't even watch the rest of the game. I tell my mother he got sick at the restaurant. I tell her it must have been something that we ate.

VIII.

We spend every Memorial Day weekend in the Florida Keys for my father's birthday. I'm twenty-six, and this will be our last year here. Today, on his sixty-eighth birthday, my father is depressed. His emphysema is making his body work too hard to breathe, causing his muscles to shrivel. His body is fragile, all bulging bones, rust-colored scabs, bandages.

He doesn't want to go fishing this year. He doesn't want to go on his boat. He cannot eat seafood for fear of his feet ballooning in a deep-purple gout. He only talks about death and money. He sleeps in the shade all the time, skips meals. He's barely my father anymore.

I'm not strong enough, he says, *to reel in. I'm an old man but I'm no Santiago.*

I take him to the swimming pool instead. The two of us dip our legs in the water, sit on the lip of the pool. When I think of my father, I think of my heart breaking in stages. A dull pain, then piercing. Electric. Still, somehow, gradual. The way his legs look in this swimming pool today—that's the first stage of my grief. Even the blue bloat of water doesn't make them look any stronger, or more capable, than a child's.

One thing I'd change, he says, *is that I never did teach my daughter to swim.*

IX.

I am twenty-one, and David and I have broken up for good this time, for real, I promise, swear it, no take backs. In Vegas, I help my father work the shoe booth in the Mandalay Bay Convention Center. *This'll take your mind off that asshole*, he says, but I excuse myself to cry in the convention center bathroom at least once an hour.

On the final day of the show, when it closes at six P.M., my father hands me a wad of cash. *Go out tonight*, he says. *Treat yourself to a date. Give yourself a time.*

My cousin Tanya rides in the cab with me.

Why do you need a babysitter? she says.

I just don't want to be alone.

Why has nobody gotten that yet?

I ask the cab driver to take us to the best of the best. The women. He knows what I mean. Tanya smokes a Marlboro out the window, says, *You're crazy, you know.*

The doormen at the Spearmint Rhino are not used to women. They want to know where our men are, who's paying. The bouncer scoots us into a small room near the entrance. *You sisters?* Cousins. *Asian Act?* Cousins. *You coming to take our business? You women are always Take Take Take Take*, and I shake my head, I say, *No*, I say, *I am here for the women I am here for the show. We're sending security near you*, he says, *to watch you because if you Solicit our fucking Men if you Take them if you are here for our Men there is going to be a Problem do you understand?*

We are not here for your men.

We are here for the women.

A security guard leads us to two seats in the front row. We order vodka and orange juice, on the rocks. Clank our glasses. Green lights dart across the stage, the walls.

Is this what you want? asks Tanya, *because you are so fucking funny you know you are so fucking weird how are we related you are so fucking funny this is so gay, you know that?*

Pick one, says Tanya. *Pick a girl. I know you want to.*

I can't choose. Instead, I pull my father's wad from the pocket of my purse. I lean back in my chair, bend my pointer finger to say, *Come here, Come.* The women—they grind on my lap and say, *You're cute which man are you with*, and I say, *Tell me about you, what's your real name, who are you?* I want them to tell the truth, but I want to give them a story.

How much?

This much, I say, shaking my father's cash. I make bills disappear in my left hand and reappear in my right. *Oh you got tricks*, they say, and I nod.

The next morning, my father asks me for change.

I gave you more than I'd meant to, he says. *All that money.*

I gave it to the women, I say.

Have I taught you nothing? he says. *Women. Those kinds of women. Don't ever look them in the eyes.*

X.

I am twenty-six, visiting my father in Boca. Tonight, he wants us to join his childhood friends for dinner. *We used to party together*, he says. *Me, your mom, and The Couple. They're my wildest friends; the greatest.*

At dinner, over oysters, The Couple asks me about a boyfriend. Is he handsome? Is he Jewish? Is his mother still alive? Does he eat meat?

A girlfriend, I say. *Hannah.*

Oh.

But you're pretty, says The Couple.

You've done so much for yourself. So much going your way.

I'm in love. That's all I ever did.

No children for you then, says The Couple. *No child should be father-less. No man will ever love a fatherless girl. She won't know how to treat him right. How to rub a man's feet.*

In the car ride home, my father apologizes on behalf of The Couple, his oldest friends.

No friends of mine, he says. *Not anymore. Out.*

Why? I ask. *Don't you feel the same about her?*

If anyone is ever going to make my daughter cry, he says, *It'd ought to be me.*

XI.

I'm twenty-seven when it happens: my mother clasps my father's gold-chain necklace around his wrist wrappings—the necklace my grandfather once gave him. The chain feels cold to the touch, heavy, like a fistful of snow. When the doctor removes the tubes from his trach, my mother and I lift the blanket all the way up to his chin, pulling his arms out and over it. With his new shave, no snakes of plastic, he looks honorable, handsome even. Like he's been napping all this time. I hold the seashell of his hand, and my brothers, mother, and I plead with him, *Let go. You're safe.* We watch the colors—lips parting indigo, the rush of grays and blues through the square patches of visible skin, red eyelids of a pigeon. And then it happens. It happens as quiet as that. The doctor, a flash in the eye. A nod. That.

My brothers clear the room, and I hold my father's body like a child, like he needs me, wrapping his slumped arms around my shoulders. Here and here and here you are, mine, you were something that was mine. My mother unclasps the necklace.

XII.

In grief, I try to become my father. My own body is not enough. I am too small for my sadness. I wear my father's striped T-shirts, his socks, even his underwear, rolled up at the yellowed elastic. I scrub my gums with his toothbrush. Spit blood. I take shots off his inhaler and wait for the rush of life. I even watch action films—karate movies, explosions, skull splatters in Italian restaurants—and replay the most violent parts.

My mother charges his cell phone every night. She uses it to call me sometimes, and swears this is a mistake. Whenever his name appears on my screen, I am hopeful. He could be on the other line this time; he could be getting through.

Hi, Daddy, I say.

I'm sorry, she says, hanging up.

Ghosts are better than nothing. Ghosts move. They want things. To haunt each other, then, is a way for my mother and I to keep him. He is more than a voice in the walls, a Ouija board movement, an iridescent cloud in the dark; he can exist here, inside us, through possession. We do our best to play the roles. Our own bodies are not big enough.

Falling in love with someone, I think, is at least like that.

XIII.

I'm seventeen, unpacking in my dorm room in New York City. I've moved here to be closer to my dad. I want to walk his streets, eat his favorite pastrami, try on a new relationship with him.

Well, he says, *let's start with a movie. Ten thirty tomorrow morning?*

Ten thirty? I ask. *On a Saturday?*

Better seats this way, he says.

Okay, it's a date.

My father is thirty minutes early to the movie. I am ten minutes early, and he tells me I am late. *I'm gonna teach you two things about life*, he says. *You better listen*, he says.

1. Early is On Time.

2. Always be early.

We share popcorn, wedge it between our cushions. We watch *Little Miss Sunshine*. I keep my legs propped up on my seat, bend them until they're numb. People in Florida have told me rats run around the theater floors here, gnawing on your shoelaces, your leftover snacks. My father shakes his legs incessantly, taps his loafers. He chews and clicks his teeth in loud smacks. I tell him to keep it down, and he elbows me, reminds me that there's nobody else in the theater. In the dark, with the light on his face, he looks the happiest he's ever looked. His face is relaxed, his mouth slightly open in awe. He gives my hand three quick squeezes.

I walk him home after the movie. Years from now, this is the part I will miss most. It's never about the movies themselves—I don't even remember them—it's about the credits rolling, our eyes adjusting to the world outside, his leather jacket leaning against the ticket booth, the walk. We pick up drooping slices of pizza and let the oil run down our chins as we make our way down Second Avenue. Soon, so soon, my father will not be able to use his legs like this. He'll take a car to meet me those few blocks away, and then to go home. But right now he does, he makes it, and I do, too. We make our Saturday morning movie for nine more years. We are always on time.

PART III

TELL THE WOMEN

I'M LONELY

KULEANA

The past is never where you think you left it.
—Katherine Anne Porter, *Ship of Fools*

* ✳ *

WINTER, 2016
PETERBOROUGH, NEW HAMPSHIRE

What we do is burn things. A Chinese New Year family tradition since before I was born—we write lists of burdens, toxins, enemies, vices, we place the strips of paper in a bowl, and we burn them. We watch our words shrivel and dissolve like a slug under salt. We burn things for luck. We burn things to move on. We burn things just to watch them burn.

I am writing my lists today. It is the year of the monkey. When I get the call from my mother, it's snowing. The whole world is the thin color of skim milk.

Hello?

A siren whines out behind her voice. A scream.

The house, she says. *It's gone.*

What house? What do you mean?

I lit the candle, says my mother. *The one by his urn. For the New Year.*

The flame caught the drapes, she says, *or the match caught the basket. I don't know.*

I am standing in the center of a parking lot. I am wearing red, for luck. It's the new year, after all. I force myself to remember the facts: I am standing in a parking lot in New Hampshire. I am alive. My mother is alive. My father is dead. My mother is in Florida. She is right here, on the phone. Something has happened.

What's happened? I say.

Grandma Mei Mei and I are fine, she says. *Just burned some hair. It's just hair.*

That's good, I say.

But the house, she says. *It's gone. I need you to understand that.*

Later that day, I begin a mental catalog of everything in that house. Boxes of photographs, yellowed horse ribbons, diaries, magic kits, dried-up nail polishes. My homecoming crown. My stuffed tiger, Tia. My mother's wedding dress. My father's leather loafers. His couch—my father's couch. His sports jackets, his backscratchers, his Yankees cap, that couch. My father. My mother's Hawaiian blanket, her crystal bonsai trees, her childhood jeans. The Spot on the floor—The Spot will be gone. This brings me some relief. I will never have to see The Spot again.

I tell my mother to get on a plane. *Come meet me here*, I say. *No fires here.*

Okay, she says. *I have nowhere else to go.*

That night, I prop wood in a pyramid in my fireplace. I stuff papers underneath—old manuscripts, receipts, napkins—before grinding the match. I watch the flames flick purple, then gold.

Home, I write on my Chinese New Year list. I circle it three times. Wad it up and toss it.

I'm not here.

My mother, Lokelani, is the oldest of four children. She's a good girl, eleven years old, punahele of the family, hiapo, the tiniest frame. Her sister Tao, my Auntie T, is one year younger than my mother, a stocky little thing, and the two sisters don't like each other much—not yet. My mother is the favorite—bright in the eyes, she works hard in school—and little Tao steals her jeans to hem them several inches so that they hit my mother above the ankle; she's jealous of her older sister. The two of them tend to two younger brothers, Makoa and Kai, but brothers are not a part of this story. Not yet, anyway. First, I want to tell you a story about sisters.

The children live on Puolo Street in Kailua, Oahu. They wear bathing suits beneath their clothing to school—Enchanted Lakes Elementary—no shoes, never. They learn to hula with the proper bend at the knees. They roast pigs with their tūtū and toss hunks of meat into the mouths of volcanoes—an offering to Pele, the fire goddess. The only house on the block with a pool and a slide, a boat out back, the children swing on banyan vines and play Gilligan's Island in the red fizz of late afternoons, throwing the rocks from their yard at the neighbor's fence.

They perform their own Hawaiian Partridge Family songs at night. Scraped knees, matching floral prints; they harmonize. Their parents applaud them, proud, beautiful, this family act, the American dream.

Sure, there are fights. Whose idea was it to wax their father's boat? Whose idea was it to push so hard, to use the *wrong kind* of wax, that white putty that clouded the boat a permanent pink? *A Pepto-Bismol pink*, my mother thinks, she is obsessed with the thought—*It was Tao's fault*—and so she feeds the chalky tablets to her younger sister—*It's candy, good for you!*—until the whole bottle is empty, until Tao's stomach must be pumped.

When the children scream at one another, they are hung in burlap potato sacks from the mango trees in the yard. Their skin matches the color of the sacks, and the snaggly fabric tears at their armpits. Their whole bodies itch. The siblings swing there until the sun comes up, until they make good on what they've done.

Or, let's move to the father. My grandfather, Al, who bought what he has named the *Frustration Release* paddle, a sleek leather body to it, a rope on the end. The children line up outside the bathroom door, oldest to youngest, waiting for their turn. Al sits on the toilet seat, pulls each of them over his lap, thwacking them until they understand. My mother apologizes right away, she is the punahele, after all, she is always let go, but her sister will not cry, will not budge, will not be sorry, not ever, *I don't even feel it*, and so the boys rarely ever get their turn.

In one of my earliest memories of my grandfather, he is about to drive me and my cousins, Tao's children—Teagan and Tanya—to dinner in Plantation, Florida. We're in matching sunflower dresses; it's the weekend of his birthday. I like it when we match like this, because people are less likely to point me out as the child who *does not fit* with these two beautiful girls—the *cousin*, not a sister. My grand-father slams the car door once we're all buckled in, but Tanya's hand is not inside the car yet, not all the way, and her finger crunches in the aluminum jaw of it. She screams out, *Please! Help!*, her face a raisin, tears and spit and a pitch so high it vibrates the air inside, but my grand-father does not move, there is no release, his face is stern outside the car window, his silver ponytail shining. *Embrace your pain*, he says, *and stop crying.* Teagan and I hold her other hand. By now, we are almost crying, too. *Calm down*, we say, or think—I can't be sure now—*keep it together.* Tanya tugs in her lip. Gasps for deeper breaths. She steadies her face, somehow, she does, before my grandfather opens the door.

But Tanya's mother, Tao, doesn't give her father what he wants. She is different, here in the bathroom in 1971, just a child, *I don't even feel it*, the paddle coming down harder. My mother waits outside the door, listening, the burn beneath her own pants, the warmer spots; she touches the places where she will bruise. She's on a plane in her mind, my mother, a flight attendant, getting off this rock in the ocean, so far from this bathroom, the line of light beneath this door, Tao's voice screaming, *I still don't feel it!*

Before my father's funeral, in my parents' bedroom on the beach, I ask my mother about that old mannequin, Uncle Nuke. I am blow-drying a pair of blue suede shoes to help the leather stretch, to fit my feet into them, when I ask her how she ever got rid of him. Where. She can't remember, not now.

I wish I could talk to him again, I tell my mother. We pull our funeral dresses over our heads—white and silk. She places a purple lei of orchids over my shoulders, kisses me on each cheek, and I do the same for her. I think we look too young for this.

Should we order some pizza for after the service? she asks. *How many people are staying over?*

Did you take him to a dump? I want to know.

Are your brothers staying over?

I wish I could know what Uncle Nuke remembers.

Why? she says. *Is today really the day for this?*

If I were giving the eulogy, I would say, "My family began with a mannequin."

You should speak today, she says, nodding. *That mannequin was the beginning.*

He wasn't supposed to die.

He wasn't supposed to die in a hospital, she says. *That's true.*

You shouldn't have thrown him away.

That's a different story.

Maybe the unfinished story is the story.

We hold the funeral at the Sands Club, in the town of Lawrence, Long Island, where my father had his senior prom. Just last month, he told me about this place, the music—*Be my little baby*—the arm wrestling and bottle fights in the parking lot. *I'll know it when I'm going to die.*

I'm buzzed on the cinnamon whiskey my brothers and I shared behind the stage curtain. My thumbnail is pressing moons into my lei orchids as people speak. I take inventory of who shows up—my father's doormen and chauffeurs, ex-business partners, Clarissa—as I hear *Gambling Man / Mad Man / Father / always the Jokes / Even Money* from the microphone. I sit on my hands. I chew on my hair. Dad, you would have liked this crowd. Everyone's dressed sharp for you. I count chandeliers. I think about sea monkeys and those mannequin legs in the corner of our first apartment and Dai Vernon shuffling cards, the weather. *Cheated on a math test / his First Wife / because that's how it Was in the Army / Ha Ha Ha Ha! / How he did it / Bet on Life / thought Invincible.* I think about the carpet of this place and my shoes are too fucking tight and that little red wagon I had as a kid, how he'd helped me paint it blue and we glued it all over with cotton balls until it was a *Time Machine*, and lobsters, the way he used to bring them home on Sundays, that was before I really knew my dad, when he was just a man who carried thrashing paper bags on his shoulders, when he was just a man who said, *I caught us some lobsters*, and I smashed them and I ate them.

Photographs are projected to the song "Free Bird." A tissue box is passed down our row. I don't know when the slideshow started, but it's ending. Dad, you loved this part of the song. You pumped the gas and brake pedals of your convertible in time with this guitar solo until my seatbelt locked and dug into my shoulder and the whole thing made me sick. The sun is in your eyes. There we are.

✳

We release my father's ashes the next day.

WINTER, 1972
KAILUA, OAHU, HAWAIʻI

See the encyclopedia over my grandfather's knee, in the study of their house, his finger finding the golden notch of the letter *F*. My mother, Tao, and the boys sitting in a semicircle at my grandfather's feet. *Florida*, he says. He stretches the syllables as if it's a healing word. *Florida—it's on the Mainland. It looks like a sock, or a gun maybe.* He points to the state on a map. *In Florida, people plug straws right into oranges, and everyone has blonde hair, and alligators sunbathe, and kids wear shoes to school.*

Shoes to school? My mother cannot believe this. She will remember it as long as she lives: *shoes to school*. What would it be like on the Mainland, away from Tūtū, away from Paulele Street, Hanauma Bay, the sweet thick pull of haupia between her teeth? Yes, she has always been curious about life somewhere else, but what gods or friends would she have in this *Florida*?

Why are we leaving? Tao wants to know, but there is no answer.

Yeah, why? asks my mother. She has a better chance.

We leave next week, says my grandfather, *so you'll need to pack your things and start cleaning.*

My Grandma Mei Mei stands in the corner of the room. She considers this conversation, this rush. Her husband—her first love, *ulua*—who had picked her up from the soda stand at the beach. She worked there, watched old mokes move chess pieces in the trade winds. One day, Al showed up. A Native Hawaiian man, through and through; he was gentle, akamai, older, a talker. Always in a sailor's cap, he was *worldly*, and so she said yes, and so she agreed, and so she married him three days after her sixteenth birthday. They exchanged vows at the Mormon Church where they would soon work—he, as a priest, and she, a Sunday school teacher. Yes, she loved this man. In this part of the story, she still does.

But here's the first moment Mei Mei questions her husband: His body leaning forward in the living room chair—this encyclopedia, open on his lap—*Florida*.

The diamond ring. She knows.

Al sold jewels to Hawaiian retailers out of the trunk of his Lincoln. Pink coral carefully arranged in velvet boxes—*so expensive kine*—all of it shipped from the Mainland. He had mentioned the ring when it went missing from his collection last month, an emphasis on his words: *Missing. The diamond ring has gone Missing.* She had noticed other leftover stock that came home with him lately— *worthless, not for sale*—out of their cases. But the diamond ring, she'd remembered that most. The value of it; he was too careful with the words. His wife had to know the exact time and day it happened, his pockets and drawers flipped, emptied—*the diamond ring has gone missing*, he'd repeated.

That red boat appeared two days later.

Yes, she knows why it's time to go.

Al and Mei Mei, 1960

H ere's what happens after death: Every object changes shape. All the little objects of hope, innocuous, gentle things: the bottles of Diet Coke saved for when he would get better, the stacks of *New York Post*s, the wedges of pineapple, the warmer socks, the protein powders, the Chinese herbs, the electro-acupuncture pens, the pictures—all the pictures, removed and naked of their frames, brighter in the corners, the pictures, gum-tacked to the hospital bed for when he would remember, he would, he would—these objects, every last one of them, become the most unbearable of all, the most acutely garish, the splintered underside of the table on which you have tried to smoothly splay out the map of your new life without this person, whom you just so happen to love most.

I am spending the holidays with Hannah and her family before I leave for New Hampshire. *Someone else's family*, I repeat, *because your father is dead*. This year, there will be no Hanukkah candles, no botched Hebrew prayers, no wads of cash, no marathon of Michael Corleone. *Dead*.

Hannah is gentle with me, and sometimes I wish she were not so gentle. That's the way other people have been treating me, the way they look at me as they quietly stir their coffee spoons, the way they creep around the facts. Hannah changes my clothes when I've been crying too hard to keep my balance. She pins my arms down when I have night terrors of tubes and machines, reminds me of where I am. When we have sex, I ask her to choke me. I want to hurt. I want flashes behind my eyes. We go on like this for weeks.

On Christmas Eve day, Hannah tacks up the mares in her yard and wraps my calves with horse polos. She weaves her hands together for my knee, lifting me into the saddle.

Up, up. Let's move, she says.

Hannah, who brought me back to horses. Hannah, who kissed me for an hour straight the first time it happened—in a dark bar full of drag queens and popcorn, her palms cradling my face—the way she called me *Thunder Snow*.

We ride through the mountains of her hometown, she and I. We spend the day like this—the yellow, protracted light of a frozen noon. Cattails, swaying. It's been fifty-two days, and this is the first time I feel like I might live.

The next morning, she kneels beside her family's tree, handing over boxes of gifts, beautiful gifts, books and scarves and blenders and stockings full of gifts. Pity gifts, I think. She keeps her arm wrapped around me as I open each one, kissing the temple of my head. It makes me sad—the degree of love I feel for her, the lifesaving power of this purity of purpose—now that I know what it feels like to lose.

Hannah's mother hands me a box no bigger than a diary. I peel open the paper. A bright-green DNA test. *You mentioned you wanted one,* she says. *Remember? At the funeral.*

For the family tree, yes, I say. I try to smile. *Thanks.*

I stack the gifts in my arms and totter up the stairs to Hannah's bedroom. I clack the blinds closed.

I am twelve years old on Christmas morning in Las Vegas. My father takes me, my mother, and the boys to Denny's, where he asks for his eggs runny—extra rye. He slides a one-hundred-dollar-bill tip to our waitress, something he will make a tradition, and the woman thanks us, wipes her cheeks, holds the bill up to the light of the window to make sure it's real.

* ✶ *

Here is a Hawaiian legend once told to me:

Sometimes the dead don't want to be dead. Sometimes souls go flit-
ting around in the air, particles of light, drifting, until a mortal crams
the soul back inside its body. The kino wailua, or spirits, can be spotted
anywhere, the face of a rock, a mountainside—a Hawaiian should
always look for facial features. It is the mortal's job to perform the
kāpuku, or resuscitation process. It is our duty to sneak the soul
beneath the toenail of a body, let the body rise up like a newly watered
plant.

WINTER-SPRING, 1972
UNITED STATES OF AMERICA

In Los Angeles, Mei Mei and Al use the cash from a second mortgage to purchase a motor home. The family will drive for the rest of the school year, five months on the road, visiting every state capital, billboard attraction, the Petrified Forest, the children's first snow. My mother and her siblings are homeschooled by Mei Mei. They visit the Grand Canyon, the gaping marble monuments of Washington, D.C., badlands of red, and Mei Mei uses the encyclopedias to tell them all about it. State bird, state fruit, state capital, state terrain—*You must learn about your world.* There is no plan, no exact destination. As long as they stay on the move.

Where you headed? a man at a gas station in Memphis asks one night. *Moving house like that, all those kids.*

Florida, says my grandfather.

Nice 'n' sunny. Where 'bouts? asks the man.

My grandfather looks at Mei Mei as if she might have the answer, as if she'd have the perfect city in mind, a star penned to the map. He had never thought of it before this moment, no, all he knew was *far away.* All he knew was *Florida.*

What do you recommend? asks my grandfather. *You have a favorite place down there?*

This stranger takes a long, hard look at my grandfather. *When you get there, just keep driving south*, he says. *Go far enough 'n' you'll disappear.*

I'm watching the Miss Florida pageant on television with my mother and Misty. In one week, I'll turn eleven. We are judging the contestants—Misty and I—in our own point system of colored penciled tallies pressed into legal pads. We give each girl a score for every round of the pageant, but we also ask our own questions: *Does the contestant seem smart? Does the contestant seem funny? Does the contestant seem like she would be nice to dogs? Would the contestant be our friend, or enemy? Does the contestant look like either one of us? If given the choice, would we choose to swap lives with the contestant forever?*

I wouldn't put your money against me, says my mother, *because today is July 11.*

My mother's favorite number combination is 7-11. She has always played it on the roulette tables in Vegas, punched it in for alarm and banking passcodes, sworn by the magic of 7:11 on a clock. When these three numbers are arranged in this order, they become charged, lucky. Contestant number two is my favorite of the beauty queens. I have her name written at the top of my pageant chart—*Marjorie, #2,*

Hollywood—but Misty likes a blonde flute player from Miami Lakes. We bet our allowance money on the girls—usually ten dollars.

Here's why I'm invested: My cousin Teagan is a pageant girl. Chinese and Hawaiian, like me. She's three years older and we look alike in the eyes, but Teagan's hair is long, her bangs trimmed ruler straight. Her adult teeth grew in perfectly and her cheeks shine like Baoding balls on the covers of magazines. In an ad for J. C. Penney, Teagan swings on a hammock with three other kids. She is the thirteen-year-old *ethnic friend*, licking chocolate cake from the prongs of a big fork, and this ad is enlarged on poster board in the corner of her room. Whenever I sleep over, I fall asleep staring at her.

Contestant number two looks related to Teagan, I say.

She's got a good walk, says my mother. *Look at her go.*

My mother, too, was once a model. After high school. She tells us about it right now, in this living room, how she modeled clothing through the lobbies of Waikiki beach hotels, tying and untying tropical wraps around her hips for haole men.

Now, she catwalks in her pajamas across the living room steady, open-lipped. She pushes her palms into her hips, each foot landing directly in front of the other. It looks a bit like hula—this grace, the exact point of her toes—before she gets to the kitchen counter, strikes a pose looking left, then right, and marches her way back to the couch.

Still got it?

How could you be a model when you're a mom? asks Misty.

You're even better than Contestant number two, I say.

We watch the contestants on television strut through several more rounds. *Go, Hapa Haole, Go!* I scream. I wonder if my mother once looked like Marjorie, number two, from Hollywood, if she once dreamed of being this very girl—her butter-colored bikini, her braid.

Contestant number two does not win the crown. Instead, she hugs the two contestants by her side, mouths *Good luck!* before smiling and waving her way offstage.

Shocker, says my mother. *Imagine that. A world that chooses white girls!*

I guess your number's off, I say.

No, it's just that Miss USA could never be a mixy mutt, says Misty. She says this sweetly. She crosses out Contestant number two on her chart.

Misty's flute player does not win either. None of us take the cash.

The world is so unfair, I say.

More than you know, says my mother.

1973–1974
PLANTATION, FLORIDA

My mother is wearing shoes to her first day of public school. Mary Janes, to be exact, with high-ribbed socks, a pale-green baby doll dress, and a lacy beige bib tucked over her chest. *The Mainland.* This school is all indoors. There are no picnics outside, no bathing suits in sight. She is the malihini in these halls, new blood, and everyone takes notice. The other students wear Peanut bell-bottoms, three buttons at the crotch, their stomachs bare and oiled. Their hair shines the color of driftwood. For the first time in her life, nobody looks like my mother.

A boy wads a spitball and pushes it into a straw. He shoots it at her. My mother spins in circles, rubbing her forehead, her dress fanning out.

Fucking Chink, says the boy, though my mother does not know what this means, and her parents do not tell her.

They called me that, too, I tell her now. *Growing up.*

My mother laughs. *Of course they did. Almost thirty years, and they can't think of something better.*

* ✳ *

She meets him in her science class. Let's call him Samuel. My mother has always looked forward to science class—the gurgling chemicals, the slick cool of test tubes, her teacher, Mr. Jackson, who looks like *the* Michael Jackson if you squint hard enough—but now science is her *absolute favorite subject* since Samuel came around. He sits behind her, and he stinks of Marlboros and pot. A haole boy with blonde hair in long waves—sometimes she swears she can feel him breathing on her shoulders.

Samuel wears rock T-shirts torn at the stomach. Bare knees through the tears of his jeans. *And his eyes, seriously, his eyes*, she says, can turn a girl into a puddle. She tells Carla this, the only girl who will talk to her, her lab partner. *Do you think he would ever . . . ?*

He's from the other side of the parking lot, she says. *You're so bad!*

It's true—there are two sides of the school parking lot. On one side, Ned Cohen and the rest of the baseball team, the football team, their rows of matching jackets, plaids and collars, shining bowls of hair, arms hooked around calendar girls. They lean back on the hoods of their cars, flared khakis crossed at the knees, none of them ever talking very much.

On the other side, the hippies. The Afros. The braids. Radios spun up. Tongues on necks. This is where Samuel has been smoking his cigarettes before and after classes, where he stubs them out in meticulous piles, the place from which he has been watching my mother for months—the way her hair flicks over her shoulders, her whinny laugh—waiting for her.

Carla scratches something into her notebook. Mr. Jackson is talking about the elegance of the periodic table when the paper is balled up, passed back and then forward, back and forward, until my mother receives it on her desk, smooths out the crinkles, squints at the smeared graphite shine of words.

Would you ever go out with Loki? Yes or No.

Samuel did not circle either word. Instead, he has written *Sure*.

My mother presses her hands into the desk until there's a pale halo of steam.

* * *

Have you heard about the shark movie with lines wrapped around the plaza? Samuel asks my mother. I imagine it was he who'd suggested it; my mother is afraid of sharks. The two of them are sitting on a bridge walkway, legs dangling.

It's impossible to get in.

My sister and I can get into any movie, any time, says my mother. *We know Ronald, the ticket guy. We're his favorites.*

The local movie theater exists inside a strip mall nearby, next door to a bookstore with carts of shriveled pages. My mother spends her summer days reading through them all, looking for the sexiest scenes. Recently, she opened up to a page describing a woman making love to a snake. She squeezed the book between her forearms, spreading the pages just enough to read the scene in that dark, electric inch.

But really, it's the movie theater that matters most to my mother. How they take her away to that numbing realm outside herself, that Other Place that she will return to, in different ways, for the rest of her life. Sometimes Ronald the ticket man will let my mother stay inside for the entire day, where she'll watch and rewatch the same scenes, hum along to the same score, the same crescendos, mouthing each word of dialogue until the words sound like something she might say.

My mother, Samuel, Tao, and her own Boy decide to try the movie. It's Friday night, and it's true—the line for *Jaws* snakes around the parking lot. My mother and her sister pull their boys by the belt loops, past the crowds of smoke and denim, all the way to Ronald. Ronald's wearing his usual blue Adidas sneakers and sagging T-shirt. He pulls my mother and Tao in for a hug—*My girls*—and tilts his head to signal them in.

In the theater, after Susan Backlinie is yanked under that freckled, gray sea, my mother leans into Samuel; she rests her head on his shoulder. She's tapping her foot on the movie theater floor—that's the way I see it now, anyway; she still does this—as the boy presses his thumb into her chin, gently turns her face, and kisses her.

Here's Samuel, with a joint behind his ear, with peeled elbow scabs and Pink Floyd T-shirts and flunking grades. But the bad boy is not bad. To my mother, he's the soft, stretched song of his stories—her ku'uipo. The way he is careful with her, a delicacy to his movements. When she stumbles, he corrects her, a hand on her back, *You okay?* It's the way he always pushes her hair behind her ear, *I wanna see you better.*

At home, after the movie, the boys ask to come inside. They want to spend the night with the girls—they'll be quiet, they promise. My mother decides against it. She says goodnight, another kiss against the wall of the house, their hips touching, a burst of warmth inside her. My Aunt Tao invites her boy in, where they will grind into their teenage love, and fall asleep in her bed.

When my grandfather finds them in the morning—crumpled sheets, their fingers clasped—he calls the police. My mother awakes to blue seesawing across her bedroom wall, the pounding of a hammer, her sister screaming, a thud. My grandfather has yanked Tao's door from the hinges, where it will never be replaced again, not as long as they all live under the same roof, though my grandfather will leave this place long before they do.

SUMMER, 1997
THE HERRINGTON INN, GENEVA, ILLINOIS

Here's how I learn about sex and babies:

It's one A.M. and I feel like a loser. I competed in National Pony Finals today and placed twenty-first in the country. I am disappointed by this placing, but my mother reminds me that there are thousands of girls and boys who wake up at four in the morning and practice every day, thousands of more expensive ponies, thousands of those kids and ponies in this very competition. I'm still at the age in which plurality is terrifying.

I hit every stride, I say. *I didn't chip once. We had speed. My jacket with the tails.*

Twenty-first out of thousands, she says. *That's pretty impressive to me.* I sit between her legs on the bed as she brushes my hair, both of us in bathrobes. She flips through channels on the hotel television as I massage my calves, not paying attention. Everything hurts.

Look, says my mother. *Look, your favorite.*

It's JonBenét Ramsey on the news again. Here she is, smiling for a camera, my favorite pageant girl. My favorite dead girl. She waves. Flashbulbs sparkle in the space behind her head.

I love her, I say.

Why do you love her so much? asks my mother. *It's very sad, what happened to her. I found her pictures torn out under your bed. What is it?*

Because she was raped and murdered, I say.

That's a very sad thing to happen, says my mother. *That's the most horrible thing that could happen to a person.*

What is rape? I ask her, *And why is it horrible?*

My mother places the hairbrush down on the bed. It's a deliberate movement for her, careful, slow. She turns me by the shoulders so that I am looking right at her, our faces close.

Rape is when someone forces sex on you, she says. *When you have sex without wanting to.*

What is sex? I ask. My cheeks are thumping. I think I might get in trouble for this question. It's a word that is always hushed in school, and my teachers get red and stuttery whenever it's mentioned.

Instead, my mother rubs her thumb over my cheek and speaks softly. She sways me a little. She breaks down the anatomy, and explains the parts that we have. *These parts belong to us girls,* she says, *but sometimes we can share.* She tells me that sex can result in a child. She tells me that it usually does.

But JonBenét's a child, she didn't have a child, I say.

That's why it's rape, she says, *and very wrong.*

So sex is when you have sex with a child?

It shouldn't be.

But this person used a rope on JonBenét, and twisted the rope around her neck, and had sex with her, too, at the same time. Is that how people have sex?

No, that's why it's murder, she says.

And rape, I say.

And horrible, and wrong, she says.

Do people usually die after sex?

No—

Does it feel like dying?

Sometimes.

Can JonBenét's body still have a baby now that she's dead?

No—

Can children have children?

They shouldn't.

If I don't look like JonBenét, will anyone ever want to rape me?

That's not the right question.

Will I want to die?

O ver spring break, the family drives to Grassy Lake. It's the little sister of Lake Placid, Florida—residential, gaping blue. On the lakeshore, wooden cabins with screened-in porches slam their doors in a smashed, metallic symphony as children run in and out, in and out, to the water.

My mother is here. She's stuck here with Tao, her brothers, and her parents. Her parents speak to each other less and less these days—her father, with his newspaper, his tiny sailboat, his heavy glasses of scotch, and her mother, in the sun, oiled arms wrapped around her knees, watching dragonflies dipping O's in the water like smoke rings. My mother is just beginning to notice this disconnect, her two parents as *people*, two people who are very different, indeed.

Let's move to my mother in her room, in the full-length mirror, tying the frayed strings of a bikini top around her neck. She ties it so tight the knot digs. Her breasts are growing—they need more support—but she hasn't mentioned this to anyone; right now, her body is still a secret. Today, she'll sail with her father on his two-person Sail-fish, but she feels different this year, his co-captain, the same bathing suit—awkward, even. She pulls her bikini bottom up, up, trying to find a smoother spot near her waistline. Her body is changing— *womanly*, she thinks—but she does not know what to do with these new twists of muscle, these new hips.

She walks out of her room, back into the patio, and takes a breath before opening the door. She feels the heat of the screen on her palm, pressing, walking out of it, *my new body*, the door slamming behind her in a crack.

How many times do I have to remind you about that damn door? says her father, as he pulls ropes through the grass toward the boat. Both he and Mei Mei take a look at their daughter, their hiapo girl, copper in the sun, like a woman. Her father squints. Her mother slides bulky, square sunglasses down her nose.

Punahele, you been eating all my sweets? asks her father. *Look at that ʻōpū on those skinny bones.*

I'm just changing, says my mother. She folds her arms over her stomach.

No more poi for you, I guess, says my grandma, winking. She knows how much my mother hates poi, the gray sludge of Hawaiian not-quite-dessert. *You look fine*, she says.

Kulikuli, says my mother in three hard blinks. She marches back into the patio, pushing the door for an extra slam.

That evening, in the shower, my mother decides to move someplace up north after graduation. She wants a place with a pale, chalky sky and winters that hurt, a place where she can wear giant knit sweaters every day, the fabric loose and her body unrecognizable, every last sweep of her skin protected.

My mother flies to New Hampshire to pick me up. Her hair is burned around the ears, curled where it has never been curly. She has a new cough from staying in the house too long. She refused to leave without our dogs.

We drive through Vermont and stay the night. On the hotel television, the news reports that new evidence has emerged against O. J. Simpson—they've found a knife on the premises. Another channel tells us about a new JonBenét docuseries.

Here we go again, says my mother.

You ever feel like history just keeps repeating itself? Never stops circling?

The next morning, we drive to Hannah's house. I am happy to see her home, which is not burned but upright, sturdy, warm. I am happy to lie in her bed; I am happy to smell her hair, her sweaters. Mostly, I am happy to see Hannah, who has been writing me letters, checking in. In the corner of the room, she's organized my things. Socks, pillows, stacks of books, the Christmas gifts. It's all still here.

Let's do those DNA tests, I tell Hannah. Her mother bought her one, too.

Do what? asks my mother.

This spit test, I say. *You send it in the mail, and this company supposedly breaks down your ancestry*, I say. *That family tree I've been planning on.*

Why would you want to do all that? my mother closes the book on her lap.

Hannah and I open the kits. We spit into the plastic tubes. I make puckering faces as I try to produce enough saliva to fill to the line, not too many bubbles. We watch the liquid settle. I punch in a blue gel to activate the test, shake the tube. I place it back in the prestamped box. Hand it over.

Later that night, in bed, Hannah asks me about the past few months. New Hampshire. The dreams about my father. My drinking. My health.

You ever sit in the car, or in a window seat on the subway, and the car or train next to you starts to move? And you think you're the one moving? And you'd swear by it? And sometimes, in your stomach, you can even feel it?

That. I say. *That's what life's like now.*

The call comes in the middle of the night, though Peter Gelb-waks is still at work. He's been working all hours lately, selling insurance to pay off the medical bills for the daughter who never came home. *Osteogenesis imperfecta.* Her name, he and his wife told The Attorney, was supposed to be Dana. Hear the phone ringing. See Sharon Gelbwaks, twenty-six years old, asleep in her bed, alone.

Hello? she picks up. *Peter?*

It's The Attorney.

I've a question for you, he says. *And answer honestly.*

Sharon is just beginning to make out the voice, its familiarity, the person on the other end of line, when The Attorney says, *If I were to tell you I found a baby, but it's biracial, would you still be interested?*

Yes, she says. *Of course I would. Of course we would.*

Do you want to ask your husband?

Sharon pauses. *Could they?* Could they really provide a life for this baby—Jewish parents, a Jewish sister—in which this child would feel comfortable? Understood? Would the child be taunted? Would she know how to cut the child's hair?

She thinks back to their last meeting with The Attorney, 150 applications slapped down on the desk, ahead of them. *This girl is young,* said The Attorney. *No prenatal care; she found out too late to do anything about it. By the look of her, I can tell how she got herself into trouble.*

Our daughter Dana had a place in our house, a bassinet, said Sharon. *I spent my whole pregnancy making this bassinet, every day I did, and then I guess I never really had to make it.*

We're good people, Peter had said. *Every bone in our daughter's body was broken.*

Sharon grips the phone harder. *Peter says of course,* she lies.

Well, that's good news, says The Attorney. *Because no other applicant was interested. If you meet me at my office tomorrow, we'll get to signing some papers.*

Congratulations, he says, and, *Goodnight.*

* ✳ *

In ancient Hawaiian folklore, the worst fate to befall someone is for their spirit, or ʻuhane, to be abandoned. Spirits should be visited, cared for, returned to, nurtured. Any spirit should be treated as one's family.

Hawaiians are told to check for the presence of ʻuhane by peering into bowls of water or lacing a trail of leaves on the ground. A human will tear the leaves with their own weight or show up, reflected, in the water. A spirit will not.

Forgotten spirits are called Kuewa. They are left to chew on mothballs, to haunt, forever, the empty dark. Sometimes, if truly angered, these forgotten spirits will visit the places they once knew, and relive their histories.

Huakaʻi pō—this is the term I was taught—*Marchers of the Night*.

SUMMER, 1997
SEVEN DEVILS, NORTH CAROLINA

I've been sworn out of the house. We are in Seven Devils, North Carolina, and my mother says, *Go now, drive down the mountain, go fishing, go.* She is baking a cake for my ninth birthday party—I know this much—but she and my father are also planning a surprise for me: a mini-horse named Tulip.

My aunts and uncles drive me down the mountain to the trout farm. My hair is still cut short, and I'm wearing my new denim overalls with a floppy, silk sunflower on the pocket. I pierce the kernels of corn, bob clumsily with my rod, while my cousins play with the worms, pretend to eat them.

My mother has always cast a line for me, and I'm unsure how to do it alone. I jiggle the release back and forth, jerk the pole up and down like I'm trying to rouse a rabbit from a hat. I fling the pole above my head, spin it in circles, swipe it like a baseball bat toward the lake, the hook flying in a tiny spark.

I don't feel the snag. I don't see it. But I hear the swarm of bees descend around my body. Wings zoom, breaking the air. My vision splits. My face vibrates all over. I swat my arms, screaming, hoping the bees don't fly into my mouth. I kick, swing, fall, cry. It seems to last forever, this buzzing, though it couldn't have been very long at all.

There are arms. My aunt's, lifting me. The hump of her steps as she is running, running, bringing me to the Trout Hut. *She might need an ambulance,* I hear her say.

Everything is burning. I don't understand what has happened.

Are you allergic to bees? she asks me, but she is already speaking to someone else.

This girl, she's allergic to everything.

My aunt is hysterical. I am playing dead. Moving hurts. My eyes don't want to open.

And then this moment. A memory that doesn't change, that needs no revision, no matter how many times I summon it: the sound of gravel rumbling under tires, the speed of Big Beau. My mother. My mother running to me, yanking me from my aunt's soft arms.

What happened? she says. *I knew something was wrong.* When I open my eyes, my mother's face is there. She's kissing my cheeks, saying, *I came fast as I could.*

According to my Grandma Rose, my mother was frosting the cake when it happened. She was smoothing the chocolate with a spoon when she felt it, that thing, dropped silver to the floor. *Something's wrong,* she said. *I have to go.* She started driving before the car door was even shut. No seat belt, no shoes.

That mother-daughter power, she'd say, for years, *it's bigger than logic.*

The bees stung my face, my eyelids, my hands, even my scalp. In the car, I stared at my thumbs swelling like dough, and I said my goodbyes. *I will die at my own birthday party. How unfair.* What I knew about bees sprung from Macaulay Culkin's body in a casket. Turns out, I was not allergic to them.

But that mother-daughter thing—I believe in it now. It's something that can spool out forever like a string between two cups. A thread that will hum when you need it.

SUMMER, 1976
PLANTATION, FLORIDA

T he Attorney wants my mother to sign the papers. She's back home now, an empty bedroom. There is no evidence of what the past nine months had meant—no baby clothes, no bassinet, no embroidered name, no pictures.

I won't sign them, she says. *I didn't even want to do this.*

But you did do this, says The Attorney. *We had a deal.*

My grandfather and grandmother look at my mother. They motion for her to go on, pick up the pen. They have already received the checks, signed their own papers.

Not unless you tell me what I had, says my mother. *A boy or a girl?*

I can't tell you, child, says The Attorney. *But I still need you to sign.*

Fifteen minutes later, my mother walks The Attorney back out to his car. She is barefoot. Her face is swollen, pale. I imagine she uses the same voice she uses now when she wants something. *Please*, she says. The mosquitos are out.

I can't tell you that, says The Attorney. *Legally, I can't.*

Please, says my mother. She holds her stomach. Flat. According to the hospital paperwork I read now, my mother is sixteen years old and ninety-eight pounds.

The Attorney opens his car door. He bends to get in, but pauses. He looks back at my mother.

When your child gets married one day, he says, *they will probably change their name.*

1976
HOLLYWOOD, FLORIDA

My baby, she's mine—Sharon Gelbwaks must get used to saying this, saying it aloud to anyone who will ask, repeating it until it goes true.

She's heard the horror stories—birth mothers changing their minds. Sometimes in the hospital, sure, but also, sometimes, later. She's heard about mothers refusing to sign the papers, refusing to let go. She's heard of mothers getting clean, realizing what they had done in that black haze of greed, coming back, *Mine*. Mothers were always coming back—what mother wouldn't? As Sharon looks at the newborn in her room, sleeping, she can't imagine it. Not coming back for her. Perfect, this baby, *her baby*, the way her head feels like velvet, the way her skin smells like paper. Oh, the noises! A real, human girl, *my baby*, it doesn't matter where she came from, what the birth mother ate during her pregnancy, what she looked like, no, the baby is *Sharon's*, whomever she and Peter would mold her to be, and they would protect this child for the rest of her life. This baby would grow up different, not looking like anyone else, *the hair*, she thinks, *look at this hair*, but Sharon feels prepared for these lessons. She feels prepared to learn.

One day, in J. C. Penney, Sharon pushes the baby, *her baby*, around in a stroller. She is looking for towels, home goods, when she sees the woman.

This woman is too old to be the mother, not a teenager—she's sure. Could it be the grandmother? An aunt? The Asian woman pauses, looks into her stroller.

An Asian baby, she says. *So cute, this baby*.

The Asian woman has two sons with her. They have dark skin— island boys. The boys tug on the leg of her jeans. These could be the brothers, Sharon thinks. They must be.

Thank you, says Sharon. *She's mine*.

Doesn't look like you.

She's mine.

How old's the baby?

Couple of months, says Sharon, before pushing the stroller through the aisle, hooking a right, and exiting the mall.

1976
HOLLYWOOD, FLORIDA

S he sees them everywhere—Asian babies, hapa babies—in her dreams, in the grocery store, at the mall. All babies look the same to my mother—like old white men, indistinguishable, really—but this baby, *her baby*, would look different. Her baby would look like an island girl, she was sure, a warm tone to her skin, tiny eyes, *the hair.*

Would her baby recognize its own mother? She is taking pills to keep her breasts from lactating, but would they drip at the sound of *her* baby's cry? There must be *something*, she thinks, between mother and child, a magnetic jolt between the two that cannot be eased apart. But how long would it take to find her? Where would she be—in which town? How would it ever happen?

What is my daughter's name? she wonders. She thinks about this all the time.

The babies are everywhere. At least, she thinks she sees them. The crescent cheek in a stroller, the black silky swirl at the top of a head. Her body will recover the connection, she thinks, the recognition of

her baby, some residuum of those blurry hours in the hospital. The eyes
may forget but the body—it remembers.

* ✳ *

When my mother graduates high school, she takes a job as a hostess at
a posh Japanese restaurant. The managers dress her in a kimono;
they don't care that she's not Japanese—*She looks close enough*. She
scans the room each night, wondering if the new parents of her
daughter might take her here. *An Asian experience*, she imagines them
saying, but she never does find them. Instead, she watches as the hibachi
chefs learn to throw knives, and she is there to bandage their fingers
after each miss. She returns home to shower off the stink of burned
onions. She falls asleep curled in a towel each night, her hair still wet.

On the weekends, she takes a job as a Floor Bunny at the downtown Playboy Club. She is weighed in each evening (an extra pound
allowed during her period) by a Mother Bunny, who has taught her
to Bunny Perch when serving men their drinks. *Breasts forward, in
their face. Left knee tucked behind right. Remember, they own you.
Remember to be pretty.*

You must move forward, Tao says. *You've got a whole story after this.*

But their mother and father have separated; my mother's baby is
gone. Her life feels pau, over before it ever started.

My mother moves back to Honolulu for one year. She moves into
Tūtū's sewing room, where flying roaches buzz against the walls.
Although this is her island, it has changed since she was a girl—she

feels malihini, new again, like a tourist—and her tūtū tries to bring back her old music, the accent on her tongue, the slow-cooked meats and body language.

During the day, my mother takes a bus to the Ala Moana shopping center, where she will try on whatever clothes she is given, climb up into a window, and pose. She is told to suck in, stretch her neck into a C, stand up straight, smile. She is good at this; I can imagine her as if I were there. I imagine her poised, eyes following each person walking by, legs buckled at the knees. I imagine my mother waiting for somebody, anybody, to stop.

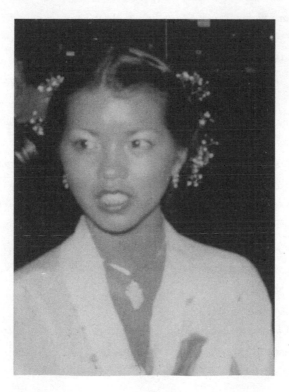

If I have the flu, I can't be around you, I say into the phone.

Get one of those nerd masks, says my father. *The ones you Asians wear on the planes.*

Tell Mom thanks for passing this on; I was up all night sweating off a fever.

Mom's making me chicken soup today, he says. *I also feel lousy.*

Good. It's her turn.

You took care of me last week; that bean stew helped. It's my turn.

I can't get out of bed, I say. *And I really can't come, with your immune system how it is.*

Have a driver get you out here—I'll pay.

I just want to sleep. I need to be home.

You sound terrible, really.

I sound like you.

You sound like me.

Well I guess we're both stuck, I say. *At least we've got the phone.*

I guess that's safe.

Drink water, Daddy.

Take care of yourself, baby.

I love you. Feel better.

Okay, now. You, too.

Later that night, when I arrive alone to my parents' dark house, the pot of water on the stove has gone cold. The chicken thighs, still pink in their Styrofoam casing. The vegetables are peeled, lined up in a row, a knife dropped with a carrot still clinging to the blade of it.

My mother responds to an ad and takes a job as a secretary. She wears an outfit that says she knows what she's doing, that she is more than an island girl, or a Playboy Bunny, or a window and hotel model, no, she is serious here—twenty years old, a *woman*—with her hair pinned back, a pencil skirt hugging her knees. She will be sophisticated, yes; she is going to make something of her life.

On her first day, a man walks through the door, combing his hair. He's wearing sunglasses, his jacket swung over his shoulder, hooked on a finger. His cologne—a velvet spice that she'll go chasing for the rest of her life. He passes right by her at first, pauses, then walks backward to her desk.

I don't believe we've met, he says. *You must be my new girl.*

Your secretary, yes, says my mother.

The man reaches for her hand and bows to her. He kisses her between the pointer and middle knuckles, peering up above his glasses. My mother crosses and uncrosses her legs beneath her desk. She does not know how to use her body in this moment, with this man. He is older, bejeweled. His hands, so certain.

I'm John Madden, he says.

See my parents, the moment they meet.

SPRING, 2016
NEW YORK, NEW YORK

She calls me first. It's one fifty-nine P.M. on a Thursday, and I'm at my desk when the phone rings. *Hello, my name is Marjorie*, she says, *from the DNA site.* It is my mother's voice, exactly, but it is not my mother on the phone. The name—*Marjorie*—is not my mother's name.

Hello, I say, to the voice of my mother. *I'm at work; let me step out for a moment.*

I exit the building and stand on the sidewalk of Twenty-Sixth Street, next to a Holiday Inn. It's an overcast day. Still a chill in the air. Men with briefcases walk in a cluster and bump around my body to get by.

Thanks for getting back to me, I say. *Like I said, I've been working on this family tree.*

Oh, of course, she says. *I hope I can help.*

So who are you? A secret cousin of mine? Or an aunt? I know it says 1706 centimorgans on the site, but I'm not sure what that means. And your picture—it's so small. I can only see your hair, really. Who are your parents?

Why did you take the test? she wants to know. This woman.

My father died six months ago, I say. *The tree—I'm just trying to fill in the blanks, I guess. There's a lot in my family—just, a lot.*

I see. I'm so sorry to hear that.

The test was a gift. A Christmas gift.

Okay, she says. We are both breathing heavily into the phone. I'm not sure why that is.

Why did you take it? I ask.

Well, she says, *I was adopted at birth.*

I watch a slouching man push a hotdog cart around the corner. I watch a woman exit the ceramic shop with a brown paper bag strangling her wrist. I scuff the sidewalk with the toe of my loafer. I'm not sure what to say to this woman.

Maybe we can both help each other?

I think we can, yes, she says.

Well, I think you may be my cousin, or aunt, I say. *I'm pretty sure. My family, there's a lot no one talks about.*

I do not want to be the one to tell her this. She must be my grandfather's—he had women on the side. I do not want to tell her that he never mentioned another child. He never went to look. I don't have a clue who the mother might be. Mostly, I do not want to tell her that my grandfather has been dead for almost twenty years.

I've seen a picture of you, she says. *On the Internet. I feel like I'm looking into a mirror.*

Everyone in my family looks alike, I say. *Island genes—they're strong.*

But it's like looking directly into a mirror, she says. *Do you understand what I'm saying?*

I think you may be my aunt, I say.

Please, help me, she says. *I've been looking all my life. Please.*

The hotdog man is gone. A girl smokes outside the Holiday Inn. She's on a bench, talking on the phone. She sips soda out of a green bottle. On her knee, half a sandwich in plastic wrap.

I'll try to help you, I say. *Tell me what you know.*

I know that for every birthday of my entire life, I've woken up wondering if my mother remembers the day. If she's thinking of me. If she looks like me. If she knows.

Let's start from the beginning, I say. *Where were you born?*

Hollywood, Florida, she says. *That's somewhere between Miami and Boca Raton.*

I know it, I say. *I was born around there, too. When?*

July 11, 1976, she says. *7-11. It's one of the few things I know.*

My sister and I speak to each other every morning and every night. We check in all day. I can't focus on anything but her. The pictures of her face, the way her voice sounds like my mother, the words that she uses to describe the moon, the descriptions of her house, her favorite movies. She leaves me voice mails singing Joni Mitchell songs—we both love Joni, we have all the same favorites—and I play them and replay them, my sister, my sister can sing, my sister. We send each other photos all day long, and I zoom in to see her face more clearly. I want to see every beauty mark. Every angle of her teeth.

At night, we go through the lists: *What is your favorite meal? What is your favorite memory? Do you like mustard? Can you drink or do you get Asia Glow? Who was your first kiss? What is your husband like? What is your girlfriend like? Did you always know you were gay? What are my nieces like? What was your childhood like? What is our mother like?*

My mom is kind, I say. *She always smells good. She writes a beautiful letter. You're going to love her.* I constantly correct myself: *Our mom. Ours.*

Marjorie Brooke Gelbwaks, Contestant #2,
Miss Florida Pageant, 1999

It is like preparation for death, I think. Describing my mother—her entire life. Who she's been as a person; who she is now. I am used to talking about my father this way—*you would have loved him*—but never my mother.

We fall asleep, one of us still talking, the other mumbling into the phone.

Are you still there? one of us will say.

Yes. Keep going, please, talk.

The relationship we have is nothing short of obsessive. Hannah is worried. She does not want me to have my heart broken. *Careful*, she says. She can already tell I am in love.

I just wonder, I say. *What do you think she looks like naked? Do you think we have the same hips? The same legs? Are our breasts the same size and shape? Do you think hers are fake? Will I look like her in twelve years?*

Why don't you meet each other first?

How long should I wait before I tell her I love her?

Meet each other, she says.

My sister has had a flight booked for months. To New York, the following week. She owes her best friend a visit, she says. My mother has a flight booked to New York, the same week. She owes me a visit, she says.

I can't tell Mom on the phone, I tell my sister. *I'll sit down with her. Explain. We'll go from there. I'm sure she'll want to meet you, too.*

My sister says, *Thank you, thank you, I'd like that*, but I can tell she does not have her hopes up.

Marjorie's profile photo, Ancestry.com.
Account created January 2014.

WINTER, 1988
COCONUT GROVE, FLORIDA

My mother has skipped her period once, twice, three times by now. She was told after the first child that she had an ovarian obstruction, twists and bumps inside her, little chance to ever be pregnant again.

I thought there was no chance, she tells my father now. She is sitting on the floor of her living room. She is trying to tell him something.

What are you trying to tell me? You said it was impossible, he says. He is pacing the room. He pumps his fist inches from the wall of her canary-yellow apartment as if he will let it go, as if he will smash this entire wall down and expose the stars, but he does not.

Get rid of it, he says.

I will not get rid of it, says my mother. *I won't.*

I'll have nothing to do with it, he says. *I have a family. Goddammit you know I have a family. I don't have the money.*

I'm keeping this baby, says my mother. *Maybe you should have considered your family sometime in the past eight years, but I haven't heard much about them till now.*

She wants to tell him. She wants nothing more than to tell this man, my father, that her stomach has been stretched this way before. Her stomach had been stretched over a living, breathing heart. Her body molded to it. She was sent away to live in an apartment complex with her fourteen-year-old sister; she pumped this baby with her own blood, fed and nurtured it. Her stomach stretched, and then it was emptied, and ever since there has been a cave behind her ribs where her daughter once lived. She wants to tell him everything, to finally tell *someone* this secret, the way her father smashed a vase when she told him, the way he drove her to one group home, then the next, before settling her into that apartment where her baby would be born, then taken. She wants to be held like a child again, but instead my father is pacing, he is shaking his fist and he is saying, *Goddamn it Goddamn you woman You did this to hurt me Goddamn this you must get rid of it, will you? Don't be such a goddamn woman. Look at me when I'm talking to you I have a goddamn family I have a wife, two children, I don't need a bastard child.*

Then leave, says my mother. *Don't see me anymore.*

What?

I'm keeping this child. I need this one thing. You can leave, she says.

She wanted to tell him. Thirty-five years together—she never did.

My mother moves back in with her sister while she is pregnant with me. The two of them watch horror movies, eat stacks of Saltine crackers (it's the only thing my mother can stomach); they match up the grooves of puzzles on the living room floor; they tend to Tanya and Teagan. My Aunt Tao rubs lotion on my mother's feet and they are girls again, young again, catching up, doing this very thing all over again. My mother is reading *The Great Gatsby*. Sometimes, she recites passages aloud.

F. Scott Fitzgerald, says my mother. *I like the sound of that. The letter in front. Powerful, yeah?*

You're right, says my aunt. *Those with the initial names.*

I want a powerful child, says my mother. *My child won't be a coward. And I'm going to put a letter in front. No other name, no abbreviation, just the letter.*

You're crazy, says my aunt. *You can't just put a letter in front.*

Maybe T, says my mother. *You're the one taking care of me, aren't you? You and these girls. My baby may be fatherless but she'll always have women. Yes, I'm gonna call her* T.

* ✳ *

Ao ʻaumākua is a place in the afterworld in which all of one's ancestors are waiting. I always liked this legend best, the idea of this place, where all family ties remain solid, intact, where nothing on Earth ever mattered. It is the place in which all family members are reunited, and I like to imagine that everyone shows up young, healthy, so much bright life in the face. In all the realms of heaven and hell, Ao ʻaumākua is most desired among the people of Hawaiʻi.

Once the family is reunited, each spirit is encouraged to visit their own idea of home. Home can be in the depths of the sea, in the tree-tops. A spirit may choose their grandmother's lap in her rocking chair, the sour smell of malasadas.

Ancient legend describes it as *the place of your greatest responsibility.*

Others define it as returning to one's rightful place, or one's greatest duty.

The Hawaiian word for this is Kuleana.

My mother opens her bedroom door, walks out, chugs water in the kitchen, walks back in, shuts the door, opens the door, shuts the door, walks into the bathroom, shuts the door, opens the door, walks back to the kitchen, drinks more water, joins me in the living room, sits on the couch, opens and shuts her eyes, opens and shuts them, says things like *Who,* and *What,* and *What will I tell your father?*

He doesn't know, she says. She is shaking. *There's so much—*

He's dead, I say. *You don't have to worry about that.*

She's not here, my mother. She's somewhere else, I can tell, replaying something, reckoning with something; she's in another time.

Don't worry about Dad, I say, *and don't worry about me.*

In the next five minutes my mother scrambles on in incomplete sentences: *Where is she? The girl? Does she hate me? Do you hate? How can you even look at me? Where is? What does she look like? Her name? Where is she? How did? Did she? Who found whom? My daughter, does she hate me? It wasn't me who let her go. I was scared. You have to understand. What happened was this. But where is she?*

I break down the facts. I repeat them several times, until she is steady, until she can hold them. Her name. Where she lives. What she does. *Here, look*, I say, offering a photograph. *She's had a good life*, I say.

I see, she says. *The girl is beautiful*, she says.

Your daughter, she's beautiful, I agree. *She looks like you. And like me.*

Perhaps, one day, maybe we could meet her? says my mother. *Maybe for the holidays?*

The next day, we decide to meet in Washington Square Park. It's two thirty P.M., New York University's graduation day, so the entire park is bobbing with purple and silver balloons. Families grasp one another by the elbows—*I'm so proud of you*—the sun throwing stripes of light between them. I am holding my mother's hand. A banjo player cries out and knocks his kick drum. We wait beneath the arc, circling, looking, my hand a visor over my eyes as my focus shifts from face to face. *Will I know?*

How will we know? asks my mother. *There are so many people.*

A child steps inside a wet circle of rope. A man lifts the rope with a stick, until the child is swallowed by a giant bubble. The girl looks calm like this, inside the wobbling rainbow. I wish I could crawl inside it, too. I'd take an extra layer of anything between me and the world right now, anything to soften the noise. The crowd thickens. The clapping, the drumming, the screaming, the stroller wheels, the voices all coalesce into a dented mirage of sound.

And then I see her. And my mother sees her. And she sees us. And we see her. It's impossible to say which comes first. It's impossible to say much more than, *We saw her.* Hair that looks blue in the sun. The shape of her. My face in her face. My mother's walk in her walk. The length of her arms. Her chin, the round cheeks. We all know it without knowing. She is mine, ours.

The bubble splats in the air—a wad of liquid, bursting. Behind my sister, a blonde is taking a video on a camcorder. She is the flute player, Contestant number four, from Miami Lakes—my sister's best friend. We all reach each other.

Hi, is all we say.

My sister.

All of our arms reach out. We dampen each other's shoulders. We don't say much more, just, *Hi, Hi*, the three of us together like that. Our hair all blending. Our height exactly the same. The way it all somehow fits.

Under a tree on the north side of the park, we sit and slide our shoes off, comparing our feet in the grass. The same unfortunate toenails. The ankles. The three of us cannot stop looking and commenting at one another's faces. The slope of the nose, the ways in which our mouths move when we speak.

Mother. Sister. Daughter. Mother.

She was there all along. How did we miss her? How many times had we opened a door for one another in our lives? How many county fair Ferris wheels? Days rotating our towels on the same beach?

Contestant number four, the flute player from Miami Lakes, takes a photograph of us on my camera.

This'll be the first photo I have where I look like the other people in it, says my sister.

We walk the streets of SoHo and Chinatown for the rest of the day, holding hands. We stop on each corner and look up at the buildings. I explain our geography, the terra-cotta, this other home of mine, the one I've made for myself. I walk hunched beneath the umbra of these buildings every day, but today they are magnificent.

That night, over dinner at a quiet restaurant, my mother begins telling my sister about Samuel. *A Good Boy,* she says, *there was so much love there. I want you to know that you came from love.*

My sister nods, listening carefully, and I think this is what she must have looked like as a child. This very expression. This is what I missed.

It's funny, says my mother, *I haven't seen him in so long, but I can see him now, in you. You have his eyebrows. It's like I can see him again.*

My sister begins to cry. My mother moves from next to me to my sister's side of the table; she wraps her arms around my sister's body.

Baby girl, it's okay, she says, rocking her. *My baby girl*, kissing her on the top of the head exactly like she would to me, like my mother had never missed any time like this, not a moment without her firstborn girl, her hiapo.

I'm thinking of calling the piece Kuleana, I tell my cousin Sarah. We're drinking beers outside Ala Moana. I've been here two weeks retracing my mother's story—her school, the banyan trees, the shopping mall windows, those rocks behind her childhood home. I held each rock in my hand, as if the light tug of their weight could somehow collapse time, tell me more. Tomorrow, I'll go back home.

That sounds right, she says.

What's your interpretation of the term? I ask. Sarah was born and raised here, in Kalihi. She has a deeper understanding of the language than I do.

When I was little, I used to think it meant chores, she says. *But it's much bigger than that. It's a person's greatest duty, or responsibility, or privilege.*

Right, I say. *I think it applies, with my mother's return to her past, her kids. The bigness of that.*

That's not what I was thinking, she shakes her head.

What were you thinking?

It's your mother's Kuleana to be with her children, yes, that's true, she says. *But that's not why the title works. That's not the point of this story.*

What's the point?

Your Kuleana, she says. *It is your Kuleana to tell it.*

✳ ✴ ✳

This is a secret of my own.

My father has been helping me write these pages. In my dreams, my father stands in our house. It is not burned or blackened or infelicitous, no melted pools of television screens, not yet. My rocking horse is still there, rocking. The air is clear. The dining room table shines. It's all in one piece—this house—the way I've always imagined it could be. So is my father.

Sometimes he says the things I wrote the way I wrote them. We play out the scenes. We have our script. Other times, he says, *No, not quite, it didn't happen like that.* My dead father is always moving. I follow him.

I wasn't standing in the living room for that part, he says. *The night of your middle school dance, I was standing right here, by the hall.* He brings me to the mouth of the hallway; the light is on. He walks me back and forth through it, buttoning his shirt, tucking it in, rushing, getting ready for something. He disappears into the wall and reappears on the living room couch.

You must get it right, he says. *Remember the details*, he says. He smooths a comb through his hair. It's still wet from a shower. I sit down next to my dead father. No one prepares you for the dreams. I want to breathe in the shoulder of his shirt.

I want to breathe in the shoulder of your shirt, I say, *but I can't remember it right. It's all gone now*, I say. *The house. The details.*

He lights a cigarette. My father is never sick in my dreams. He is not plugged into tubes; he has no oxygen mask. Here, we are both breathing.

What's missing is always there, he says. He taps the center of my forehead three times.

Relax, he says.

There are so many ways to lose a person. There are so many revisions.

*B*ut wait. *There's something else*, Hannah says.

We're sitting in her truck in her driveway upstate. It is midnight, just after my twenty-ninth birthday, and the engine is turned off, the air soured with hay.

It's not what you think, she says. She rubs at the back of her neck.

Hannah, who'd spent the past month with my family, housing two of my teenage cousins while I'd traveled through July. Hannah, who'd overheard something she should not have heard while I was gone, who'd jerked across a freeway to the side of the road when she'd heard it; she'd stopped and listened again. Hannah, who'd wanted to wait until after I came home to tell me herself, my hands in hers; she'd wanted to wait until after my birthday.

I'm glad she found her sister, is what she'd heard, *but where is the brother?*

What are you talking about? I say.

I'm still trying to figure it out, she tells me.

That night, in her driveway, I punch the truck's window until I feel bone.

✳ ✳ ✳

Let me try this again.

My family, we began with a mannequin.

He was a full-bodied jewelry mannequin: fancy, distinguished. Those were the words we used. When I was two years old, my mother and I lived alone in a canary-yellow apartment in Coconut Grove, Florida. See my mother, single, the crimson-mouthed mistress of my father, a white man in downtown Miami who has been promising to leave his artist wife, his two handsome boys. *We needed a man in our home, a figure bigger than us, to scare off all the other men who would come.*

This is the story I know.

But let me go truer.

Before my father arrives at our apartment, my mother sits the mannequin in a rocking chair near the front window. My mother and I like to change his socks together. We pull the bright patterns over his club feet, roll the bands up his calves. We'll do this again years from now, for my father, just before he dies.

Merit cigarettes, orange juice and vodka, money. I miss the grind of his voice. I miss the word when it was still golden: *father.*

This here is your father.

Hello, little one, I'm your father.

My mother, a Chinese, Hawaiian, pocketknife of a woman, shot a man once. She's already lost her own father, her islands, Samuel, a daughter, the gift of naming that daughter and holding her and tossing her into the air, the joy in that suspension.

But then, there was another.

There is always the point at which a story changes. A good story must always change its terms.

I'm glad she found her sister, but where is the brother?

Another missed period. Another month of nausea. Another month. Another talk on the living room floor between my mother and father as I squirmed in a crib.

You can't keep him, my father says. *We've done this before.*

I can.

We can't.

That's how I imagine the scene going. That's what I've been told.

My mother kept carrying that baby. She thought my father would change his mind. The mannequin—he'd had a greater purpose. He protected me and he protected my mother as she grew, as she listened for noises at the window. I don't remember pressing my ear to her stomach, saying *Hello*, but I did that.

Sometimes we choose what to believe, sometimes we know it.

Like this: Uncle Nuke was left on our curb one Christmas wearing a Santa hat. I was six. My mother went back out for him, the trash bags still waiting for pickup, but he was gone already. Off to another family, or little girl, who needed him. The truth is, I hadn't missed him till now. I never even knew he was gone.

I thought your father would change his mind once the boy was born, says my mother. *I'd waited for that.*

These hushed years. These secrets of the body. To whom did they belong first? I want to find where it began and say, *I'm here now, listening.* I want to reach through the years and tell the women I've been lonely.

My father stopped breathing on a cold, clear afternoon. October. The sun was out.

My mother was making him soup.

The story I'd rather tell: I make it out to the beach that day. My half brothers are there. And my half sister. My baby brother, too. We are all familiar to one another. We're a family.

Truer.

My brother was born on January 27, 1990, in Miami, Florida. Before he was adopted, my parents named him. I was sent to Disney World when he was born, though I will never remember that. Baby boy. Beautiful, I know it. I never got to meet him.

You could have told me, I say now, to my mother, *all of this.*

My father, he married her. I wore a yellow dress. They kept me.

Son, my father used to say.

There once was a girl on a flying horse and everybody loved her.

That's the unfinished story.

That's all.

ACKNOWLEDGMENTS

Billie, it's with you I start—I didn't write that, Evan "Billie" Rehill did, and though Evan does not appear in this book, he's spent years walking me over every bridge in New York to safer places. Thank you, EBR, for the matchbooks, the guts, every rabbit in every hat, and your unwavering belief and love.

To Anne-E. Wood, for teaching me how to draw a house in that first writing class I ever took. I've been doing my best to live inside of it ever since.

To Jin Auh, who is so much more than my agent and Spice Girls manager. Since the day we met you've reminded me that words are power, and the work you do to translate and advocate for that power is nothing short of sorcery. Thank you for always feeding me sweets, for your great laughs and wisdom. Thank you, too, Alexandra Christie, Jessica Friedman, and the superb Wylie Agency.

To my editor, Callie Garnett. The way you have seen me and this book is a greater magic trick than any deck of I AM's. Thank you for the privilege of seeing you, too—an acolyte, a poet, a precious stone, a dear friend. This book will always feel like *ours*. My sincerest gratitude to Barbara Darko, Nancy Miller, Marie Coolman, Cindy Loh, Sarah New, Nicole Jarvis, Laura Keefe, Tree Abraham, and the whole Bloomsbury family, for believing in a book that couldn't be summarized easily or packaged sweetly.

To those who have provided the time, space, warmth, and support to write these pages, I am so grateful: the MacDowell Colony (my safe haven in the darkest days, and the place this book was born), Hedgebrook, *Tin House*, Yaddo, New York Foundation for the Arts, the Fine Arts Work Center (who treated a bedfellow like family), Todd Lawton and Jeff LeBlanc, and especially Cynthia LaFave and Paul Rapoli, for providing so many literal and figurative homes for me to write in, and for loving me like your own.

To my beloved teachers, for your friendship and mentorship and words both in and out of the classroom: Suzanne Hoover, Nelly Reifler, Noy Holland, Jo Ann Beard, Lidia Yuknavitch, Jeff Parker, and Claire Vaye Watkins. To Mary Morris, who taught me everything from peeling a potato to structuring a story.

Sometimes we *are* lucky enough to choose our family. That's been the case with Ian "PTP" Carlos Mormeneo, Randie Kutzen, Jana Krumholtz, James Question Marks, Marisa Lee, Michaela Basilio Batten, Rick Moody, and Laurel Nakadate, all of whom have stood with me through every fire.

I am so moved each day by the ferocious minds of my *No Tokens* family, including Rowan Hisayo Buchanan (for all the wonder), Justine Champine and Molly Tolsky (for Taco Trio, the best writing group in history), Annabel Everest Graham (for the saudade), Janelle Greco (for shaking 'em up), Lauren Hilger (for the heat, the poems, the oracles, the girls), Ursula Villarreal-Moura (for never forgetting me), Hannah Mulligan (for the ponies), Leah Schnelbach (couchmate, soulmate, purple blazer dream machine), Carina del Valle Schorske (for the moves and the nudes), Samantha Turk (for every sacred word), and Scout Woodhouse (for the missives).

To those who have listened, who have supported this book and supported me through the writing of this book by reading drafts and writing blurbs and offering me beds to sleep in and fish to eat, by sending postcards and saying *Yes* to every long walk and always asking *How can I help?* when I've needed it most, my gratitude is profound and enormous: Benjamin Schaefer, N. Michelle AuBuchon, Chelsea Bieker, Genevieve Hudson, Ruthie Crawford, Tatiana Ryckman, Jonathan Dixon, Mary Gaitskill, Allie Rowbottom, Kristin Dombek, Vincent Scarpa, Adam Dalva, Tony Fu, Shelly Oria, Melissa Febos, Meakin Armstrong, Karissa Chen, Bükem Reitmayer, Che Yeun, Alisson Wood, Cal Morgan, Brigitte Hamadey, Jack Woods, Sarah Gerard, Kimberly King Parsons, Alex Marzano-Lesnevich, Julie Buntin, Lauren Groff, Matt Bell, Laura Lampton Scott, Gabriel Jesiolowski, Alexandra Ford, Kyle Kolomona Nakatsuka, and Team Jo Ann Beard. And to those who may or may not appear in this book, who gave me a past and helped me make my way back through it, thank you: Alyssa Banker Hiller, "Gabrielle," Graham Heyward, Jennifer Abrams, Lisa Mendoza, Karen Purcell, Nicki Alpern, Nicole Polat, Paige Newberry, Maxwell Burns, and Nicole Betty.

To Jac Martinez, for the light and shadows. For leaving flowers on the dashboard.

To John Bean for the French lessons, the metaphors, and for always reminding me that *No* is a complete sentence. You've helped me find and therefore love myself in ways I had forgotten.

Excerpts of this book have appeared in *Guernica, Black Warrior Review, Minola Review,* and *Go Home!,* thanks to the generous and vigilant editors who have stood behind my story: Eryn Loeb, Hillary Brenhouse, Kayleb Rae Candrilli, Robin Richardson, Jisu Kim, and

Jyothi Natarajan. Deep thanks, as well, to the photographers who have allowed me to reprint the moments they've captured in these pages: Bob Lasky, Don Seidman, Sherrie Helms Kukulski, and Jac Martinez. Aurore DeCarlo and Team Carrie Goldberg—this book is full of bad guys, but you good ones give me hope. Thank you for your tremendous dedication to justice, to truth, and to my safety during the writing of these pages.

To Lynda Barry, Grace Paley, and Heather Lewis, whose work shook me alive and made room for the rest of us. Yours is the lake I most wish to feed.

To my 'ohana, both near and across oceans: the Maddens, the T's, the Hedges, the Schaefers, the LaFaves, the Beresfords, the Gonzalezes, the Kamakawiwo'oles, and the Lindenmuths (especially Mary-Beth, for the deep ruts). To Jeanne Kam and Tammie Anthony, for staying on the phone until I got it right. To Sarah Kamakawiwo'ole, for your joy and your islands and all the right words. To Nikki and Kaitlyn "Kidd Jackson" Hedge, my lifelines and the most non-piece-of-shit humans in the world—I love you.

Sharon and Peter Gelbwaks—you didn't know that adopting my sister meant adopting me, too, but you're stuck with me now. I'm so grateful for this new iteration of family.

To my sister and first star, Marjorie Hokulani, for always finding me, and my beloved nieces, Katherine Ailani, Victoria Ululani, and Kensington Kamaya.

To my brothers, the best men I've ever known: Shawn D. Madden and Blake Madden. For the laughs and the crabs and the jams and all those winding streets. Shawn, this book will always be titled *Ghost Ride That Rainbow Whip* in your honor. Blake, forever my hero and

Soup King. Sweet love and fierce admiration to Tricia Murphy Madden, Tabitha Murphy Madden, and Tiffany Vergara Madden.

To Alexander, for turning the hourglass over.

To Petra and Chuck, for making the call and inviting me in.

To Chaplin, Ruby-June, and my first best friend, Cloud 9: I've always said I'd never be the writer to thank pets, yet here I am. Feeling guilty. The truth is, you've saved me from my sadness in ways both small and large.

To my parents, John Laurence Madden and Sherrie Lokelani Madden, to whom this book is dedicated. For this Big Life. For the greatest love of all. To Mom, especially, for facing these pages with unfathomable grace and understanding, for your fearless and wild and gorgeous heart, for all the handwritten cards, and for letting our story go on.

This book was written because once, a little girl needed more stories like her own. My greatest dedication and gratitude to every other drop-dead-lonely, queer-as-hell, bucktoothed loserly outcast reading a book under the covers with a little light, for anyone with a story to tell and a will to rise. Write it down. You are not alone; you are the champion of my heart.

To Drew Barrymore, for saving this kid's life with a book.

And to my wife, Hannah Beresford, for every draft, every mile, every kiss, and every day. They say happy endings don't make for good stories but you have given me both, at once, in equal measure.

A NOTE ON THE AUTHOR

T KIRA MADDEN is an APIA writer, photographer, and amateur magician. She is the founding editor in chief of *No Tokens*, and facilitates writing workshops for homeless and formerly incarcerated individuals. A 2017 NYSCA/NYFA Artist Fellow in nonfiction literature, she has received fellowships from the MacDowell Colony, Hedgebrook, *Tin House*, DISQUIET, Summer Literary Seminars, and Yaddo, where she was selected for the 2017 Linda Collins Endowed Residency Award. She lives in New York City and teaches at Sarah Lawrence College.